Russia Ris

Russia Rising

Putin's Foreign Policy in the Middle East and North Africa

Edited by
Dimitar Bechev, Nicu Popescu, and
Stanislav Secrieru

I.B.TAURIS
LONDON • NEW YORK • OXFORD • NEW DELHI • SYDNEY

I.B. TAURIS
Bloomsbury Publishing Plc
50 Bedford Square, London, WC1B 3DP, UK
1385 Broadway, New York, NY 10018, USA
29 Earlsfort Terrace, Dublin 2, Ireland

BLOOMSBURY, I.B. TAURIS and the I.B. Tauris logo are trademarks of
Bloomsbury Publishing Plc

First published in Great Britain 2021
Reprinted 2021 (twice)

Cover design by Holly Bell

A catalogue record for this book is available from the British Library.

A catalog record for this book is available from the Library of Congress.

ISBN: HB: 978-0-7556-3663-1
PB: 978-0-7556-3664-8
ePDF: 978-0-7556-3666-2
eBook: 978-0-7556-3665-5

Typeset by Newgen KnowledgeWorks Pvt. Ltd., Chennai, India
Printed and bound in Great Britain

To find out more about our authors and books visit www.bloomsbury.com
and sign up for our newsletters

Contents

Illustrations

Contributors

Julien Barnes-Dacey is director of the Middle East & North Africa program at the European Council on Foreign Relations. His work focuses on European policy toward Syria and the wider Mashreq. He has worked as a researcher and journalist across the Middle East, including in Syria from 2007 to 2011 where he reported for the *Wall Street Journal* and the *Christian Science Monitor*.

Dimitar Bechev is a nonresident senior fellow at the Atlantic Council in Washington, DC, as well as a fellow at Europe's Futures program at the Institute for Human Sciences (IWM), Vienna. He is the author of *Rival Power: Russia in Southeast Europe* (2017). He has held positions with the University of North Carolina at Chapel Hill, University of Oxford, and the European Council on Foreign Relations (ECFR) and has published widely on Turkey, Russia, the Balkans, and the Eastern Mediterranean.

Timofey Borisov has been a research fellow at the Centre for Analysis of Strategies and Technologies (CAST) in Moscow since 2016. He previously worked as a market research analyst in the Russian defense industry. He holds a master's degree in international relations from the Higher School of Economics in Moscow. He is a regular contributor to Eksport Vooruzhenii (Arms Exports) and Moscow Defense Brief.

Dmitriy Frolovskiy is a political analyst and consultant. He is a contributor to the Carnegie Moscow Center, Middle East Institute, and many other think tanks. He is currently a private consultant on policy and strategy in the Middle East with official and private entities. He has also written extensively about Russia's foreign policy toward the Gulf Cooperation Council states.

Florence Gaub is the deputy director of the European Union Institute for Security Studies (EUISS), where she is in charge of research coordination. In addition to her work on the Middle East, she focuses on foresight and future studies. She holds degrees from Munich University, the Sorbonne, the Institut d'études politiques de Paris (Sciences Po) and a Ph.D. from the Humboldt University of Berlin. She was previously employed at NATO Defense College. Her latest coauthored book is *The Cauldron: NATO's Campaign in Libya* (2018).

Dalia Ghanem is a resident scholar at the Carnegie Middle East Center in Beirut, where her work examines political and extremist violence, radicalization, Islamism, and jihadism with an emphasis on Algeria. She has been a guest speaker on these issues in various conferences and a regular commentator in different Arab and international print and audiovisual media.

Mark N. Katz is a professor of government and politics at George Mason University in Fairfax, Virginia. He was a Fulbright Scholar at the School of Oriental and African Studies (SOAS) in London during January–March 2018 and the Sir William Luce Fellow at Durham University during April–June 2018.

Alexey Khlebnikov is an expert on the Middle East at the Russian International Affairs Council and a strategic risk consultant. He received his master's degree in global public policy from the Hubert H. Humphrey School of Public Affairs at the University of Minnesota and both bachelor's and master's in Middle East studies from Lobachevsky State University in Nizhni Novgorod. He was a research fellow at Johns Hopkins School of Advanced International Studies (SAIS) in 2013. He has published on international relations topics, in particular on the Middle East, in academic journals and media sources in Russia, Europe, the United States, and the Middle East. His research interests are focused on the "Arab Spring" failure, current intraregional tensions (within GCC, intra-Sunni, Sunni-Shiite), and great powers' policies in the region.

Anton Lavrov is a graduate of Tver State Technical University. He is an independent defense analyst affiliated with the Moscow-based Center for Analysis of Strategies and Technologies (CAST). His major fields of expertise are Russian military reform, the Russian defense industry, the 2008 Russian-Georgian War, the Russia-Ukraine conflict, and the recent Russian operation in Syria. In 2018 he was a visiting fellow in the Washington-based Center for Strategic and International Studies.

Carole Nakhle is the founder and CEO of Crystol Energy. She specializes in international petroleum contractual arrangements, fiscal regimes and regulations; sustainable development of the petroleum sector including revenue management and governance; capacity building; energy policy, security, investment, and market developments. Dr. Nakhle has worked with oil and gas companies (NOCs and IOCs) at the executive level, governments and policy makers, international organizations, academic institutions, and specialized think tanks on a global scale. She has published two widely acclaimed books: *Petroleum Taxation: Sharing the Wealth* published in 2008 and reprinted in 2012 and used as a primary reference in leading universities and industry training courses; and *Out of the Energy Labyrinth* (2007), coauthored with Lord David Howell.

Nicu Popescu is director of the Wider Europe program at the European Council on Foreign Relations. In 2019 he served as minister of foreign affairs and European integration of Moldova. Prior to becoming a minister, Dr. Popescu worked as a senior analyst at the EU Institute for Security Studies (2013–18); senior advisor on foreign policy and EU affairs for the prime minister of Moldova (2010, 2012–13); head of program and senior research fellow at ECFR in London (2007–9, 2011–12), and research fellow at the Centre for European Policy Studies in Brussels (2005–7). He holds a Ph.D. in international relations from the Central European University in Budapest, Hungary. He is the author of *EU Foreign Policy and Post-Soviet Conflicts: Stealth Intervention* (2010) and coeditor of *Democratization in EU Foreign Policy* (with Benedetta Berti and Kristina Mikulova) published in 2015.

Carol R. Saivetz is a senior advisor at MIT's Security Studies Program. Additionally, she is a lecturer in political science, also at MIT, and a research associate at Harvard's Davis Center for Russian and Eurasian Studies. She holds an M.I.A. and Ph.D. from Columbia in political science and a Certificate from the Russian Institute (now the Harriman Institute). She is the author and coeditor of five books and has written widely about Soviet and now Russian policy in the Middle East. Professor Saivetz has also written about Russian policy toward the other Soviet successor states. She is a contributor to the Lawfare blog and has appeared on PBS's "Great Boston." Her current research focuses on Russian policy toward Syria, including Moscow's relations with Teheran and Ankara.

Stanislav Secrieru is a senior analyst at the EUISS, where he covers Russia and the EU's eastern neighborhood. His research interests focus on EU-Russia relations, Russia's foreign and security policy in the post-Soviet region. Before joining the EUISS, Dr. Secrieru was a senior research fellow at the Polish Institute of International Affairs (2014–16) and a policy analyst at the Open Society European Policy Institute in Brussels (2016–17). He also previously had been a research fellow at the NATO Defence College in Rome (2006), the Institute for European Politics in Berlin (2009–10), and the New Europe College in Bucharest (2011–12).

Dmitri Trenin has been director of the Carnegie Moscow Center since 2008. He joined the Center in 1994 after having served in the Soviet/Russian army from 1972 to 1993. He is the author of several books on Russia's foreign relations, including *What Is Russia up to in the Middle East?* (2018).

Introduction

Dimitar Bechev, Nicu Popescu, and Stanislav Secrieru

In 1984, the US Department of Defense ran its annual assessment of Soviet power in the Middle East and, more generally, the Third World. The report fretted about the inexorable rise of Moscow's influence.

> The USSR has greatly increased its offensive military capability and has significantly enhanced its ability to conduct military operations worldwide … Since invading Afghanistan 4 years ago, the USSR has established bases within striking distance of the Persian Gulf oil fields. The Soviets continue to deliver a growing arsenal of weapons to Syria, Libya, Cuba and Nicaragua. The number of Soviet personnel in Syria has grown from 2,000 to 7,000 … The USSR has increased its influence in the Third World through the presence of over 21,000 military advisers and technicians in nearly 30 countries. An additional 120,000 Soviet troops are stationed in Afghanistan, Cuba and Syria. The result is that the Soviets are able to cultivate pro-Soviet sentiments and influence local military policies.[1]

At the time, such a doom-and-gloom perspective appeared warranted. The same year, the United States, France, and Italy were forced to withdraw troops from Lebanon after Hezbollah militants bombed their barracks with help from Syria and Iran. USSR, having been dislodged from Egypt, was cementing ties with Hafez al-Assad, while sending military aid to Iraq in its war against Iran, an ally of Syria.[2] Meanwhile, relations between America and its allies across the Atlantic were going downhill. The United States threatened sanctions over a Soviet natural gas pipeline built with discounted credits from Western European banks.

Soon enough, it would transpire that fears of resurgent Soviet influence were overblown. Moscow's capacity to project and sustain power overseas turned out to be rather narrow. Instead of focusing on costly geopolitical expansion, the leadership in Moscow shifted attention to domestic consolidation and reform. The USSR withdrew from Afghanistan, cut out aid to its clients in the Middle East, and ultimately imploded as forces unleashed by *perestroika* and *glasnost* swept through the country. The so-called unipolar moment ensued. For two decades, US hegemony shaped the region's politics. Current debates on Russia's growing role in the Middle East echo the early 1980s.[3] For the past several years, Russia and Vladimir Putin have ruled the headlines.

Military intervention in Syria, without precedent in the post-Soviet period, elevated Russia to a power broker in the war-torn country, once a regional power, and in the Middle East. Moscow has rebuilt links to former friends and found new partners. It benefits from strong ties to top-tier regional players such as Iran, Turkey, Israel, and Saudi Arabia. Egypt, the largest Arab state, has stepped up military and economic cooperation with the Russians as well. Russia has inserted itself in regional flashpoints such as Libya and even in Yemen. At the same time, Moscow has managed to keep at an arm's length from local rivalries. It is in the unique position of being on good terms with both the Israelis and the Iranians, Turkey and the Kurds, Saudi Arabia and Qatar, Libya's government of national unity and its adversary, General Khalifa Haftar, Algeria and Morocco, and so forth. In consequence, Russia has been reaping strategic and commercial benefits: Russian arms exports are up; state-owned energy firms like Rosneft and Gazprom are on the lookout for lucrative deals; Turkey's purchase of S-400 missiles is fracturing its relationship with the United States— to the Kremlin's advantage; Riyadh and Moscow manage in tandem, not without hiccups, global oil prices.

Russia's spectacular return to the Middle East raises lots of questions. What is behind Moscow's renewed interest in the Middle East and North Africa? How sustainable is the "comeback"—and are we not bearing witness to another short-lived surge as in the late Cold War? Is Russia to remain an arbiter in regional affairs, or will it eventually decide to pull back? Can it avoid becoming bogged down in local squabbles? How is the foray into the Middle East affecting relations with the United States, still the leading global power, at present as well as in the future? What are the consequences of Russian activism for local players and how does it impact the balance at the regional level? In order to address these issues, *Russia Rising: Putin's Policy in the Middle East and North Africa* provides a snapshot of the Russian involvement in the region, maps the drivers and political dynamics at work, and explores future trajectories. The initial impulse for this volume came from a Chaillot paper on Russia's surge in the Middle East published by the European Union Institute for Security Studies (Paris) in 2018.[4] While based on this paper, the book significantly widens and deepens the research scope.

Russia's Return: The Backstory

Many analysts took note of Russia only with the onset of the Arab Spring, or even the intervention in Syria. In reality, the so-called return to the Middle East had been in the making for a decade or more. In the late 1990s, Foreign Minister (and later Prime Minister) Yevgeny Primakov, an Arabist by training, argued for an alliance with Iran and Iraq to balance against US unilateralism.[5] Russia deepened economic ties with Turkey, a key ally of America. In 1997, Ankara and Moscow agreed to lay the first gas pipeline across the Black Sea. Links with Israel grew closer, too, as around 1.6 million Russophone Jews from across the former Soviet Union immigrated, leaving their mark on Israeli society and politics. Throughout the 2000s, the Russian Federation doubled down on the Middle East. President Putin was the first Russian leader to officially visit the Jewish state in 2005. Moscow also began to build bridges and set diplomatic and intelligence back channels to the Gulf, eager to curb support for Chechen insurgents. Vladimir Putin visited Saudi Arabia in February 2007, another first. Russia became an observer in the Organization of the Islamic Conference, an acknowledgment of Islam as part of its cultural and historic heritage. The new Chechen leader Ramzan Kadyrov, who cultivated a pious Muslim image, became the face of Russian diplomacy in the Middle East.[6] Russia cleaned up books converting Soviet-era debts into new arms deals and investment ventures. In 2005 Russia agreed to write off 73 percent of Syria's dues, estimated at $9.8 billion, in exchange for new arms contracts and access to the facility at Tartus once used by the Soviet navy.[7] Moscow pushed for institutionalization of the Gas Exporting Countries Forum headquartered in Doha and sought to redress relations with wealthy oil producers from the Gulf. Freed from the constraints of ideology, post-Soviet Russia focused on strategic and economic gains, reviving old contacts and forging new partnerships across the Middle East and North Africa.

Engagement provided Russia with a hedge against the United States. The opening toward the region coincided with a downturn in relations with Washington during Putin's second term as president (2004–8). The initial enthusiasm in the Kremlin with regard to the post-9/11 "war on terror" gave way to opposition to US unilateralism. This was not only a response to the "colored revolutions" in Georgia and Ukraine that Moscow blamed on Western meddling. Having backed the US campaign in Afghanistan, Putin deplored the 2003 invasion of Iraq by the Bush administration. To him, it fractured regional order and posed a grave threat to stability in the Middle East and beyond, an argument that was to resurface during the Arab Spring some years later. In his famous speech at the 2007 Munich Security Conference, Putin observed:

> And let's say things as they are—one hand distributes charitable help and the other hand not only preserves economic backwardness but also reaps the profits thereof. The increasing social tension in depressed regions inevitably results in the growth of radicalism, extremism, feeds terrorism and local conflicts. And if all this happens in, shall we say, a region such as the Middle East where there is increasingly the sense that the world at large is unfair, then there is the risk of global destabilization.[8]

On the one hand, Russia portrayed itself as a champion of the status quo, adamantly opposed to regime change. On the other, Putin deployed Soviet-era rhetoric portraying Western neocolonialism as the source of social and political ills bedeviling the Middle East. However, by holding the West responsible, the Russian leadership overlooked the ferment brewing within local societies, which eventually led to the upheaval in the early 2010s.

Yet, as in the Cold War, tough talk did not rule out cooperation with the United States on issues of common interest. Russians made inroads in post-Saddam Iraq, agreeing to write off debts as early as 2004. Moscow did not block at the UN the establishment of a special tribunal to try suspects of the 2005 assassination of Lebanese prime minister Rafiq Hariri linked to the Syrian government.[9] Starting from 2006, Russia supported UN Security Council resolutions calling on Iran to halt its nuclear program and, in June 2010, it voted in favor of Resolution 1929 introducing sanctions against the Islamic Republic. It furthermore froze the delivery of S-300 missiles to Tehran. Cooperation on the Iranian nuclear file marked the peak of the policy of reset (*perezagruzka*) pursued by President Dmitry Medvedev and the Obama administration.[10] Ultimately, Russia became one of the signatories of the so-called Joint Comprehensive Plan of Action (JCPOA) negotiated by Iran and the West. Back then as now, Russia looked at the Middle East as a source of geopolitical currency to be used in dealings with America.

The Arab Spring ushered in a new chapter. Russia was no longer an outsider in the Middle East, with economic and security links to countries such as Libya and Syria. But it was certainly seen in such light by the United States and the Europeans, as they struggled to craft a response to the popular upheaval across the region. The Russian leadership, in turn, interpreted the Arab Spring as an extension of the Bush-era doctrine of regime change. Libya proved to be the inflection point. In March 2011, then prime minister Vladimir Putin upbraided President Medvedev for bandwagoning with the West over the imposition of a no-fly zone and indirectly endorsing the intervention by Britain and France, with the United States "leading from behind." "The [UN Security Council] resolution is defective," Putin told workers at a defense plant in the Russian provincial town of Votkinsk. "It resembles medieval calls for crusades."[11]

The sense that Russia had been tricked over Libya informed its dogged defense of the Assad regime in Syria. Moscow vetoed all attempts of the UN Security Council to impose an arms embargo. Russia sent to the regime military hardware, including twenty-four MiG-29 fighter planes. Between 2011 and 2013, Russian deliveries accounted for 85 percent of all arms sales to Damascus.[12] At the same time, Russia kept diplomatic channels open and options on the table, taking part in the Geneva talks on Syria and, in 2012, supporting political transition.[13] Putin scored a diplomatic coup in August 2013, taking advantage of President Obama's reluctance to enforce his red lines in reaction to the use of chemical weapons by the Syrian regime. The Russian president mediated a deal under which Assad agreed to give up his chemical arsenal and accede to the 1992 Chemical Weapons Convention. Moscow positioned itself as a power broker, a foretaste of what was to come.

Russian Policy Deciphered

Russia's involvement in the Middle East reflects a variety of factors at the international, regional, and domestic levels.

First, Russia pursues status. As the chapter by Dmitri Trenin reminds us, recognition as an indispensable power with a stake in issues of global concern has always been at the forefront of Russian foreign policy. Influencing a key region, just like the Soviet Union in its day, signals Russia is back in the game—and is capable, with limited investment, to mount a challenge to US dominance. In the wake of the annexation of Crimea, President Obama dismissed Russia as a regional power bound to decline.[14] While his assessment might not be entirely off the mark, the intervention in Syria and Russia's subsequent diplomatic activism across the Middle East testify to its ability to project power and influence beyond the post-Soviet region. In addition, Russia has gained clout thanks to its partnership with Iran and Turkey, two pivotal regional players that have replaced traditional Arab powers such as Egypt, Syria, and Iraq, as well as thanks to closer ties with Saudi Arabia.

Second and related, Russian policymakers see their country's foothold in the Middle East as a bargaining chip vis-à-vis the West. Though Russia has failed to win any concessions in Ukraine or with regard to Western sanctions, it faces no threat of diplomatic isolation. Both the United States and the EU are concerned about radical Islam and transnational jihadi groups such as the self-styled Islamic State and al-Qaeda originating from the Middle East. In Russia's view, that provides the basis for engagement and geopolitical give-and-take. And at the same time, as Florence Gaub convincingly demonstrates in this volume, Russia's calls to set up an international anti-terrorist coalition do not prevent its strategic communication machine to blame the West for the upsurge of radicalism.

Third, the Middle East and North Africa offer economic opportunities. As Timofey Borisov and Carole Nakhle show in their chapters, the region holds particular attraction to Russia's arms exporters and energy giants. According to the Stockholm International Peace Research Institute (SIPRI), arms imports in the region doubled between 2014 and 2019. More than half of the US arms exports went to the Middle East, and Russia is eager to compete, as it has seen demand by crucial clients like India and Venezuela shrink and its exports in the global market go down by 17 percent.[15] The Gulf, the subject of Dmitriy Frolovskiy's chapter, is a prospective export destination, in addition to traditional customers such as Algeria and Syria. From Turkey to Iraq to Egypt, Russian companies have been pursuing projects related to the extraction and trade of oil and natural gas as well as the construction of nuclear power plants, an area where Moscow is keen to become a global technological leader.

Fourth, the Middle East is connected to the Caucasus and Central Asia, which Russia considers its "soft underbelly." These two regions were even known as the Soviet Middle East during the Cold War.[16] Initially, the war in Syria worked as a safety valve. According to Russian government estimates, two thousand people had left the North Caucasus to join various militias by 2015, some of them apparently not without covert assistance from Moscow's security services.[17] Of those, a fair number were killed in action, but others would no doubt have headed home. Currently, the Russian authorities are implementing a repatriation and de-radicalization program for family members of IS fighters. While there are 16 million Russian Federation citizens who profess Islam—close to 12 percent of the overall population (not counting migrants from the ex-Soviet states of Central Asia)—past decades have seen a rise of xenophobia and anti-Muslim sentiment in Russian society. The return of ethnic tensions presents a challenge for a leader like Putin who draws part of his legitimacy from his success in reducing instability originating from Chechnya, Dagestan, and other parts of the North Caucasus.

The Limits of Moscow's Influence

Back in 2015, the Russian incursion into Syria bred expectations that, sooner rather than later, Putin's gamble would lead to a quagmire scenario. One of the proponents of this theory was President Obama who described Russia's conduct as a "recipe for disaster."[18] The Russian military's performance on the battlefield proved skeptics wrong. At the same time, initial assessments in the West set the bar for assessing Moscow's policy very low. With time, analyses have veered to the other extreme. The longer Russia stays in Syria, the greater the tendency to exaggerate its power over local actors.

In fact, Russia's influence is not as extensive. In Syria, for instance, it has not been able to kick-start a political process leading to a settlement, partly because its interests are at variance with those of the Assad regime and its Iranian backers—a point argued by Julien Barnes-Dacey in his chapter. Egypt has deepened security and economic links to Moscow but, at the end of the day, is more closely aligned with the West and the Gulf, as Alexey Khlebnikov shows. Turkey and Iran remain Russia's "frenemies," not allies, even if cooperation with both is thriving. And as the chapter by Mark N. Katz points out, should Iran and Israel clash head-on, Russia's stock in the Middle Eastern market will plummet as the United States will have to step in politically and militarily.

Moscow is well aware of the limits and constraints it faces. It also has learned its lessons from the Cold War when Soviet clients oftentimes proved unreliable, put Moscow's own interests at risk, and frequently defected to its adversary, the United States. Russian policy nowadays is based on the desire to limit exposure while maximizing the payoff from engagement. This is one of the reasons the intervention in Syria has been kept within certain bounds. As Anton Lavrov demonstrates in this volume, it involves primarily the Russian air force rather than "boots on the ground," part of the operation shouldered by Iran, its proxies, and Hezbollah. Russian deployment pales in comparison to the war in Afghanistan in the 1980s or even Soviet naval and ground presence in the 1970s. Moscow has put on display its upgraded conventional capabilities, but it is unwilling and, in likelihood, unable to scale up its operation.

All this calls for a realistic appraisal of Russia's role in Middle Eastern affairs, exposing its assets as well as weaknesses and taking into account the regional landscape and the strategies pursued by local players. Russia has become a pivotal player and aspiring intermediary in a fractious, multipolar Middle East. The argument we make in this book is that Russia is neither willing nor able to replace US primacy. It definitely desires a seat at the Middle Eastern table, and its pugnacious approach combined with its agile and skillful diplomacy proves just that. At the same time, it does not want and cannot take over the burden of managing a volatile region from the United States, which is trying to extricate itself. In this respect, President Putin's comment, replying to a question on the collapsing JCPOA, that "Russia is not a firefighting rescue crew. [It] cannot save things that are not fully under [its] control,"[19] speaks volumes.

Outline of the Chapters

The book is organized into three sections—exploring Russia's motivations, its impact on select issue areas, and relations with key regional actors.

The first section opens with a chapter by Florence Gaub, Nicu Popescu, and Dimitar Bechev on the Soviet Union's involvement in the Middle East and North Africa during the Cold War. Authors highlight the ambivalence in ties between Moscow and its allies in the region and explain the reasons behind the failure to project ideological influence and mount a robust challenge to the United States. Nationalist regimes who took power in Egypt, Syria, Iraq, Algeria and elsewhere took inspiration from the Soviet model but asserted their autonomy, often at the expense of Soviet strategic interests.

The Soviet era may bear on present-day Russia's perspective on the region but there are significant discontinuities, too. Freed from the shackles of communist ideology, Moscow acts with greater flexibility in the pursuit of strategic and economic objectives. Dmitri Trenin assesses the drivers and motives shaping Russian policy in the Middle East. To him, the intervention in Syria has been a springboard for global influence and a test for relations with the United States. "Russia has learned the art of establishing and managing 21st century alliances, which is very different from the past Soviet and current U.S. experience." Trenin offers a reality check, too, pointing out the constraints faced by Russia.

The second section explores various facets of Russian presence in the Middle East and North Africa. Anton Lavrov looks at the Russian military in Syria. In his view, not only did the campaign bolster Moscow's geopolitical standing but the experience in combat will chart the way forward for the country's military, intervention in regional conflicts, and competition with the United States and NATO. Florence Gaub takes a different angle, zooming in on Russia's "nonwar" with Islamic State/Daesh. Under the cover of a campaign against jihadi terrorism, Moscow helped Assad crush an array of militias opposed to the regime. Russia manipulated the international revulsion over the atrocities committed by Daesh for essentially three purposes: to achieve its strategic goal of ensuring the Syrian regime's survival; to discredit Western efforts not just in Syria but in the region more generally; and to bolster support for its strategy and policies. Yet, while the Kremlin's strategic communications apparatus did the job internationally, Gaub contends, it failed to shape the narrative in the Middle East.

Russia sees the Syrian war as an opportunity to sell its weapons as well as monetize political ties through trade and investment. Timofey Borisov takes a deep dive into Russian arms exports to the region and shows that, following a slump in the 1990s, Moscow has expanded its market share. Sustaining that share in the longer run might prove challenging, however. Though local rivalries and arms races pump up demand, competition among suppliers is fierce as is the pressure to innovate technologically. Borisov is furthermore skeptical that sales of weapons could open the door for Russian business in other, civilian areas. Energy certainly commands central interest. It is the subject of Carole Nakhle's contribution to the volume. The OPEC+ deal struck in December 2016 on managing global oil prices strengthened Russia's ties with hydrocarbon-rich Gulf countries, although temporary collapse of the OPEC+ deal in

2020 and a brief oil price war between Russia and Saudi Arabia revealed the limits of these relations. Still in the last decade, from Algeria all the way to Iraq, Moscow has bagged lucrative contracts in upstream oil and gas as well. Nuclear technology is a promising area, with projects in Turkey, Egypt, and possibly the Gulf following the plant built by Rosatom at Bushehr in Iran.

The last section is dedicated to Russia's relations with regional actors. Carol Saivetz sheds light on Iran, not only Moscow's ally in Syria but also a principal interlocutor on a range of security issues in the Middle East, South Caucasus, and Central Asia. The chapter highlights the complex interplay of Russia and Iran's interests vis-à-vis the Caspian Sea, the Persian Gulf, and the Iranian nuclear program. Julien Barnes-Dacey then takes a look at the Russian policy vis-à-vis the so-called "resistance axis" bringing together Iran, the Assad regime, and Hezbollah. In his analysis, Moscow's objectives are often at odds with those of the Islamic Republic and its regional clients. Assad has successfully sabotaged attempts at reaching political settlement in Syria, working at cross-purposes with the Russian diplomacy. At the same time, the behind-the-scenes competition between Moscow and Tehran and their divergent views of Israel, in Barnes-Dacey's assessment, are unlikely to derail the power duet. Ambivalence is the central theme in Dimitar Bechev's chapter on Russian-Turkish relations. From bitter rivals in Syria, Vladimir Putin and Turkish president Recep Tayyip Erdoğan have become partners thanks to the confluence of interests. Cooperation between the two former imperial powers has deeper roots going back to the late 1990s. But the current honeymoon does not rule out the fact that Moscow and Ankara are still at odds on a number of issues, from Syria to security in the Black Sea and the Southern Caucasus.

The Russia–Iran–Turkey triangle may be at the forefront of Russian policy, but there are other actors and relationships that also loom large for policymakers in Moscow. In his contribution on the Gulf, Dmitriy Frolovskiy observes that past tensions and distrust between Russia and countries such as Saudi Arabia, United Arab Emirates, and Qatar have given way to ever closer political and economic cooperation. At the same time, Moscow is eager to avoid embroilment into the Gulf's power rivalries. The chapter highlights—in the light of tensions between Moscow and Riyadh over the oil price management in March 2020—Russia's gains in the region are not irreversible. Egypt is one country where Russian and Saudi policies intersect, as well as the subject of Alexey Khlebnikov's chapter in the volume. Since 2013, ties between Moscow and Cairo have been, once more, on an upward trajectory, with Egyptians purchasing Russian-made arms worth billions, staging joint military exercises, and discussing large-scale investment projects. However, the United States and Europe, as well as the Gulf monarchies, remain the focal point of Egyptian foreign policy. Russia, Khlebnikov opines, will not overinvest in links that, in the past, has proven rather mercurial. The section continues with an overview of Russia's relations with three countries of the Maghreb, Algeria, Morocco, and Tunisia, by Dalia Ghanem. Russia is striking a fine balance between Algeria, a long-standing customer of its arms industry, and its neighbor and rival Morocco. Unlike the Soviet Union that sided with the Algerians in the West Sahara dispute, Russia is opting for positive neutrality. Moscow has worked to develop economic and diplomatic links with post–Arab Spring Tunis, as well. Russian-Israeli ties have blossomed too, since Putin's advent to power two decades ago. In his chapter, Mark N. Katz describes them as resilient and "remarkably friendly," despite the Russian coupling with Iran over Syria and Israel's steadfast alliance with the United States. Spoilers at the regional level make the future of the relationship less than certain, yet Katz argues cooperation between the two states could endure in some shape or form.

Part I

Russia in the Middle East:
From the Soviet Union to Putin

2

The Soviet Union in the Middle East: An Overview

Dimitar Bechev, Florence Gaub, and Nicu Popescu

Geopolitics is back in fashion. Three decades after the Cold War ended, commentators eagerly speculate on the rise and fall of great powers on the global stage. Parallels to the past highlight the rivalry between the United States and Russia along with other emerging players, the quest for clients and allies, and political, security, economic, and ideological competition. Yet the invocation of historical precedents and grand narratives often blurs local nuances and variations. The Middle East and North Africa illustrate the point. At the global level, the Cold War was both an old-school contest for power and a struggle of ideas on social organization and economic development, pitting Soviet communism against Western democracy and capitalism. In the Middle East, however, the former aspect prevailed. In addition, the superpowers' scramble for dominance often empowered local actors. As Yezid Sayigh and Avi Shlaim put it eloquently, "[Middle East states had] a narrower range of interests and much more at stake and [might] therefore be expected to work more energetically and single-mindedly to protect these interests. Moreover, the greater the competition between the external powers, the greater the scope for local initiative and direction."[1] Regional politics imposed costs on both the USSR and the United States. The Cold War in the Middle East was characterized by dramatic shifts and realignments. Fluid boundaries between the two blocs in the region increased the risk of confrontation. Local tensions translated into tensions between Washington and Moscow, a consideration that bore heavily on Soviet policymakers' attitude. On multiple occasions, the two opted for cooperation, driven by the need to avoid risky entanglements which could set in motion dangerous escalation, all the way to a nuclear showdown. In short, the "lessons" of the Cold War for the policymakers of today, whether in Moscow, Washington, Europe, or further afield, are ambiguous.

This chapter looks at Middle Eastern politics, Russia's presence in particular, from a longer historical perspective. Underscoring the importance of factors at the regional level, it aims to shed light on the motivations informing the local responses to Soviet policy.

The Soviets in the Middle East

The early Cold War was mostly fought in Europe and East Asia, with the Middle East and North Africa taking a back seat. The "frontline countries" in the northern tier, Iran and Turkey, were partial exceptions. Yet, both the so-called Azerbaijan crisis of 1946 and the frictions between the Soviets and Turkey over the status of the Straits found relatively speedy resolution, in US favor. Turkey, which had cooperated extensively with the USSR in the interwar years, was admitted into NATO. Together with other pro-Western states such as Iran, Iraq, and Pakistan it signed the 1955 Baghdad Pact, a British initiative whose purpose was to contain the USSR.

Moscow turned to the region as a result of the reshuffle of regional order with the rise of Arab nationalism and the waning of British and French power in the Middle East. Lenin had famously appealed to Muslims to rise against colonialism worldwide in December 1917, communist ideas had made some inroads, for example, the Tudeh Party in Iran, and the Soviets had opened diplomatic legations in Arab countries toward the end of the Second World War. However, around 1950 the region did not appear ripe for revolution. Soviet ideology held limited attraction for Arab nationalists even if they saw, much like Moscow, the old colonial powers as their adversary.[2]

The tide began to turn after the ouster of the Egyptian monarchy by the Free Officers in 1952. Although non-communist, the new regime's anti-bourgeois and anti-imperialist rhetoric chimed with Marxism–Leninism. Furthermore, the Soviet socioeconomic model based on state-driven modernization appealed to populations struggling with underdevelopment, poverty, and quasi-feudal structures. Agrarian reform was one of the first policy priorities of Gamal Abdel Nasser and his comrades in a country where, as of 1947, 6 percent owned more than 65 percent of the land.[3] Demands for land redistribution were on the rise in Syria and Iraq, too.

It was the failure by the United States to engage with emerging political movements and revolutionary regimes that gave the Soviets an edge. By contrast, the new leader in the Kremlin, Nikita Khruschev, identified Third World anti-colonial movements as a key ally in the global struggle waged by the Soviet Union. America's refusal to deliver weapons to Nasser made his turn to the Soviets almost inevitable. In 1955, Egypt secured arms worth $250 million, including 150 MiG fighter jets, from Moscow via Czechoslovakia.[4] This, plus the nationalization of the Suez Canal, led British Prime Minister Anthony Eden to the conclusion that "Nasser, whether he likes it or not, is now effectively in Russian hands, just as Mussolini was in Hitler's," as he wrote to US president Dwight Eisenhower.[5] In an attempt to push back, France and Britain engineered the Suez crisis. The outcome was the exact opposite to what they intended. Both European powers suffered a humiliation, lost regional influence, while the Soviet Union gained influence and prestige as did Nasser's model of socialism and Pan-Arabism.

The USSR benefited from the unraveling of the ancien régime across the region, which had aligned with the United States following Britain and France's departure post-Suez. By the early 1970s, more than half of Middle Eastern monarchs had been toppled and replaced by republican governments keen on root-and-branch change under the banner of Arab nationalism and socialism. In 1971, the Soviets concluded friendship agreements with both Syria, where a radical wing of the Ba'ath Party had seized power in 1966, and Egypt. Iraq, ruled by another offshoot of Ba'ath, signed such a treaty the following year.[6] Such links added immensely to Soviet political influence. Egypt hosted more than 20,000 Soviet military advisors (arriving in civilian clothing to switch to local military uniforms) in the late 1960s and 1970s. Their task was to bolster Egypt's air defenses against Israel, which they did so successfully, thereby denying much of Israel's air advantage.[7] Under an agreement signed in January 1970, Moscow obtained access to Egyptian support bases at Alexandria and Mersa Matruh. The Soviets established naval base in Tartus, Syria, the year to follow.

The Soviets attracted allies beyond the core of the Middle East. Algeria, Sudan, South Yemen, and later Libya gravitated toward Moscow. USSR backed the National Liberation Front (FLN) in the Algerian War, as did the members of the local communist party and Egypt's Nasser. That vindicated the Leninist doctrine of the anti-colonial movements in the Third World as the vanguard in the fight against Western capitalism. Following independence in 1962, Algeria received technical and financial assistance, as well as several loans for the purchase of military equipment. The USSR found another fellow traveler in Colonel Muammar Gaddafi who, upon seizing power in Libya in 1969, promoted his own version of socialism with Arab flavor. It did appear that the Soviet Union was succeeding in making regional states increasingly dependent on its economic and political support. Even NATO member Turkey, cornerstone of the US containment policy, engaged in mass-scale commercial and industrial development projects with the Soviets throughout the 1960s and 1970s.

Yet the perception of rising Soviet influence was largely misleading. Middle Eastern clients did their best to take advantage of Moscow. Being geographically removed from the USSR they had room to maneuver. When US secretary of state John Foster Dulles allegedly warned Nasser about becoming too close to the USSR in the light of Soviet military takeovers in Eastern Europe, Nasser's self-confident reply was "but how can they get at us? They went into Eastern Europe because they had common frontiers, so they could send their armies in. But the Red Army is a long way from Egypt."[8] Unlike the "northern tier" countries such as Turkey, Iran, and eventually Afghanistan, Egypt had fewer reasons to fear Soviet interference.

Unwanted Wars

For the USSR, involvement in the Middle East was a mixed blessing. Arab leaders were both a geopolitical asset and a cause of trouble. Sure enough, they helped the Soviets advance their objectives: build presence in the Middle East, undermine US power and achieve strategic parity in a vast region from the East Mediterranean to the Indian Ocean, and nudge countries on a "noncapitalist" development path. Yet USSR risked being sucked into local rivalries and conflicts that had little to do with either communist ideology or its strategic interests.

Nasser, along with the great majority of Arab secular nationalists, viewed the Soviet Union as an ally in the struggle against Israel. All the way into the early 1970s, they hoped that Soviet weaponry, military training, as well as direct help on the battlefield would help them tip the balance of power in their own favor. Though initially skeptical, the Soviets eventually developed close ties with the Palestine Liberation Organization (PLO), declaring it in 1972, "the vanguard of Arab liberation."

The Soviet Union stance on Israel diverged from that of the Arabs. For one, despite its early disillusionment with the notion that Israel, led by left-leaning Jews from Eastern Europe, could become an ally, it did accept its right of existence as a state. Moscow severed diplomatic relations with Tel Aviv only in 1967, as a result of the Six-Day War. Yet it backed UN Security Council Resolution 242 (November 22, 1967) establishing the "land for peace" principle and guaranteeing "the sovereignty, territorial integrity and political independence of every State in the area." The Arab coalition's defeat in the conflict dealt a blow to Soviet prestige, too. An US ally, equipped with American-made hardware and technology, decimated the armies of Egypt and Syria, Soviet clients armed and supported with advice and military intelligence by Moscow, as well as that of Jordan. Last but certainly not least, the Soviet leadership did not want regional wars provoked by Middle Eastern rulers' penchant for brinkmanship to escalate into superpower conflict or put in jeopardy the *détente* with the United States.[9]

The 1973 Arab-Israeli war offers another good example of the tail wagging the dog. In the run-up to the conflict, Moscow tried—in vain—to dissuade the Arabs from going to war.[10] In fact, Egypt hoped that the presence of Soviet troops in Egypt would drag the USSR into the fight should things turn sour for Cairo. When the Soviets refused to fight Israel directly, Cairo was disappointed. In Egyptian eyes, the 1973 war left a "legacy of mutual distrust and suspicion. The Arabs accused the Russians of coming to their aid during the fighting with too little and too late, both in respect of arms and diplomatic support" while the Soviets thought the Arabs failed to fight.[11] Even though the Soviet Union had troops on the ground in Egypt and up to forty Soviet soldiers were killed by Israel in the years before that war, they refrained from taking part in the fighting (though they supplied the Arabs with arms). The 1973 war also threatened to spill over in a direct clash between the superpowers, as the United States also ramped up its assistance to the Israelis. The US Sixth Fleet and the Soviet Mediterranean Squadron faced off in the open sea. On October 24, 1973, US nuclear forces across the world were put on high alert, the worst escalation since the Cuban Missile Crisis eleven years earlier.

Syrian-Soviet relations provided ample proof of how Middle Eastern leaders ignored Soviet interests. Seizing power through a coup in November 1970, Hafez al-Assad sought military assistance from Moscow and met Leonid Brezhnev several times. However, in 1976, he intervened in Lebanon against the PLO, another Soviet ally, putting his superpower partner in an embarrassing position. Assad acted on the premise that a Palestinian victory against the Maronite militias, backed by Israel, would provoke an invasion from the south and harm Syria's own security. Regional power politics prevailed over Cold War alignments. Assad, ever the pragmatic, turned back to Moscow only after the signature of the 1978 Camp David accords, which broke apart the Syrian-Egyptian axis opposing Israel. In 1980, after declining to do so, he signed an agreement with USSR stipulating that "if a third party were to invade Syrian territory, the Soviet Union would become involved in the events." The USSR sent in five thousand to six thousand military advisors (roughly equal to the number of Russian deployment in 2016–17) and massive amounts of weaponry. The agreement came at a time when Assad was weakened internally by the rise of the Muslim Brotherhood, culminating in the Hama massacre carried out by the regime in February 1982, as well as the challenge posed by his brother Rifaat al-Assad. Yet the Syrian leader made sure he did not go all the way to the Soviets and alienate the United States.[12] When Moscow requested a naval base in Latakia-Banias (in addition to their facility in Tartus), Syria refused.[13]

The Syrians could also be disrespectful in other ways. An anecdote related by Arkadii Vinogradov, a Soviet diplomat in Damascus and senior advisor to the Syrian defense minister, tells the story of Mohammed Suleiman, a cadet at the military academy in Moscow in the 1980s.[14] Suleiman was sentenced for killing three Russian girls in a drunk driving incident. In response, Syrians staged a road accident to frame the deputy to the chief Soviet military advisor in Damascus. The Soviet army captain was jailed and then exchanged for Suleiman. Upon his return to Syria, Suleiman was made a colonel and appointed advisor to the president. He went on to become a brigadier general and one of the most influential aides to Bashar al-Assad. (He was killed by snipers during a party at his seafront villa in Tartus in 2008. Some suspected the Israelis,[15] while a WikiLeaks cable linked his murder to factional struggles in the regime.)[16]

Superpower Self-Restraint

While competing in the Middle East, superpowers acted with self-restraint and even opted for cooperation. For the USSR, stability at the systemic level came before commitment to partners and regional interests. After the ceasefire in the Yom Kippur War, Leonid Brezhnev allegedly inveighed against Arab allies in the following terms:

> They [the Arabs] can go to hell! We have offered them a sensible way for so many years. But no, they wanted to fight. Fine! We gave them the latest technology. They had double superiority in tanks and aircraft, triple in artillery, and in air defence and anti-tank weapons they had absolute supremacy. And then what? Sadat woke me up twice in the middle of the night over the phone, "Save me!" He demanded that we send Soviet troops, and immediately! No! We are not going to fight for them. The people would not understand that. And especially we will not start a world war because of them.[17]

The Soviet Union's overtures toward the United States harmed its credibility with Egypt. The Egyptians complained when in 1969 "Gromyko produced yet another proposal for a settlement which bore remarkable similarities to an American proposal."[18] Despite a lot of mutually hostile rhetoric between the United States and the USSR, the two superpowers tried to avoid entanglement into a direct military confrontation through the scheming of their regional allies. When the United States and France launched their military interventions in the Lebanese civil war in 1982, Syria tried to persuade the USSR to do the same, but Moscow refused (although individual Soviet officers embedded with Syrian army units still ended up in Lebanon). Superpower *détente* signaled to regional actors, be it Egypt, Syria, or the PLO, that the Soviets would put relations with the United States first.

How Soviets Failed

Soviet presence started shrinking in 1972, when Egypt's president Anwar Sadat expelled the military advisors. Although Moscow preserved ties with Syria, Algeria, South Yemen, Libya, and so on, it never managed to export its political system, secure the political dependence and allegiance of the Arab states, and ultimately contain the United States in the region. By contrast, America's alliances with the conservative monarchies of the Gulf, Israel, and Turkey persisted. The United States lost Iran but managed to forge a partnership with Egypt. There were four reasons why the USSR failed.

First, Arab states had just gained independence after a long period of imperial rule—by France, the British Empire, or the Ottomans. They were not eager to submit to another foreign overlord. More importantly, as independence had been largely won under a nationalist banner, these states were implicitly at odds with Soviet ideology. After all, communism prophesized—though never practiced in earnest—the withering away of nation states and the advent of classless society. But although communist parties sprang up in every Arab country, they failed to gain traction. Arab nationalism exerted a far stronger appeal and it had a complicated relationship with communists. As Patrick Seale explains in the case of Syria, "Ba'thist leaders remained wary of communism at home. They knew that Marxist internationalism was the enemy of Arab nationalism and they had little interest in a 'world proletarian revolution.' Ba'thists had on occasions allied themselves tactically with the communists in battles against 'reactionary' enemies, but they never forgot that the communists were dangerous rivals."[19] Tunisian president Habib Bourguiba noted in an op-ed for *Foreign Affairs* in 1957, "the struggle for national independence served as a restraint and a deterrent" against communism.[20] The intervention in Afghanistan in 1979 dealt the coup de grâce to the Soviet Union's claim that it was the standard bearer of national liberation and the fight against imperialism.

Second, although communism appealed to lower strata, its focus was on the working class. But at this point, the latter was too small to count politically. Though the Second World War had given industrialization a strong boost, the urban proletariat was small in number and incapable of giving rise to a cohesive movement. The vast majority of lower-class Arabs worked in the agricultural sector, as small-scale peasants or land laborers. During the Cold War, many leftists in the region drew inspiration from Mao's teachings of preindustrial agrarian society as the basis for socialist revolution. It was China, rather than the Soviets, that provided the strongest backing for PLO in the 1960s. The People's Democratic Republic of Yemen was a rare example of an orthodox

Marxist party taking over. Tudeh, the only mass communist-influenced political force, never managed to come on top in Iran. The Turkish left was internally split, with Maoists and pro-Moscow factions in competition, and kept in check by the military and the state establishment.

Third, communism's opposition to religion sat ill with conservative Islamic societies. The Soviet experience in the Caucasus, Central Asia, and other areas populated with Muslims seemed of little relevance. At one meeting of the Non-Aligned Movement, Libya's Gaddafi settled the matter by explaining that the Quran was the source of Libya's socialist model, rather than Marxism–Leninism.[21] It was around this time, in the late 1970s, that Moscow was forced to recognize that other nations might follow their own path to Marxism, separate from the Soviet Union. Ultimately, Islamism crowded out socialism by taking aboard social justice as an issue. The Iranian revolution of 1979, originally supported by the left, went a long way in establishing the notion of a third way, different from both Western capitalism and Soviet communism. It begot a new crop of social movements across the Middle East, which also presented a challenge to the Arab nationalism and socialism embraced by the incumbent regimes whose promise of modernization, growth, and social welfare faltered.

Lastly but most importantly, the Soviet Union failed to become the region's patron because of its unwillingness to take sides in the conflict with Israel. Although Israel never became the communist state Moscow had originally hoped it would, the Soviets hesitated to take a hard line against it. Its policy stressed peaceful conflict resolution through the UN Security Council, that is, through cooperation with the United States. The Soviets failed to support other allies, just the same. Although Moscow condemned American strikes on Tripoli in 1986, it did not do much more to help its ally Libya.[22] Palestinians, too, kept lines of communication open to the United States, not unlike Syria or other Soviet partners.

Conclusion

Soviet Union's lasting presence in the Middle East during the Cold War has distorted perceptions as to the extent of its influence. Neither Egypt, nor Syria, Algeria, Libya, or the PLO, turned out to be faithful clients for the Soviet Union. By the mid-1970s, Moscow's geopolitical "offensive was in a state of total collapse," in the words of Nasser's friend and onetime propaganda minister Mohamed Heikal.[23] Relations with friendly regimes did not lend themselves to the export of Soviet-style communism to the region or, for that matter, the consolidation of a bloc of satellites and vassal states. By the time Mikhail Gorbachev came to power and launched the so-called new political thinking prioritizing rapprochement with the West, USSR was well on its way out from the Middle East and North Africa. The Soviet model had lost its former glimmer as the superpower's economy decayed from within and lagged far behind in growth rates, productivity, and innovation from the industrialized West. Indeed, Western allies in the Middle East—the oil-rich Gulf monarchies, Israel, and Turkey—outperformed the likes of Egypt and Syria.

Even so, the Cold War has left a powerful legacy. Russia's opening to the Middle East and North Africa from the 2000s onward benefited from old ties across the region. Local actors look at Moscow as a partner and counterweight to the West. But unlike its Soviet predecessor, the Russian Federation is not bound by ideology and acts with greater flexibility. Its ambitions are less far-reaching too and resources more limited. Still, the formative experience of the Cold War sets a benchmark and, arguably, informs Moscow's perceptions and objectives in the present.

3

What Drives Russia's Policy in the Middle East?

Dmitri Trenin

Russia's policy in the Middle East is important in its own right—Moscow has made a spectacular comeback to an extremely volatile region. Yet it matters even more as a crucible of the country's emerging new global foreign policy, which is very different from both the practices of the last quarter-century and from those of Soviet times.

This chapter builds upon a short book published in late 2017.[1] It argued that Russia's reentry into the Middle East, culminating in the military intervention in Syria, was essentially part of its endeavor to return to the global chessboard as a great power. Other motives—reversing the dynamics of the Arab Spring, stemming the surge in Islamist radicalism, physically eliminating extremists hailing from Russia itself, or indeed turning Syria into a geopolitical stronghold and military base in the region—were secondary.

The book also highlighted what appeared to be new and distinctive features of Moscow's foreign policy, which manifest themselves in its actions in the Middle East. These were essentially pragmatism and political realism, characterized by a willingness to deal with all relevant players, treating no one wholly as an ally or wholly as an adversary; an ability to straddle conflictual divides, whether between the Israelis and the Iranians, the Turks and the Kurds, or the Sunni and Shia; and maintaining a clear focus on Russia's own national interests, whether linked to setting the oil price or promoting arms sales, ensuring technology transfers from Israel or investment from the Gulf states.

This chapter allows the author not to plough the same ground again but instead avail of the opportunity to take up the analysis where it was left off.

Russia and the Middle Eastern Conundrum

In December 2017, Vladimir Putin, on a flying visit to the Russian air base in Kmeimim, Syria, famously proclaimed victory in the military campaign against Daesh and the opponents of Bashar al-Assad's regime. The aftermath of that victory, of course, has demonstrated the many difficulties involved in making peace among Syrians and of managing the diverging interests of the regional players involved in the conflict. In April 2018, the US strikes in Syria, provoked by the alleged use of chemical weapons in the town of Douma,[2] raised for the first time in several decades the specter of a direct military collision between Washington and Moscow. In May 2018, the Trump Administration's withdrawal from the Joint Comprehensive Plan of Action (JCPOA) raised the prospect of a war between the United States and Iran. Suddenly, the Europeans found themselves closer to the Russian position on an important issue than to that of their transatlantic ally. Shortly before that, Israeli prime minister Binyamin Netanyahu conferred with Vladimir Putin in Moscow on Russia's sacred Victory Day, just before launching a massive attack against Iranian targets in Syria, both countries being Russian allies.

The Middle Eastern conundrum seems tortuous and intractable. Yet, there are ways of negotiating the region's difficult geopolitical terrain, and, at the time of writing, Russia is continuing its diplomatic and military foray. As it proceeds, there are valuable takeaways at each turn of events, which help inform Moscow's policy in the region and beyond. To identify the "lessons learned," the chapter examines several key issues: the management of a Syria where the war has ebbed but peace remains elusive; the emerging rules of engagement between Russian and US military forces in the Middle East; and the careful balancing between regional antagonists who are all valuable partners for Russia.

War after Victory in Syria

There was little doubt in serious observers' minds that the victory announced by President Putin at Khmeimim was a victory in a military campaign confirming Damascus as the main winner, rather than an harbinger of peace in the war-ravaged land. Triumphing on the battlefield, Moscow immediately faced the wrath of the defeated parties and their sponsors.

The "peace congress" in Sochi, which Russian diplomacy had painstakingly sought to prepare within the so-called Astana process as the diplomatic platform for political negotiations between the Syrian government and the armed opposition, proved a failure.[3] In Moscow's view the Syrian opposition, its Arab sponsors, and Western countries were united in their determination not to let Russia convert the fruits of its success on the battlefield into a lasting political dividend.

The setback in the peace process must have disappointed Russian diplomats, but it only boosted the resolve of the military and eventually the Kremlin to press the opposition even harder. Russian forces helped Bashar al-Assad to eliminate a major pocket of resistance in the Eastern Ghouta province in April 2018. This enclave, so near to the Syrian capital, had been a major irritant and a source of real danger. Even the Russian embassy in Damascus had been repeatedly targeted by Islamist rebels from positions as close as only 10 km away. Thus, the Russian response to the diplomatic blockade was to do "another Aleppo": help the Syrian government forces to clear out a rebel stronghold. As in Eastern Aleppo in late 2016, the regime succeeded in winning back control over a strategically vital area, evacuating the surviving rebel fighters to the biggest remaining enclave, Idlib on the Turkish border. Having accomplished this, the Russians went on to help Assad win control over the insurgent-held areas in southwestern Syria, close to the Golan Heights.[4]

With the peace process stalled and the political settlement as originally anticipated by Moscow in doubt, Russia switched from Plan A (power-sharing among the parties in some new all-Syrian arrangement) to Plan B (helping consolidate Damascus's control over the most important parts of the country). The main political problem it now faced was no longer the opposition's recalcitrance, which was taken as a provisional "no" to a negotiated settlement but rather Bashar al-Assad's now greatly enhanced ambition to restore his regime's rule over all of Syria. An emboldened Bashar was clearly playing the Russians off against the Iranians, his other major ally and sponsor. Moscow was not amused.

Indeed, Moscow had entered into a situational alliance with both Tehran and Ankara since late 2016, but right from the start that alliance was very different from either the NATO model or the Soviet-era Warsaw Pact. Russia acknowledged and de facto accepted what it considered the legitimate national security interests of its notional allies. Thus, it agreed with Ankara that allowing the Kurdistan Workers' Party (*Partiya Karkerên Kurdistanê*, PKK) bases and training camps in the Kurdish-held Syrian territory along the Turkish border would constitute a threat to Turkey's security and stability. Putin, who hosted Recep Tayyip Erdoğan in Sochi in January 2018 and made a point of traveling to Ankara on his first foreign trip after his reelection as president in March 2018, must have privately given the nod to Erdoğan's military invasion of Afrin in northwest Syria. Yet Putin must have also extracted a pledge from Erdoğan that the invasion would remain limited, and that Turkey would refrain from attempting to undermine the regime in Damascus. As for the Kurds, while taking the risk of facing a Kurdish outcry over the Turkish operation, Russia continued to support Kurdish autonomy within Syria[5]—against the preferences of its ally in Damascus.

The situation in Idlib, the last major enclave in Syria still held by extremists and radicals, illustrates Russia's dilemma regarding Turkey. In September 2018, Putin and Erdoğan agreed on a plan to deal with Idlib, which had become a base for jihadists' forays into the Syrian government-held areas, and even for drone attacks against the Russian bases in Latakia. Under the agreement, Russia was content to leave isolating and neutralizing Hayat Tahrir al-Sham (HTS) within the enclave to Ankara, while restraining Damascus from launching an offensive that would have resulted in numerous civilian casualties. Yet, when Turkey proved unable to fulfill its commitment, Russia did not allow the Syrians to move in, but exercised strategic patience instead. Russian warplanes occasionally engaged targets in Idlib, but Moscow decided to tolerate the situation for a while, believing it to be the lesser evil. The other options—risking a breakdown of relations with Turkey or a European opprobrium as a result of the Syrian offensive—were rejected as unpalatable.

Yet, when by the end of 2019 the tactics used by Damascus and supported by Moscow, of chipping away parts of Idlib, provoked a military pushback by Ankara, the Russo-Turkish relationship was put to the hardest test since the downing of the Russian warplane in November 2015.

In February–March 2020, President Putin had to engage again in diplomatic heavy lifting with President Erdoğan. For both leaders, staying engaged, while having to bicker from time to time, was preferable to breaking off the relationship. Half-hearted and lacking real trust, cooperation between the two countries has been restored and continues.

With regard to Iran, Russia understood Tehran's need to maintain a land link to its Lebanese ally Hezbollah. Moscow regarded the Shia movement as a legitimate politico-military actor in the region rather than a terrorist organization. Yet it also looked askance at Iranian attempts to threaten Israel from within Syria. While Russia acknowledged Iran and Hezbollah's role in achieving the very victory announced by Putin—the Russian military has never believed that any war could be won by air campaigns alone—it never supported Tehran's ambition to control Syria in league with the Assad regime and the Alawites. Russo-Iranian competition for influence has been a fixture of Damascus politics since the beginning of the Russian intervention in 2015—a factor often exploited by Bashar al-Assad to his advantage. It is likewise telling that within the Lebanese body politic Russia has come to be regarded as a potential guarantor of the country's unity since 2018. Locals point at Moscow's close ties to the principal outside players with antagonistic interests in Lebanon: Iran, Syria, and Israel.

US–Russian Rules of Engagement

In February 2018, Moscow was confronted with an embarrassing situation when a number of Russian mercenaries, recruited by Wagner, a private Russian military company operating in Syria, got into trouble as they tried to wrestle control of an oil well from a US-backed Kurdish militia. The Russians, acting on behalf of pro-Damascus business interests, reportedly ignored US warnings, came under attack by the American forces, and suffered substantial casualties.[6] It is not clear why the US warnings had been ignored, or what kind of a relationship actually existed between the private company, still illegal under Russian law, and the Russian forces in Syria. In any event, Moscow replaced its top military commander in Syria, but abstained from retaliating against the United States, probably recognizing that Wagner had gone too far. This recognition must have contributed to establishing the rules of engagement between Russia and the United States in Syria.

A much more serious episode happened exactly two months later, as the United States launched missile strikes in response to an alleged chemical attack by Assad's forces against civilians. Weeks before the incident, General Valery Gerasimov, chief of the Russian General Staff, warned about a coming "provocation" in the form of a fabricated chemical weapons attack near Damascus, which would then be used as a pretext for massive US strikes against the Syrian government's forces. Should that happen, Gerasimov warned, and if Russian personnel or assets were affected, Russia would not only intercept the incoming US missiles but also launch counterstrikes against American troops.

This was, in a nutshell, the scenario of the first US–Russian military showdown since the Cold War era. When the incident accepted by Washington as a chemical attack launched by the Syrian regime happened in April 2018, and President Trump vowed to retaliate, the two states found themselves closer to a direct military confrontation than they had been for over half a century. However, despite all the bombast coming from Trump, the actual strikes turned out to be very limited. The United States, supported by Britain and France, destroyed just three structures described as Syrian chemical weapons facilities and incurred no casualties—either Syrian or Russian, military or civilian. In the run-up to these strikes, James Mattis, the US Secretary of Defense, and General Dunford, the chairman of the Joint Chiefs of Staff, expressly pleaded for the utmost restraint. Deterrence had worked. The United States and Russia, despite their highly adversarial relationship, have de facto agreed to refrain from action that would result in a head-on clash between their militaries. The deconfliction mechanism, first established between Russian and US forces in Syria in 2015, was tested and found effective.

It has also expanded beyond the regional commanders in the Middle East to include the defense ministers and defense chiefs of the two countries, as well as the supreme commander of NATO forces in Europe. The "hot line" between the Kremlin and the White House is in regular use as well. In early 2018, the three Russian intelligence chiefs, heads of the Federal Security Service (FSB), the Foreign Intelligence Service (SVR), and the Military Intelligence Directorate (GRU), made an unprecedented visit to the United States. This is a far cry from the situation in 1962 when there was a sole channel of communication involving the KGB station chief in Washington and Robert Kennedy, the US president's brother. Unlike in 1962, however, deconfliction these days does not necessarily lead to de-escalation of the wider US–Russian conflict.

Indeed, it is the security chiefs' channel that has become virtually the only place for a dialogue of sorts between Russia and the United States. The Middle East features prominently there among the topics. In June 2019, the secretary of the Russian Federation's Security Council Nikolai Patrushev conferred in Jerusalem with the US national security advisor John Bolton and the head of the Israeli National Security Council. The three discussed at length the situation in Syria and Iran-related developments related to Iran.

Managing Antagonists

On May 9, 2018, the million-strong Victory Day procession in Moscow, with people carrying portraits of relatives who fought (and in many cases died) in the Great Patriotic War, the so-called march of the "Immortal Regiment," included a rare participant, Binyamin Netanyahu. The Israeli prime minister carried a photo of a Jewish Soviet colonel, a hero of the Soviet Union. Netanyahu, however, had come not only to mark the anniversary of the victory over Nazi Germany. Having just revealed documents describing Iran's nuclear program, he meant to engage Putin in a discussion of what to do about the issue as well as about Islamic Republic's growing—and, from Israel's perspective, menacing—presence in Syria.

The details of the conversation will remain unavailable to the general public. However, within hours of the leaders' meeting, the Israeli Defense Force hit scores of Iranian targets in Syria. Moscow issued only a pro forma statement calling on all sides to show restraint and avoid escalation. The Russians have long been trying to straddle one of the most serious lines of fracture in the Middle East, that between Israel and Iran. They were probably unimpressed by Netanyahu's Iranian disclosures, whose aim was to give Donald Trump a fresh argument for leading the United States out of the JCPOA. At the same time, the Russian leadership took Israeli concerns about the Iranian presence on the ground in Syria much more seriously. As noted already, Moscow and Tehran do share some important interests in Syria, but certainly not all. When the Iranians launched their missiles into the Israeli-held Golan Heights, they, in the Russian analysis, went too far. Occasionally, the Russians believe, Israel also oversteps limits. The Iranian missile strikes were in retaliation for an Israeli attack against an Iranian base in Syria, code-named T-4. By publicly revealing the identity of the attacker, Russia probably sent a signal to Israel. The ensuing missile exchange between Iran and Israel, which did not escalate further, probably yielded a situation of mutual deterrence. As for Moscow, it will continue looking for a balance between what it regards as the legitimate security interests of its situational ally Tehran and its valuable partner Israel.

Regarding President Trump's decision in May 2018 to withdraw from JCPOA, Russia vowed to support the accord even without United States being part of it. As a result of Washington's move, UK, France, and Germany found themselves, uneasily, closer to Russia than to the Trump Administration. From Moscow's perspective, this opens a window for productive cooperation with US European allies that it does not see as Russia's actual opponents—unlike the United States, again the main adversary. Yet, so far little has been achieved in this field.

The Middle East as a Springboard for Russia's Global Influence

Engagement in the Middle East since 2015 has contributed greatly to the perception of Russia's expanding global influence. There are a number of good reasons for this. These include:

— With the intervention in Syria, Russian foreign policy stopped being largely defensive and limited essentially to the former USSR. While in Ukraine, Moscow went onto a counteroffensive—against, as the Kremlin saw it, Western encroachments in its strategic glacis—in Syria, Russia undertook an offensive operation and succeeded, as Putin later admitted,[7] beyond its own expectations. As a result, Russia markedly improved its standing across the Arab world, from Libya to Egypt to the Gulf; cemented its relations with Turkey and Iran;
— Russia adopted a more flexible approach in its foreign policy, compared to the Soviet period. It ignores no relevant actor, but keeps close contacts with all. Moscow can partner with anyone, provided interests align sufficiently and the terms of interaction are right. Russia does not take sides but simply follows its own self-interest. It has learned to manage adversaries, like Iran and Saudi Arabia, and even antagonists, such as Israel and Iran. It can employ this approach in other contested areas, from Afghanistan to Central and South Asia;

— During the Syria campaign, Russia has learned the art of establishing and managing twenty-first-century alliances, which is very different from the past Soviet and current US experience. These alliances are dynamic rather than static. They should be flexible, limited in time, territorially circumscribed and have precise objectives. Moscow's alliances with Ankara, Tehran, and Damascus, none of them perfect, have proven themselves rather effective as geopolitical and military instruments;

— The Syrian operation has highlighted the difference that Russia's successful military reform has made. For the first time since the withdrawal from Afghanistan in 1989, the Kremlin again has usable military power at its disposal. Russia's comeback to the world stage via Syria was only made possible by its military victories. As a result, the prestige of Russian arms has grown both in the region, including in the Gulf, and beyond it, from Turkey to India, which decided to buy major Russian weapons systems ignoring US warnings. Russia has also established itself as a security partner in several African countries, from Sudan to the Central African Republic to Congo;

— Kremlin's strong political will, its resolute action and successful execution from Crimea to Syria, and its effective support for its allies such as Assad or Nicolas Maduro in Venezuela have earned it a reputation for high impact on modest investment. This strikes a sharp contrast with the ongoing warfare within the US political elite, the self-defeating behavior of the UK ruling class over Brexit and the lingering inability of the European Union to get its act together in the foreign policy realm, or even to deal effectively initially with the spread of the coronavirus;

— Russia's world influence has grown also against the background of the widespread disillusionment with globalization and with the liberal democratic model that underpins it. The crisis provoked by the COVID-19 pandemic has further aggravated the situation. Russia offers no social model of its own, but it is putting on display the powers of a strong and self-conscious state, which appears consistent with the current global trend.

Russia's foreign policy, of course, is not without flaws, some fundamental. One obvious one is the narrowness and relative weakness of the Russian economic base. Falling back technologically, not only vis-à-vis the West but also the rising states such as China, is another major problem. One needs to add to that Russia's stagnant to negative demographics. For the time being, Russia is certainly punching above its weight both globally and regionally.

Russia's Limitations in the Middle East

This chapter's largely illustrative overview highlights the salient features of Moscow's foreign policy in the Middle East. Russia engages militarily and diplomatically abroad in support of its claim to great power status. It continues to use its newly revived and rebuilt military power, still very modest by Pentagon standards, judiciously and overall quite effectively. It takes a *Realpolitik* approach to international relations, which works well in the Middle East. It has been able to deter the United States and has accepted the need to exercise restraint in its own actions. It has been ruthless to its opponents on the battlefield, but has found managing its own allies, like Bashar al-Assad, every bit as challenging. It has also been able to work across the challenging divides in the Middle East while promoting its own interests.

It is unclear whether this situation is sustainable in the long run. Russia is not the region's dominant power and its recognized security overlord, nor does it harbor ambition of becoming one. If push comes to shove, and Israel and Iran do engage in a real war, which would probably mean Israeli airstrikes on Iranian territory and retaliatory action by the Islamic Republic or proxies such Hezbollah, Russia would probably have to step aside. Relations with both Jerusalem and Tehran are bound to suffer. Moscow's current efforts, however, are aimed precisely at preventing such a situation from arising and helping establish a crude mutual deterrence between the two antagonists. On important, though less conflictual issues, such as the future of the 2020 agreement among the OPEC+ group on oil production, Russia has to deal with difficult players such as Saudi Arabia and Iran bearing in mind its own national interest.

Of course, Russia has to contend with a number of limitations. The economic and financial base of its foreign policy overall, and in the Middle East specifically, is still inadequate for a country that projects itself as a great power. Currently, Russia obviously punches above its nominal weight, measured in gross domestic product (GDP) terms, but skillfully compensates this with diplomatic activism and military successes, as well as its strong position as a major oil producer. However, its rather weak standing in the region's foreign trade landscape—where it does not feature prominently except as the exporter of a few key items, such as weapons, grain, and nuclear technology—limits its influence. Its information resources—including the RT Arabic television channel— fall far short of those of Western countries, and thus Moscow is virtually unable to correct the highly negative view of its policies in the Middle East that is prevalent in the Western media. And lastly the extremely pragmatic, "piecemeal" approach that has characterized the Russian handling of the region's issues has so far impeded a more strategic approach to the Middle East. Such an approach would require developing a long-term view of the region's place and role in Russia's twenty-first-century global foreign policy; devising a set of sub-strategies toward various countries, ranging from an eventual settlement in Syria to a future management of Iran's nuclear program after the 2018 US withdrawal from the JCPOA to stable partnerships with Turkey, Israel, and Egypt; and harmonizing those policies within a broader region-wide approach. With luck, Russia may manage to develop such a strategy in the future.

Part II

Russian Policy in Action

4

Russia in Syria: A Military Analysis

Anton Lavrov

Russia's armed intervention in the Syrian civil war has been the first large-scale military operation that it has undertaken so far abroad since the fall of the Soviet Union. It has already had lasting political and military consequences reverberating throughout the entire region. In order to gauge the intervention's success, it is necessary to identify Russia's goals and motivations in the Syrian conflict. Generally, the operation has provided a unique opportunity to observe Russia's reformed military and new capabilities in action, shedding light on both strengths and weaknesses. As a result, Moscow has been able to draw valuable lessons from the performance of its armed forces.

Russia's Aims

The official goal behind Russia's military operation was to fight internationally recognized terrorist groups—the so-called "Islamic State of Iraq and Syria" (ISIS) and al-Nusra. Moscow had reason to be concerned about the rise of Islamic extremism: the newly proclaimed "Islamic Caliphate" affected it directly. By the end of 2015, up to five thousand to seven thousand people from the Russian Federation and the post-Soviet states had joined the ranks of ISIS (or Daesh).[1] In June 2015, most jihadi terrorist groups in the Russian Caucasus, Chechnya, and Dagestan had switched allegiance from al-Qaeda to Daesh.[2] But from the very first days of the Syrian intervention, Russia's air force began strikes against other anti-Assad rebel groups, including even militias supported by the United States and Turkey.[3] In fact, most targets initially were groups separate from Daesh.[4] This did not come as a big surprise, since even before sending troops to the region, Russia had firmly backed Assad's efforts to crush the uprising. And at this stage of the war, the insurgents, rather than the Daesh militants occupying the remote desert regions, threatened the very existence of the Syrian regime.

Russia launched its intervention in pursuit of strategic but also immediate, practical objectives. It aimed to interrupt the cycle of regime change that had swept through the Middle East in the wake of the 2011 Arab Spring and to ensure the survival of the Assad regime. Russia acted to preserve order. In the view of the Kremlin, a strong, united, and functioning state is a necessary condition to suppress terrorism. In a TV interview conducted on the day before Russia's military operation in Syria started, Vladimir Putin said: "we are trying to prevent the creation of a power vacuum in Syria in general because as soon as the government agencies in a state, in a country are destroyed, a power vacuum sets in, and that vacuum is quickly filled with terrorists. This was the case in Libya and Iraq; this was the case in some other countries."[5]

In addition to these obvious goals, Russia also had another, less conspicuous reason for intervening in Syria. Many Western politicians and analysts believed that the Russian leadership aimed to deflect attention from the Ukraine conflict. Latvian president Rajmonds Vejonis remarked in a television interview that "at the time when Russia began to scale down its efforts in Eastern Ukraine, the Kremlin began to use the situation in Syria to improve its domestic reputation and to divert international attention from Ukraine."[6] Russian foreign minister Sergey Lavrov dismissed such allegations as "something which sick minds are presenting to the media."[7] But there was at least some truth in the Latvian president's take. Though large-scale fighting in the Donbass region of Eastern Ukraine had ended in February 2015, the political consequences of the conflict for Russia were still grievous. The Ukrainian question continued to overshadow its relations with the West. Moreover, the US-led attempt to politically isolate Russia from the rest of the world was a blow to Putin's pride.[8]

In this sense, quite plausibly, Russia settled on Daesh as a convenient enemy. Having entered the fight against the terrorist organization, Russia wanted to demonstrate that it could be a useful partner for the West, capable of resolving the most pressing international problems. Speaking at the United Nations General Assembly, President Putin called for the creation of "a genuinely broad international coalition" to fight Daesh.[9]

The intervention in Syria was a dangerous gamble. But it enjoyed a certain success from the very beginning. Days before the start of the Russian air campaign, the United States was forced to restore military-to-military contacts with Russia, after a break of a year and a half, in order to avoid incidents.[10] The first meeting between Vladimir Putin and Barack Obama since the annexation of Crimea also took place on the sidelines of the UN General Assembly in late September 2015.[11] But while contacts with the United States remained very limited, relations with most of the countries of the Middle East dramatically improved.[12] Russia managed to break out of its political isolation, and the Ukrainian question was put on the back burner even in Europe.

The Russian Military Footprint in Syria

Initially, the Russian leadership did not plan to be drawn into a prolonged conflict. Moscow's deployment of modernized aircraft and new precision weapons was expected to deliver a quick victory for Assad. Alexey Pushkov, chairman of the Foreign Affairs Committee of the Duma, anticipated that Russian operations in Syria would last "three or four months."[13] One year down the line, Russian deputy foreign minister Mikhail Bogdanov recalled: "when our active actions began, and our airforce joined the fight against terrorists, we expected that the operation would last for several months."[14] Such assessments were to prove overly optimistic. But Russia was able to adapt to the new reality of prolonged conflict and successfully support a small expeditionary force in Syria over an extended period of time.

Depending on the strategic situation, the number of aircraft at the Russian base in Syria fluctuated from more than forty warplanes in early 2016 and at the end of 2017 to just twenty to twenty-four during a lull in summer 2016. The absolute minimum was recorded in November 2018, with only eighteen warplanes. There were also about twenty Russian attack and transport helicopters in Syria at any given time. In addition to the forces stationed in the country, navy ships and submarines attacked targets in Syria with cruise missiles from the Mediterranean and the Caspian Sea. Russia deployed a squadron of a dozen Tu-22M3 long-range bombers at the border air base in Mozdok (North Ossetia), which delivered massed strikes in Syria with free-falling bombs. The strategic bombers Tu-160 and Tu-95MS were used in small groups, flying from their bases in Russia and attacking targets with cruise missiles. But their missions were not numerous, the purpose being training and power demonstration.

The intervention involved small contingents of ground troops—for the protection of external perimeter of two Russian bases. Only the experimental artillery group and the groups of Special Operations Forces fighters took part in active combat. Also, Russian military advisers were assigned to almost all Syrian regular army units from battalion level upward. They consisted of several staff officers, artillery spotters, aviation controllers, translators, and support personnel.[15]

Russia for the first time deployed its military police abroad. It was formed just a few months before the start of the Russian operation, in March 2015. As Russia helped government in Damascus to retake parts of territory, the contingents of Russia's military police increased and the role they played expanded. Reportedly, by mid-2017 there were 1,200 Russian military policemen in Syria.[16] This contingent has been beefed up with extra three hundred servicemen in 2019.[17] If before the military police largely ensured inner security of the Russian military facilities, from 2016 onward these units were also involved in security of convoys, distribution of aid in government-controlled areas, and monitoring of the de-escalation zones. Used to boost Russia's soft power, on several occasions Russia's military police came under attack and had to employ lethal means.[18]

In a more proactive role, military police were used during the Turkish Peace Spring operation in 2019. At first, it helped the Assad government establish partial control over the Kurdish territories. Then, by agreement with Ankara, it launched joint patrols with the Turkish military in the security zone in the Kurdish areas along the border between Turkey and Syria. In March 2020, Russian military police was used to stop the advance of Turkish-backed militants in Idlib.[19]

The Russian Ministry of Defense did not and still does not disclose the total strength of the Russian contingent. But judging from indirect information, even at peak times, it only consisted of about five thousand people. After the number of Russian forces was reduced in December 2017, it became even smaller. In the presidential elections in Russia in March of 2018, voter rolls listed 3,840 Russian citizens in Syria.[20] Most of them were military, but this number also included an insignificant number of civilian contractors and diplomatic personnel.

As in previous conflicts, Russian authorities have not released official casualty numbers. But losses have remained small, given the fact that the Russian military is almost not involved in direct ground combat. It is known that 109 Russian servicemen have been killed in Syria in the first three years of operation. About half of these deaths were combat-related—among the victims were the crews of crashed and downed aircraft, elite Spetsnaz soldiers, who directed close air support (CAS) and conducted forward air control, and advisory officers who worked on the front line. Most of the rest were killed in two major aviation incidents: in the crash of the An-32 during landing on Khmeimim and in an IL-20 reconnaissance aircraft shot down by Syrian air defense.[21] Losses at this level remain acceptable in the Russian public opinion. Furthermore, only professional military personnel—officers and contract soldiers—have been killed. Conscripts are not sent to Syria.

To date (from September 2015 to April 2020), the Russian military has lost eight planes and twelve helicopters during the intervention.[22] Out of more than forty-five thousand combat sorties, only one Russian plane was shot down by hostile fire from the ground. Another bomber was lost in an incident with Turkey in November 2015.[23] The remaining five (including two carrier-borne fighters) crashed due to technical problems and crew errors. Striking almost exclusively from an altitude of more than fifty-four kilometers, Russian combat planes have remained immune to man-portable air-defense systems (MANPADS) and the fire of small-caliber antiaircraft guns.

Helicopters flew fewer sorties than aviation, but they had to operate at low altitudes and mostly during the day. Their losses from hostile fire are therefore higher. Six of the fleet of twelve helicopters were shot down or destroyed on the ground by missiles. Four Russian attack helicopters were burned after a mortar shelling of the forward airfield at the T4 airbase by Daesh militants in May 2016.[24] Losses of land equipment remained insignificant, with just several trucks being destroyed. One armored car, "Tiger," was lost in a rare ambush-style attack in which four Russian officers were killed.[25]

Apart from the official involvement of the Russian regular forces in Syria, Russian mercenary military companies are also present. They are a fairly new phenomenon that emerged in 2014–15 during the fighting in the east of Ukraine.[26] The legal status of such "companies" remains ill-defined even in Russia, and their very existence until very recently has been refuted by the Russian authorities. In Syria, they have acted with the unspoken blessing of the Russian Ministry of Defense and sometimes in cooperation with it, but outside of the military chain of command.[27]

They are mercenaries in the old-fashioned sense, reminiscent of Renaissance Italy more than of today's Western private military companies (PMCs). They obtain money and even heavy military equipment from Syrian and Russian oligarchs and fight to protect their business interests.

One of the tactical commanders described their initial role as expanding zones of influence rather than engaging in full-scale military operations: "They take territory under control—as a rule, oil and gas fields—and then guard these territories. They are paid for this … But it is impossible to control an oil field if there are hostile fighters 500 metres away, so they have to force them out."[28]

In 2017 Russian mercenaries took part in offensive action to capture towns and oil fields from the crumbling "Islamic Caliphate."[29] The participation of such "contractors" in close combat has led to much bigger losses than in the "official" Russian military contingent. But there are no exact figures, and estimates fluctuate wildly from dozens to thousands. The most reliable estimates put casualty figures among them in the hundreds. Public outcry for losses of those "volunteers" is even less than for the staff of the Ministry of Defense.

Limited military losses indicate that Syria did not become a "quagmire" for Russia as Barack Obama had predicted, even if Russia did not achieve the quick victory for which the Kremlin had initially hoped.[30] Moreover, it was not a too costly intervention for Russia. Boldest estimates put the total cost of the first twenty months of the military operation in Syria at only around $2.4 billion.[31] This has not put a huge strain on the $50 billion annual budget of the Ministry of Defense. It seems that the Russian military presence in Syria can be sustained without too much difficulty, especially after the force reduction.

A much more challenging question is what to do after the end of the war? The astronomical cost of rebuilding Syria is clearly beyond the capacity of the Russian Federation's budget.

Achievements and Lessons Learned

By mid-2018 after the series of victories Russia had fulfilled its mission to shore up the Assad government. Before the Russian intervention, the regime's eventual defeat seemed preordained. In 2015 only one-sixth of the country's territory remained under the government's control.[32] As of spring 2020, Assad is in charge of more than 70 percent of the territory of the country where over 70 percent of its prewar population lived and has seized control of the principal rebel strongholds—Eastern Aleppo and Eastern Ghouta.[33] He extends some control over another quarter of Syria, controlled by Kurdish forces and threatening the last rebel-controlled province of Idlib.

But despite several attempts, Russia failed to create effective government fighting forces capable of acting independently. This was demonstrated in April–June 2019 during the attempt of the best Assad forces to launch new offensive on Idlib and North Hama in the area of the al-Ghab plain. The operation was conducted with minimal support from a significantly scaled down Russian force and, despite heavy losses sustained by the Assad troops, failed to make significant headway.

Anti-Assad rebels and radical Islamic groups in Idlib, such as the Hayat Tahrir al-Sham (successor to al-Nusra), combined hold less than 11 percent of the territory.[34] But even in the event of a complete military victory over them, Syria will remain fragmented into three–four zones controlled by different foreign powers. Almost a quarter of the country is controlled by the Kurdish-dominated Syrian Democratic Forces (SDF) units, supported by the United States.[35] Several large areas are occupied by Turkey and its proxy army of rebels and Islamists. The prospect of reuniting Syria therefore seems remote. Russia prevented the fall of Assad but has not been able to restore the whole country to him.

Initially, Russia did not insist on keeping Assad in power and was ready for some form of political transition in line with the 2012 Geneva Communique on Syria it endorsed.[36] But now, after the string of government military victories, Russia seems strongly committed to Assad remaining in power.

In return for Russia's assistance, Damascus signed a deal with Moscow allowing Russia to use air and naval bases in the country for another forty-nine years. To preserve these, which are its only bridgeheads in the region, Russia must be sure that the civil war will end either with the complete military victory of Assad and his coalition or with a diplomatic solution accompanied by conditions favorable to Russia. And maintaining Assad in power seems like the most straightforward way to preserve Russian influence and bases.

The length of the conflict has enabled the Russian military to acquire valuable insights and skills, with Syria becoming an ideal testing ground for new Russian weaponry and tactics. Many new-generation weapons have not only been used in Syria for the first time in real combat conditions but also subsequently been improved by manufacturers after an assessment of their performance, and then retested again. To date more than 359 new weapons have gone through tests and evaluations in Syria.[37]

This number includes many samples already accepted into service, such as a new generation of precision ammunition for combat aircraft and helicopters. But it also involved numerous examples remaining at the stage of development and prototypes: Su-57 fighters, medium-altitude long-endurance (MALE-class) drones, small unmanned aerial vehicles (UAVs) with laser target designators for artillery and aviation, modernized air defense missiles, and electronic warfare (EW) equipment. Even more exotic designs were tried, such as the heavily armed twelve-ton robot Uran-9 and passive exoskeletons for combat engineers.

Russia's military operation in Syria was conducted for the first time by the Joint Operational Headquarters. From Russia's Khmeimim airbase, it simultaneously controls land, air, and naval assets in Syria, as well as coordination with foreign allies on the ground. At the strategic level of command, the operation was supervised by the new National Defense Center in Moscow (*Natsionalnyi tsentr upravleniya oborony*), which was established only in December 2014. The new control system radically improved the interaction between troops, which historically has been a weak point in the Russian military.

Russian military officers are able to hone their combat and tactical skills in Syria. They work in the country on short two- to three-month shifts. This has allowed more than 68,000 officers and professional soldiers to gain experience in Syria in the space of three years. So, for example, all the commanders of the military districts of Russia took turns to be commanders of the Joint Operational Headquarters at Khmeimim. By early 2019 around 60 percent of Russian military police has been rotated in Syria.[38] Around 87–97 percent of combat aviation crews have also operated on shifts in Syria at least once.[39]

In the Syrian war theatre, probably the most serious challenge faced by the Russian armed forces has been in the area of tactical reconnaissance. With modern high-precision weapons, locating targets is a more difficult task than actually hitting them. Russian satellite reconnaissance capabilities are still not very impressive. This was partially compensated by using many light but long-endurance drones, such as the Orlan-10 reconnaissance drone. In Syria, several dozen were deployed. UAVs performed more than a thousand sorties a month and spent many more hours in the air than piloted aircraft.[40] They were used not only for reconnaissance but also for evaluating the results of airstrikes in real time and for adjusting artillery fire. Still far from perfect, Russian tactical intelligence capabilities have grown significantly thanks to UAVs.

Russian aviation has demonstrated radically improved capabilities when it comes to hitting stationary targets. This is due to the use of the new Gefest digital targeting systems for dumb bombs and the greater use of precision weapons. But it still has difficulties with the search-and-destroy missions against small-sized mobile objects. In the first months, there were huge problems even with CAS on the battlefield. Since 2017, there has been a marked improvement, but it is still not enough. Russian bombers and fighters are still not equipped with sufficiently sophisticated sights or reconnaissance containers to independently locate small-scale targets. A serious drawback is also the lack of MALE-class armed drones. Of the three heavy drones under development, only a one-ton Orion was ready to battle-test in Syria in 2019 in the weaponized version.

In the Russian military, striking such targets and providing CAS to the ground forces on the front line remains the specialized task of helicopters. But even the newest Mi-28N and Ka-52 helicopters, deployed to Syria, did not prove to be very successful at night missions. This led to an emergency program to accelerate their modernization.[41]

The unsuccessful deployment of the Russian aircraft carrier Admiral Kuznetsov to the shores of Syria in the winter of 2016/17 was a source of deep disappointment to the Kremlin. This was the first time in decades that the Russian navy had the opportunity to prove itself in real combat and confirm the need for aircraft carriers in its ranks. But the effectiveness of its deck aviation was considerably less than that of shore-based Aerospace Forces. Moreover, out of only 154 sorties launched from the carrier,[42] two fighter jets were lost in accidents.

The navy managed to redeem its reputation somewhat with the successful launch of over a hundred Kalibr cruise missiles from frigates, small corvettes, and diesel submarines. This new weapon was tested in battle for the first time in the course of Russia's intervention in Syria. With it, ships were now able to attack ground targets up to 1,500 kilometers from the coast—a useful capability which the Russian Navy did not previously possess.

Even though the contingent deployed by the Russian military was small, it was necessary to deliver in first two and half years over 1.6 million tons of cargo to Syria by sea and by air.[43] This pushed Russian military logistics to the limit: the navy even had to purchase old civilian vessels for military transport.[44] This shows that Russia's expeditionary capabilities remain severely limited. It is not clear if Russia could, if necessary, maintain an overseas contingent in Syria of more than a few thousand people and half a hundred aircraft.

Syria and the Future of the Russian Armed Forces

The combat experience gained in Syria will determine how the Russian armed forces evolve in the foreseeable future. The adoption of a new State Armament Program

(*Gosudarstvennaya programma vooruzheniya*) was delayed and not signed until February 2018, in order to take the lessons learned from the Syrian campaign into account. It is known that it will place more emphasis on the development and purchase of large quantities of precision weapons,[45] increasing the accuracy and effectiveness of artillery, and that there will be a substantial investment in upgrading the ground forces' outdated fleet of armored vehicles.

Priority is given to the strengthening of strategic aviation, which can now use long-range non-nuclear cruise missiles. Financing of the navy procurements, in comparison with the previous program, is significantly reduced. In view of the new military budget constraints, investment in a "blue-water" ocean fleet was considered not to be cost-effective. In the next ten years, there are no plans to begin construction of new aircraft.[46] Preference is given to the air force, rather than the navy, as a tool for projecting force beyond Russia's borders. Also, there are no indications of a major expansion of expeditionary capabilities beyond two planned amphibious assault ships. Russia's conventional forces will still be focused on defending Russian territory and projecting power on the "near abroad."

The civil war in this Middle Eastern country has become an opportunity for Moscow to closely observe the military actions of the United States and NATO countries. This has allowed Russia to get a close look at modern Western tactics and weapons, gauge their effectiveness, and compare the performance of its own weapons with those used by rival powers against the same targets. Also, the Russian military has been able to closely monitor several massed cruise missile strikes launched by NATO countries and gain first-hand experience of the effectiveness of Soviet-era and more modern Russian air defenses against such a threat. The duel between Turkey's attack drones and the Russian-made air defense systems deployed by Assad during the Idlib offensive of February–March 2020 held important lessons in that regard. The acquisition of such insights and information is of critical importance for the successful future development of the Russian armed forces and weapons.

5

The Nonwar on Daesh

Florence Gaub

Russia's military campaign in Syria has been a masterpiece in strategic disinformation. Moscow showed up late to the international fight against Daesh—the so-called Islamic State in Iraq and Syria (ISIS)—a full year after the US-led coalition had been launched, following an official request from the Syrian government for it to intervene. The military campaign that Russia subsequently conducted in Syria actively undermined the campaign waged by the international coalition. Although only months earlier President Putin had declared somewhat boldly that Daesh "does not pose a direct threat to Russia,"[1] Russia now stated that its objectives in Syria were to give "exclusively air support to the Syrian armed forces in their fight against ISIS."[2]

The military intervention in Syria was presented in the Russian media as a war on Islamic terrorism, in glaring contradiction of the way in which Russia actually conducted operations on the ground. Extensive evidence, gathered through crowdsourcing and open source analysis, disproved Russia's claim that it was bombing Daesh: in fact, more than 90 percent of its airstrikes targeted non-jihadist rebels. Not even Daesh's nemesis, the al-Qaeda-affiliated Nusra Front, was targeted. If that was not evidence enough, Daesh was losing territory only in areas where Russia was not militarily active.

Instead of defeating Daesh, Moscow was helping the Syrian regime crush the only viable political alternative left, the vast array of militias operating under the umbrella of the Free Syrian Army. Backed by Russian air cover, Syrian troops were finally able to push back into territory in the west of the country that had previously been lost and ultimately retake Aleppo. As this was the real objective of the campaign, it was perhaps only logical that Putin declared "mission accomplished" in spring 2016, when Daesh still held an area equal in size to the territory then controlled by the Syrian regime.[3] Of course, Russian operations continued, and Putin announced, on two further occasions, that the objectives of the mission had been accomplished, declaring victory against Daesh in December 2017.

Despite all the evidence to the contrary, Moscow maintained the narrative of its anti-Daesh fight—and not merely to cover its operations in international legitimacy. Constant repetition of lies, so the exercise shows, will yield results eventually, regardless of how many times they are disproved thanks to the well-documented "illusory truth effect" whereby repeated exposure to false information leads to the acceptance of it as truth—or at least creates a strong element of doubt (Map 5.1).

Russia struck more rebel than ISIS targets

Approximation of Russian airstrikes in Syria, September 30–October 28 2015

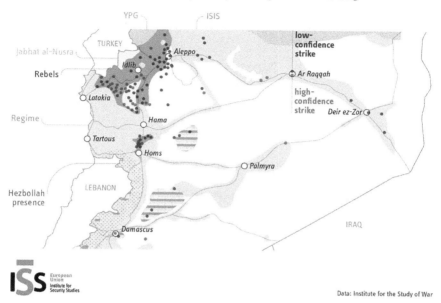

Map 5.1 Approximation of Russian strikes in Syria.

Source: EUISS and Institute for the Study of War.

Repeating endlessly that the Syrian opposition was colluding with Daesh, that the options in Syria were either Assad or Islamist terrorists at the helm of the country, that Daesh was a Western creation in the first place and has enjoyed Western support throughout the Syrian conflict—and that Russia was the only country willing to face it down—definitely had a strategic impact: it discredited the Syrian opposition; it reduced the complexities of the Syrian war to a binary choice between the Assad regime and a takeover by Islamic extremists; it hollowed out European and American public support for regime change in Syria at a time when refugees were streaming into Europe; and it portrayed European and American governments as responsible for the bloodshed. In sum: this was a stratagem designed to change Western policy on Syria—and toward Russia itself, which had languished in isolation following the annexation of Crimea in 2014 and the war in Donbas.

Step One: Opposition? Which Opposition?

The first victim of Russia's Daesh narrative was and is, of course, the Syrian opposition: but the target of the campaign was the public in Europe and the United States—and indeed in Russia, whose public also needed to be convinced.[4]

Although the Kremlin's statements on Russia's military campaign clearly identified Daesh as the target, official language used by both the government and the media soon began to blur the lines, referring to all militias active in Syria as "extremists," "Islamists," and "terrorists."[5] Even organizations such as the White Helmets, dedicated to the rescue of civilians from combat zones, became the target of a campaign accusing them of having links with al-Qaeda.[6] This was in stark contrast to language that had previously been used: in the early years of the war, neither Putin nor other Russian officials defined the entire opposition in those terms. Although the Kremlin's objectives diverged from the opposition's goals from the outset, the narrative was then about protracted instability and peaceful change—and clearly aimed at preventing a Western intervention in Syria, which would only lead to terrorism, as Putin noted in an op-ed. At this point, the Russian narrative was at odds with the regime's narrative that, from the beginning of the conflict, portrayed the uprising as the work of terrorists.[7] But the emergence of Daesh on the Syrian battlefield led to a change in rhetoric in Moscow; from 2014 onward, all armed opposition groups were regarded as either Islamist or collaborating with Islamists. This served two purposes: it tapped into international sentiment and revulsion against Daesh and, by the same token, discredited those forces that could pose a threat to the Assad regime as they represented a credible political alternative.

Around the same time, a second line of narration emerged: the portrayal of the Syrian conflict in almost Manichean terms as a choice between the Assad regime and Daesh. The Syrian opposition, now eliminated from the discussion through having been amalgamated with Daesh, no longer featured as an option in this vision of things. "People are not fleeing from the Bashar al-Assad regime—they are fleeing from the Islamic State," Putin stated.[8] His foreign minister, Sergey Lavrov, even claimed that "all of our Western partners, without exception, are telling us that they understand perfectly well the nature of the main threat in the Middle East and North Africa. It is not the Assad regime, but the Islamic State."[9] Neither statement was true, but as always with disinformation, this was not the point.[10] Instead, this discourse was aimed at removing the opposition from the equation and presenting the Syrian war as a battle between a secular regime and a brutal terrorist entity. "Syria's Bashar Assad is not a perfect leader, but certainly better than the Islamic State," Russian media outlet RT noted.[11] The Russian narrative also had the effect of portraying Western leaders as hypocrites, saying one thing in private and another in public.

The persistent repetition of this discourse eventually did have an impact on European and American opinion regarding the Syrian conflict. By October 2015, 70 percent of the American public stated that the government had no strategy for Syria, and 53 percent considered that "Putin has the upper hand in Syria." Some Western media even uncritically adopted the Russian narrative: the British Express for instance noted that 71 percent of people who responded to a poll organized by the newspaper said that they "support Vladimir Putin's bombing campaign in Syria, which is blitzing a large number of Islamic State owned buildings and vehicles"—when Russian sorties were, in fact, not "blitzing" Daesh.[12]

Originally supportive of the Arab uprisings of 2011, policymakers and public alike began to echo the Russian narratives. For example, François Fillon, former French prime minister and candidate for the presidency in 2017, declared that Bashar al-Assad was a bulwark against Islamist terrorism and the protector of Middle Eastern Christians.[13]

An American state senator endorsed the notion that all opposition groups in Syria could be lumped together as terrorist: "I travelled all around the country and repeatedly Syrians are offended by this idea of rebels or opposition. To them, they are all terrorists"[14]—chiming with the views expressed by President Putin who in October 2015 declared: "There's no need to play with words and split terrorists into moderate and not moderate. I would like to know what the difference is."[15] French far-right leader Marine Le Pen joined the chorus: "The question comes down to the choice: do you want there to be at least some form of state or Daesh?"[16]

This unnuanced, black-and-white view of the conflict soon permeated Western public opinion as well. American media outlets repeated the Russian narrative: "Supporting Assad remains the only realistic path that will return us to the relative stability of the pre-Arab Spring days, and that will defeat ISIS. No one is more motivated to defeat ISIS than Assad."[17] When a French MP called for rapprochement with Assad in the fight against Daesh, a leading national newspaper wondered: "Do we have to choose between Assad and ISIS?"[18] Think tankers, too, began to argue in favor of a policy accepting that Assad remain in power[19]—and ultimately, even the United Nations Syria envoy Staffan de Mistura conceded that Assad was "a crucial part of the solution"— when originally, he had been identified as a crucial part of the problem.[20] Both France and the United States began to relent on their original demand for Assad to step down even before the transition in Syria began—of course, not solely as a result of Russian disinformation but adhering to Russia's presentation of the situation as boiling down to a choice between Assad and the jihadists.

What had disappeared from the discussion was the root cause of the Syrian conflict—which had nothing to do with Daesh and everything with Assad.

Step Two: Blaming the West

After the Syrian opposition, Europe and the United States were the second target of Russian propaganda attacks. As with the campaign against the opposition, this narrative comprised two main strands: it accused the West of having created Islamists in the first place and of covertly cooperating with them.[21] Both lines of narrative tap into certain perceptions that both Middle Eastern and Russian audiences tend to have anyway, and are therefore probably designed mainly for their consumption.[22]

The first, the notion that Islamism is a phenomenon created by Western countries, is spun around the "original sin" of American support to the Taliban during the Soviet invasion of Afghanistan. While it is true that Western powers aided the mujahideen opposition to Moscow at the time, it was the USSR that plunged Afghanistan into four decades of civil war, destabilizing the entire country and mobilizing Islamist networks of all sorts across the region. However, this notion fits neatly with the view that since it was the invasion of Iraq in 2003 that paved the way for the emergence of Daesh, it was the United States that created Daesh, as President Putin claimed—letting it be understood that they did this intentionally. With regard to Syria, this narrative was reinforced by claims in the Russian media that the Obama administration funneled weapons to "an insurgency they knew was linked to al-Qaeda in order to overthrow the Syrian government. Al-Qaeda has built its largest affiliate in history as a direct result of this reckless U.S. regime change policy." In the same article, RT claimed that Western states "prolonged the slaughter and empowered al-Qaeda."[23] Such accusations gradually had an impact on European public opinion, too: an opinion poll suggested that some 31 percent of French citizens believed that "jihadist terrorist organisations like al-Qaeda and ISIS were in reality manipulated by Western intelligence services."[24]

The second part of the narrative is that the West did not just unleash the beast, but that it colludes with jihadists in Syria too, as claimed by Russian foreign minister Lavrov. According to this interpretation of events, it does this by refraining from targeting them in airstrikes and obstructing the Syrian regime's efforts to fight Daesh.[25] For instance, Putin claimed that the coalition's bombing of Raqqa, Daesh's self-declared "capital," was designed not to defeat Daesh but to obstruct progovernment forces.[26] In December 2017, after the fall of Daesh strongholds Mosul and Raqqa (neither of which Russia had bombed), Putin declared: "we defeated ISIS." In fact the opposite happened. While Russia barely bombed Daesh, most of the fighting that succeeded in wresting Syrian and Iraqi territories from the terrorist organization's control was done by Kurdish forces, the Iraqi government with close Western air and intelligence support, and even some Western special forces on the ground. Only when French foreign minister Jean-Yves Le Drian expressed his surprise at this claim did Russia backpedal, stating that it was the Syrian regime that had defeated Daesh (still giving no credit to Western efforts).[27]

A Convincing Narrative?

Russia manipulated the international revulsion over the atrocities committed by Daesh for essentially three purposes: to achieve its strategic goal of ensuring the Syrian regime's survival; to discredit Western efforts not just in Syria but in the region more generally; and to bolster support for its strategy and policies. Russia's "ISIS narrative" was accepted mainly in Russia itself; its impact in Europe and the United States was not as profound but still important enough to create cracks in a previous near-consensus on the Syrian war as a morally justified uprising against a repressive and brutal regime. Nevertheless, Russian strategic communication did not succeed in changing either European or American policies on Syria—for the time being. It did, however, bring international efforts for a negotiated transition in Syria to a near halt.

Where Russia failed, however, was in convincing Middle Eastern audiences of its storyline: according to different surveys, two-thirds of Arabs see Russia's role in the Syrian conflict as negative. On average, three out of four Arabs are of the view that Russia is a major source of instability in Syria—ranking it just a few points behind the United States, regarded as the main culprit.[28] Overall, 66 percent of Arab citizens have a negative perception of Russia (while 75 percent have a negative view of the United States), and 69 percent say Russia poses a threat to Arab stability.[29] Although much has been written about Russia's "return to the Middle East," this seems to be more about power projection than about reality.

In sum, some important lessons can be drawn from Russia's use of Daesh as a strategic communication tool: the first is that repetition alone is often enough to create an illusion of truth, and efforts to refute such assertions are often of no avail. This poses challenges to Western policymakers who seek to counteract fake news with real news. The second is that while communication alone is not enough to change a state's policy, it can undermine its efforts significantly; although ultimately not as successful as feared, Russia's Syria narrative has changed the dynamics of the war's storytelling to its advantage. Third, the Russian narrative builds on historical grievances such as alleged Western support to the Taliban during the USSR–Afghanistan war in the 1980s, the invasion of Iraq, and NATO's campaign in Libya to strengthen its argument and build a larger, anti-Western case. As a result, its story is more believable and hence has greater resonance. Fourth and lastly, Russia used Daesh to reduce the complexities of the war in Syria to a stark choice between the Assad regime and Islamist terrorism—a version of events which an audience weary of war was eager to believe. The cumulative effect of these factors was that while Russia presented its intervention in Syria in the autumn of 2015 as an antiterrorist operation that was supposed to lead to an alliance with the West (and hence to Russia's de-isolation after the war in Ukraine and the relaxation of sanctions), Moscow's nonwar on Daesh ended up heightening, not alleviating, its tensions with the West.

6

Russian Arms Exports in the Middle East

Timofey Borisov

Russia has been one of the most active players in the Middle East and North Africa (MENA) armaments market since the mid-twentieth century, using arms exports as an important foreign policy instrument.

The first major breakthrough in this field was the Czech-Egyptian arms deal of 1955 that provided for the supply of a large batch of Soviet weapons worth $250 million to Egypt.[1] During the same period the USSR began sales to Syria. By the 1970s it had significantly expanded its presence in the regional arms market, adding a group of Arab socialist countries as customers: Algeria, Iraq, Libya, and South Yemen. At the time, those five states surpassed the Warsaw Pact members in terms of transfers.[2] Russia's MENA client base also included Jordan, Kuwait, and Sudan (until the early 1970s).[3]

The general state of the economy and internal political issues in Russia after the collapse of the Soviet Union inevitably led to a sharp decline in arms exports in all directions, including the MENA region. Defense industry companies suffered from the lack of investment and domestic procurement, and many of them had to switch their production lines to civilian goods or even go into liquidation. Despite the contracts for supply of BMP-3 infantry fighting vehicles (IFVs) and Smerch multiple launch rocket systems (MLRS) to Kuwait and the United Arab Emirates (UAE), which were important from the political and marketing perspectives, the Russian presence in the MENA arms market from the 1990s until the mid-2000s was insignificant. Moscow looked elsewhere. During that period, China and India together accounted for 60 to 80 percent of all Russian supplies.[4] However, that started to change a decade or so ago.

Russia's Comeback

The first major arms deal with a MENA country after the breakup of the Soviet Union took place in 2006. Moscow signed a $7.5 billion package of agreements with Algeria, which nowadays buys its weapons primarily from Russia. By 2009–11 Algeria had procured more Russian weapons than China, and this included 34 MiG-29SMT/UMT light fighter aircraft, 28 Su-30MKI(A) heavy multipurpose fighters, 16 Yak-130 advanced jet trainers, 8 battalions of the S-300PMU-2 (SA-20) long-range surface-to-air missile systems (SAMs), and 185 T-90SA main battle tanks (MBTs). It also signed contracts with Russia for the modernization of 250 T-72M tanks and 400 BMP-1 IFVs, and the delivery of Metis-M1 and Kornet-E anti-tank guided missile systems (ATGMs).[5]

The Algerian deal gave a significant boost to post-Soviet Russian arms exports, although it did not immediately lead to the strengthening of Russia's position in the MENA market. Moreover, several developments over which the Kremlin did not have entire control hindered Russia's ambitions in this respect. During 1989–91 Russia and Iran signed several contracts to the tune of $5.1 billion. Over the following years Tehran received a large amount of weapons including MiG-29 fighters, Su-24MK strike aircraft, S-200VE (SA-5) SAM systems, and the original Kilo-class submarines[6] (Project 877EKM). Russia had also agreed to help organize the licensed production of T-72S tanks and BMP-2 IFVs in Iran, but in the late 1990s under US pressure the Russian government pledged to complete all shipments according to existing contracts by the end of 1999 and then to cease arms sales to Iran. The cooperation was resumed to a limited extent after the year 2000; however, in 2010 Russia once again decided to cut off arms supplies to Iran as part of the implementation of the United Nations Security Council Resolution (UNSCR) 1929 (adopted on June 9, 2010) and to freeze the previously concluded agreement for delivery of PMU2 (SA-20) SAM systems.[7] Later in 2011 Moscow also voted in favor of the UN arms embargo on Libya (UNSCR 1970), which led to the loss of expected profits amounting to $7 billion.[8] Apart from the financial losses incurred, these episodes tarnished Russia's reputation as a reliable arms supplier.

Nevertheless in recent years the MENA region has become one of the largest recipients of Russian weapons. This is due in some measure at least to the success of Russia's military campaign in Syria. In 2015 the region accounted for 36 percent of all Russian arms exports, becoming the second most important market after Asia-Pacific, which represented 48 percent.[9] In 2017 exports of Russian military hardware exceeded $15 billion.[10] The MENA region now ranked as the largest recipient of Russian armaments, taking almost 50 percent of the total exports. Furthermore, according to Alexander Mikheev, the director general of Rosoboronexport, Russia's state arms exports agency, there are contracts with twenty-three MENA countries worth $8 billion or 20 percent of the order portfolio.[11]

In February 2019 Dmitry Shugayev, the head of the Federal Service for Military-Technical Cooperation, told the *Kommersant* newspaper that MENA market was very important for Russia and that there were ten countries (primarily from the Middle East) interested in purchasing S-400 systems.[12] Later the same month at IDEX 2019, International Defense Exhibition in Abu Dhabi, Rostec CEO Sergey Chemezov said that in 2018 Russian arms exports to MENA countries had reached $6 billion.[13] This figure was probably attributed to Rosoboronexport sales only, while the total volume including spare parts and service amounted to $7.2 billion or about 45 percent of all Russian arms sales during that year.[14] Aircraft and air defense systems account for approximately 40 percent of the total Russian arms exports to the region, according to Shugayev.[15]

Algeria is one of the biggest importers of Russian arms in the MENA region. In 2007–9 it received twenty-eight Su-30MKI(A) multirole fighters under the $1.5 billion contract of 2006, and in 2011–12 it acquired sixteen more aircraft worth $0.9 billion. In 2015 the third contract for fourteen Su-30MKI(A) fighters was signed, the first eight of which were delivered in December 2016.[16] During recent years Russia has also supplied Buk-M2E (SA-17) medium-range SAM systems, Pantsir-S1 (SA-22) short-range SAM/gun systems, Mi-28NE attack helicopters, and Mi-26T2 heavy lift cargo helicopters to Algeria. The importance of the Algerian arms market for Russia might be illustrated by the fact that it was the second country to procure the Iskander-E (SS-26) short-range ballistic missile system after Armenia, which is a member of the Collective Security Treaty Organization (CSTO) along with Russia.[17] Another example is the contract signed in 2014 on licensed production of two hundred T-90SA MBTs with an estimated cost of $1 billion, which makes it one of the biggest deals in the world market regarding this type of weaponry.[18] In total since 2006 Algeria has received more than five hundred T-90SA tanks. (In contrast France, Germany, and the UK have between 200 and 250 tanks each.) In December 2019, *MENA Defense* reported that the Algerian air force had allegedly singed contracts for the procurement of fourteen Su-57 fifth-generation stealth fighters, fourteen Su-34 bombers, and fourteen Su-35 multirole fighters with deliveries that should be completed by 2025.[19] All in all, Russia sells to Algeria technologically advanced hardware that brings not only larger revenues but also prestige and geopolitical clout in the region.

Who Else in the Region Buys Russian Weapons?

Another major recipient is Iraq, although in the period 2003–12 it was mainly oriented toward arms imports from the United States. But in 2012 it signed a package agreement worth $4.2 billion with Russia, which was Moscow's biggest arms deal in the MENA region back then. In 2014 the country even became the second-biggest importer of Russian military equipment after India. During that year Baghdad received nine Su-25 attack aircraft, twelve TOS-1A heavy flamethrower systems, six Mi-28NE, and up to ten Mi-35M attack helicopters; also the deliveries of Pantsir-S1 systems began—all amounted to $1.7 billion.[20] In total Iraq received fifteen Mi-28NE and twenty-eight Mi-35M attack helicopters. In 2014 the contract for the supply of BMP-3 IMVs was signed, but its implementation was delayed due to various problems and the first deliveries took place only in August 2018.[21] According to Albert Bakov, the vice president of Concern Tractor Plants (BMP-3 producer), the total number of vehicles ordered was five hundred.[22] In February 2018, Iraq purchased thirty-six T-90S MBTs and thirty-seven more were expected to be delivered by late April.[23] Now it is also considered to be one of the potential recipients of S-400 (SA-21) SAM systems.[24] In May 2019, the ambassador of the Republic of Iraq to the Russian Federation Haidar Mansour Hadi announced that the Iraqi government had made a decision and it wanted to purchase S-400s, but there was no signed agreement or any other official document clinching the deal.[25]

Egypt, which had an extensive arms deal with the United States as part of its Camp David accord with Israel, is yet another important partner for Russia. In 2013 countries signed agreements worth more than $3 billion for the supply of Tor-M2E (SA-15), firearms, and ammunition. In 2015 another contract for forty-six MiG-29M/M2 at an estimated cost of $2 billion was signed.[26] Egypt was also the first country to order Ka-52 attack helicopters: it signed a contract for forty-six Ka-52s in 2015, and the first deliveries were carried out in June 2017. In March 2018, *Kommersant* reported citing two senior managers from Russian defense industry that Russia and Egypt had signed agreement for the supply of more than two dozens of Su-35 multirole fighters worth approximately $2 billion. The deliveries were expected to begin in 2020–1. Later Rosoboronexport officials refuted this information saying that Russia was ready to supply the fighters, but there was no contract signed.[27]

Does the Syrian Campaign Help Russian Arms Exports?

The Syrian campaign also has an impact on how Russia perceives and pursues its arms export strategy in the Middle East. This impact is not immediately quantifiable but it exists. Russia's involvement in the Syrian conflict has had several consequences with respect to the promotion of its military and dual-purpose products.

The first and the most evident one is the marketing of Russian weapons systems. During its intervention in Syria Moscow had tested about three hundred new types of weapons and military equipment in real combat conditions.[28] President Putin emphasized the Russian military's success in its first use of long-range high-precision weapons, namely the sea-launched Kalibr and air-launched Kh-101 cruise missiles.[29] Several systems have demonstrated good performance, which is likely to have increased their attractiveness for potential buyers. These have included the Su-34 bombers, Su-30SM and Su-35 multirole fighters, Mi-28N and Ka-52 helicopters, to name just a few. At the same time the operation has occasionally revealed deficiencies in certain weapons systems and provided information in the light of which Russian engineers can make further improvements.

The second, probably more significant effect is that Russia has shown that it is an important security actor impossible to ignore. Moreover, Russian political and military support for the Syrian government in such a difficult period might be perceived by the political leaders of other regional powers as an indicator that Moscow is a responsible and reliable partner.

Taken together, these factors could contribute to the promotion of Russian arms and military hardware throughout the region. One of the first signs of this impact had been seen in December 2015: almost eight years since they began, negotiations on the supply of Su-32 bombers (an export version of Su-34) to Algeria were ramped up, as reported by the media, though by the end of 2019 this contract has not been signed. The estimated cost of twelve Su-32 aircraft was about $500–600 million.[30] In April 2018, Rosoboronexport's director Alexander Mikheev described the effects of the Syrian campaign on Russian arms exports the following way:

We feel the increased interest from our foreign partners in armaments and military equipment which have proved its performance characteristics in combat conditions during the anti-terrorist operation in Syria. This applies to combat aircraft, helicopters, armored vehicles, sea, air and ground-based weapons. Yes, there is an interest in almost all Russian weapons systems. Are there any specific requests and does our portfolio of orders grow? Both are true, but let's not run ahead.[31]

Prospective Clients

Saudi Arabia, which is a traditional recipient of US arms, has also expressed its interest in cooperating with Russia. During the visit by Saudi Arabia's King Salman bin Abdulaziz Al Saud to Moscow in October 2017 the countries reached a preliminary agreement worth $3.5 billion that included the S-400 SAM systems, TOS-1A systems, Kornet-EM ATGMs, automatic grenade launchers, and the production of Kalashnikov AK-103 assault rifles in Saudi Arabia.[32] In April 2019, Saudi Arabia received the first batch of TOS-1A systems under the abovementioned contract. According to Russia's Federal Service for Military-Technical Cooperation spokesperson Maria Vorobyeva, all other projects in this sphere including the most difficult issue of licensed production "are carried out in accordance with previously reached agreements."[33] There is certain skepticism among Russian experts regarding the success of the negotiations on S-400s, since the purchase of these systems seems excessive taking into consideration the significant amount of American-origin air defense systems Saudi Arabia already has in its arsenal.[34] But the rest correspond with the current demands of the country's armed forces' needs and have good chances to be materialized. Moreover, after the drone attack on Saudi Aramco oil processing facilities at Abqaiq and Khurais in September 2019 the interest of several MENA countries, namely Saudi Arabia and UAE, to the Russian air defense systems increased, said Dmitry Shugayev, avoiding further details.[35]

Russia is eager to enter the previously almost inaccessible market in the Gulf. Cooperation with the UAE has already borne fruit. In August 2000 the Emirates signed an agreement for the purchase and partial financing of Russian research and development efforts in the Pantsir-S1 (SA-22) project, thus helping it to create a modern and commercially viable weapons system. Today countries are discussing the possible modernization of the previously delivered air defense systems and the creation of the specialized maintenance centers.[36] In 2017 UAE signed a letter of intent on the purchase of Su-35 fighters, and the two countries also agreed to jointly develop a new fifth-generation fighter based upon the MiG-29 twin-engine fighter aircraft.[37] During the same year Russian defense minister Sergei Shoigu visited Qatar where the Intergovernmental Agreement on Military-Technical Cooperation was signed: Moscow had concluded a similar agreement with Bahrain in 2016. Russia and Qatar are also holding talks on the possible delivery of Su-35 fighters.[38] In February 2019, it was reported that there were ongoing negotiations between Russia and Qatar on S-400 systems as well.[39] In June 2019, Vladimir Putin signed a decree setting up military attaché office at the Russian Embassy in Qatar.[40] This move is aimed at improving military-to-military contacts between the two countries and might also contribute to the promotion of Russian arms in general.

One of the most notable developments in the field of Russian arms exports in recent years has been the emergence of Turkey as a large customer, despite all the political tensions that have occurred between the two countries. In 2017 Moscow and Ankara signed a contract on the delivery of four batteries of S-400 systems worth $2.5 billion, with Russia providing loans to cover 55 percent of the total sum.[41] This contract was in large part driven by political factors that resulted from the 2016 Turkish coup d'état attempt against President Recep Tayyip Erdoğan and the deterioration of US–Turkey relations. At the same time Turkey is actively developing its own defense industry and its arms exports are growing, mainly to Muslim countries like Qatar, Bahrain, and Tunisia. The long-standing cultural and diplomatic ties between Turkey and MENA countries together with the competitive products of the Turkish defense industry might become a challenge for Russia aiming to enter this new market.

Iran is another attractive partner. In 2015 President Vladimir Putin signed a decree lifting the self-imposed ban on the delivery of S-300 SAM systems to Tehran. That marked an important milestone in bilateral relations.[42] Moreover, UNSCR 2231 stipulates the lifting of the ban on conventional arms sales to Iran by 2020. Russia is eager to benefit from that window of opportunity and has already been negotiating the possible intensification of arms transfers.[43] "We are open for discussions on delivering S-400 Triumph air defense systems, including to Iran. Especially given that this equipment is not subject to restrictions outlined in UN Security Council's resolution, issued on June 20, 2015. We have not received an official request from our partners on this matter yet," a representative of the press service of the Russian Federal Service of Military-Technical Cooperation told in June 2019.[44]

Hindrance Factors

There are two major factors that might impede the Russian arms exports worldwide and in the MENA region in particular: these are oil prices and the US sanctions. In recent years there were several periods of extremely low oil prices, which negatively affected the ability of several Russian clients to pay. Thus, in 2015–16 there were cases of delays in payments of such oil-dependent importers as Iran and Azerbaijan.[45] The sharp decline in oil prices also provoked an escalation of the economic and political crisis in Venezuela, which for a long time was one of the largest Russian importers, undermining its ability to acquire new weapons. But this factor is especially relevant for the MENA countries as many of them depend on the hydrocarbon export revenues.

Another big issue for Russian arms exports is the implementation of Countering America's Adversaries Through Sanctions Act (CAATSA), passed by US Congress in 2017. Section 231 of the Act requires the president to impose sanctions with respect to persons engaging in "significant transaction" with the intelligence or defense sectors of the Government of the Russian Federation.[46] In March 2019, Kuwaiti Army Head of Armament and Equipment Authority Anwar Al Mazidi said that the purchase of T-90MS/MSK tanks from Russia was postponed (though not canceled), supposedly because of the possible CAATSA sanctions.[47] In April 2019, reacting to the previously mentioned report on the possible sale of Su-35 fighters to Egypt, US secretary of state Mike Pompeo warned that "if those systems were to be purchased, statute CAATSA would require sanctions on the regime."[48] Another case is the US–Turkey dispute over Ankara's acquisition of Russian S-400 systems. Washington removed Turkey from the Lockheed Martin F-35 Lightning II fighters production program.[49] Turkish pilots also are no longer trained by the United States to fly the new stealth fighter.

In sum, CAATSA might have a significant impact on Russian arms exports to MENA in the medium term, but its effectiveness will depend on the bargaining power recipient states hold vis-à-vis the United States. Russia on its part will try to get around this law. In September 2018, the Deputy Prime Minister Yuri Borisov said that Russia had already switched to national currencies in some of the arms export contracts.[50] For example, Russia and India agreed on the mechanism of payments in national currencies, which will unblock arms deliveries temporarily suspended in 2018.[51] Later, in June 2019, it was reported that Russia abandoned dollar and SWIFT in defense deals.[52]

Conclusion

All in all, having successfully overcome the hurdles and setbacks of the 1990s, Russia has significantly expanded its presence in the MENA arms market in recent years. This seems to be in line with the general thrust of Russia's foreign policy, aimed at improving its image as a reliable partner, increasing its influence and establishing long-term partnerships with MENA countries. Moscow is concentrating on further development of military and technical ties with major regional powers and is expecting to enter new markets, seeing arms sales not as the end goal but as an instrument to boost other spheres of cooperation such as oil and gas, nuclear energy, trade in commodities, and so on. But this strategy will certainly not be easy to carry out. The global arms market is becoming more and more competitive and Russia will be exposed to fierce competition in the MENA market. The recent developments in relations with countries that have traditionally imported arms from the United States and Europe do not necessarily signify they are switching to Russia for good but reflects their aspiration to benefit from this competition between the major arms exporters and mitigate their exposure to political risks by diversifying their arms suppliers. Thus, while a window of opportunity has opened for Russia, of which it has already taken full advantage, the rapidly changing political environment in the region might yet make its own adjustments.

7

Russia's Energy Diplomacy in the Middle East

Carole Nakhle

The "Energy Strategy of Russia for the Period up to 2030," published in 2010, highlights "the strengthening of foreign economic positions of the country" as one of the Russian government's key priorities.[1] The Kremlin has pursued energy diplomacy more actively since, particularly with major hydrocarbon-producing nations, in an endeavor to achieve that aim.

Energy diplomacy typically refers to efforts by a consumer country to access energy resources from a producer country, with a view to ensuring *security of supply*. The EU–Russia energy relationship falls under this paradigm, with Russia often accused of leveraging its gas resources to achieve political goals in the European continent. Energy diplomacy may also refer to a producer country's endeavors to secure access to markets, with a view to attaining *security of demand*. In this sense, from the perspective of producers, energy diplomacy takes on a different meaning: after all, producers sell the same product and compete for market share; what one economic actor loses is usually captured by a competitor.

The growing *rapprochement* between Russia and the Middle East and North Africa encompasses the two forms of energy diplomacy. It is manifest in enhanced interaction and coordination among oil- and gas-producing countries pursuing common interests, on the one hand, while nuclear energy, on the other hand, falls under the conventional category of producer–consumer diplomacy. In both cases, closer cooperation facilitates and supports Russia's wider commercial and political aspirations.

Common Challenges

Together, Russia and the Middle East and North Africa sit on 60 percent and 63 percent of the world's proven oil and natural gas reserves, respectively, and produce half of the world's oil and nearly 40 percent of its gas.[2] Any cooperation between these two giant players will therefore have significant implications for global energy markets.

Today, Russia and the region's oil producers are facing similar challenges that make the case for cooperation particularly appealing. In the short term, they are having to contend with a relatively lower price environment, compared to only a few years ago: in 2011–14, for example, oil prices hovered around $110 per barrel/bl. Furthermore, the ascent of, and growing competition from, US tight oil[3] has created new dynamics in the market, given its ability to respond swiftly to price changes. When oil prices increase, for instance, there is a corresponding rise in tight oil production, thereby helping to keep a lid on any further price increases. In contrast, with conventional oil (produced by Russia and the Middle East and North Africa), delays of several years between investment decision and first production are the norm. This is what economists describe as an *inelastic supply*. Conventional oil producers thereby continuously face the risk of losing market share to a more agile supplier, whenever oil prices increase enough to boost investment and tight oil production.

In the longer term, aggressive climate change policies, if successfully implemented, can render hydrocarbon resources in the ground valueless irrespective of how extensive these may be. For instance, at their annual summit in 2015, the G7 leaders agreed (though the US position has changed since then) to phase out the use of fossil fuels by the end of the century, while countries like France and the UK announced that they would ban the sales of petrol and diesel engines from as early as 2040. As the fight against global warming intensifies and development of alternative sources of energy and technologies rapidly expands, the outlook for oil demand becomes increasingly uncertain. For economies that are heavily dependent on oil and gas, such changes threaten their long-term stability. In Russia, oil and gas account for about half of federal budget revenues; in the Middle Eastern countries like Iraq that dependence can exceed 90 percent.[4]

Taking these challenges into consideration, the dilemma for these producers then becomes: how to produce enough oil to safeguard such an important revenue base while protecting market share and maintaining prices at "appropriate" levels that limit the expansion of tight oil, extend the longevity of their valuable asset as long as possible, and deter the growth of alternative energy sources. The answer ultimately resides in cooperation, which is facilitated by energy diplomacy.

Favorable Timing

Although Russia is no stranger to the Middle East and North Africa, its footprint there has become increasingly visible over the last ten years, and this trend looks set to continue. In 2014, two consecutive events accelerated Moscow's pursuit of *rapprochement* with the regional countries, as it sought to diversify its energy relations and exports due to deteriorating relations with the West.

First, the annexation of Crimea in March 2014 prompted Western governments, led by the United States and the European Union, to impose sanctions on Russia, targeting state finances, the energy, and arms sectors. These sanctions restricted a selective list of Russian banks and firms' ability to raise capital and their access to international financial markets.

Second, between June and December 2014, oil prices plummeted from more than $110/bl to less than $60/bl. The combination of the sanctions and the collapse in oil prices hit the economy hard. In 2015, Russia's gross domestic product (GDP) contracted by 2.8 percent and the economy was plunged into recession.[5]

**OPEC members crude oil production
in mb/d and share within OPEC (January 2020)**

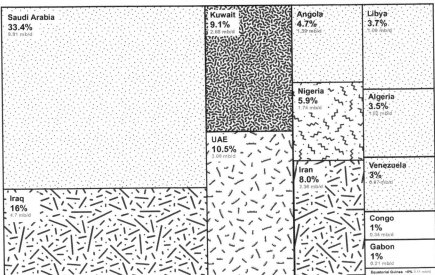

Figure 7.1 OPEC crude oil production share by country (January 2020).

Source: IEA Monthly Oil Market Report, January 2020.

These developments prompted Russia to introduce new policies to stabilize its economy. The devaluation of its currency, the ruble, for instance, facilitated the country's economic recovery. But due to the sanctions, some major Russian banks and companies were no longer able to raise capital on the global markets, and so an alternative was needed; and for this, an increase in the price of oil would of course be most helpful.

The Middle East and North Africa partly held the answer, primarily through the Organization of the Petroleum Exporting Countries (OPEC). Half of OPEC's thirteen members are from the region,[6] representing nearly 83 percent of the organization's oil production and most of the spare capacity, with Saudi Arabia ranking as the largest producer among them (Figure 7.1).[7]

OPEC+ Deal

For years, Russia played with the idea of collaborating with OPEC in public, but its support remained limited to sympathetic statements that fell short of policy delivery. That position changed post the 2014 events.

After a long period of negotiations, the historic agreement between OPEC and non-OPEC producers, which became known as OPEC+, was announced in Vienna in

December 2016. Its stated aim was to "rebalance" the market. However, markets can always take care of this themselves, as economists assert. What OPEC+ wanted to do, by contrast, was rebalance the market to benefit signatory countries, that is, at higher prices than what a fully freely functioning market would have set at the time.

Originally the agreement required a cumulative cut of 1.8 million barrels per day (mb/d) (1.2 mb/d from OPEC and additional 600 kb/d from non-OPEC), effective as of January 2017 and set for six months. Azerbaijan, Bahrain, Brunei, Equatorial Guinea, Kazakhstan, Malaysia, Mexico, Oman, Sudan, and South Sudan committed to reduced production in concert with OPEC members, but the key contributor that made the agreement possible was Russia, which pledged to cut its production by 300 kb/d.[8] Furthermore, it is believed that Russian mediation at the highest level contributed to Saudi Arabia and Iran putting their differences aside, thus ensuring the success of the deal.[9]

Over the next three years, that deal was modified, extended, and modified again on several occasions, partly to absorb the buildup of inventories in previous years of low prices and partly to offset continuous increase in US tight oil. Despite initial skepticism among market observers, Russia proved to be a reliable partner until the short-lived fallout in March 2020.

Up until 2020, the OPEC+ production cut strategy worked well: the oil price recovered from its 2016 lows. The cooperation successfully put a floor under oil prices. Prior to the agreement, prices were heading to below $40 a barrel. Following the OPEC+ deal and up until early 2020, they traded at above $60. For OPEC as a whole, however, this did not come cheap or easy. Most of the cuts had been carried out by the organization's members whose market share shrunk significantly over this period, though the market shares for Saudi Arabia and Russia remained rather stable (around 13 percent).[10]

For Russia, the benefits were clear. Within a year, the Russian economy stabilized, turning from "recession to recovery," as formulated in the title of a report by the World Bank.[11] According to the Bank, Russia's GDP went from a decline of 2.8 percent in 2015 to a growth of 1.7 percent in 2017. Its federal budget went from a deficit to a surplus over the first nine months of 2017, and higher oil tax revenues were generated thanks to a royalty tax imposed on a sliding scale that changes (primarily) with the oil price. These numbers played well ahead of the presidential election in 2018. Furthermore, the deal increased Russia's influence in the Middle East. Thus, the OPEC+ agreement paid off both economically and geopolitically.

Throughout 2019, there were talks about institutionalizing OPEC+ into a formal organization bringing together Russia and OPEC. Several challenges acted against such an ambition. Chief among them is the fact that OPEC+ strategy may become increasingly untenable in the view of the continued expansion of US production: the more successful the 2016 agreement is in keeping prices alleviated, the faster the growth of US production. This mechanism presents an existential challenge to cooperation under OPEC+. Additionally, the commercial interests of Russia and OPEC, particularly Saudi Arabia, are increasingly diverging, further questioning the future of the alliance. Politics, however, may prove to be more powerful.

The fallout between Russia and OPEC in March 2020 is a good illustration of the risks facing their partnership, though it was overshadowed by the COVID-19 crisis.

In March 2020, OPEC leaders convened in Vienna and proposed an additional cut of 1.5 mb/d for the remainder of the year. Russia refused to accept and for the first time since its formation, OPEC+ did not reach an agreement. Saudi Arabia immediately announced that it was going to put in the market an additional 2.6 mb/d above the March numbers (with total production reaching 12.3 mb/d in April) and drastically cut its export prices. (The UAE also immediately announced it would increase production by around 1 mb/d to 4 mb/d.) The media labeled the move a price "war," variously perceived as launched by the Kingdom against Russia, or US shale, or—in one of many conspiracy theories—by the Kingdom and Russia jointly against American shale.[12] It was, however, too short-lived to justify the label, or the energy put in explaining it. With hindsight, it seems that both Russia and Saudi Arabia surprised each other and overlooked the consequences of their actions.

The combination of price war and emerging pandemic proved toxic. As a result, oil prices were in free fall, crashing by more than 50 percent between March 1 and March 18, 2020, and reaching a low of $20/bl on April 1—the lowest since late February 2002.[13] The United States, the world's largest oil producer, stepped in and called on OPEC+ to reconvene at a time when both Saudi Arabia and Russia played hard to get. The unprecedented challenge posed by the COVID-19 pandemic forced Saudi Arabia and Russia to reconsider. A deal was reached in April.

Under the April 2020 agreement, OPEC+ would cut 9.7 mb/d over two years effective from May 2020. This equates to 23 percent for each member of the alliance except for Russia and Saudi Arabia, where the numbers were artificially equalized (the assumption was that they would both cut 2.508 mb/d from an assumed production of 11 mb/d).[14]

Economics vs. Politics

The partnership between Russia and Saudi Arabia is the foundation that has supported the OPEC+ strategy (for more on Russian-Saudi relations see Frolovskiy's chapter in this volume). While the interests of the two countries have been aligned so far, fundamental differences remain:

- While Russia and Saudi Arabia have similar production capacity, Moscow lacks the Saudis' ability to rapidly and cheaply change output levels due to complex reservoirs and a hostile climate. For this reason, Russian production cuts have always been implemented gradually over a period of months rather than weeks—a true swing producer it is not. A swing producer has the capacity to add or withdraw volumes from the global market quickly in order to balance fundamentals. Over the last decades, this role has traditionally been claimed by Saudi Arabia. The de facto leader of OPEC has long ago made a strategic choice to maintain significant spare capacity,[15] which allows the country to manage the market by scaling production up and down within a matter of weeks.

- Russian oil reserves are dwarfed by those of Saudi Arabia and other key OPEC members: at 106 billion barrels, Russian proven reserves represent only twenty-six years of remaining production (the so-called reserves-to-production (R/P) ratio) compared to sixty-one for Saudi Arabia and eighty-five for OPEC as a whole.[16] This implies that Moscow's focus is by necessity of shorter term than that of its OPEC partners (Figure 7.2).
- The Russian economy is not as dependent on oil revenues as those of Saudi Arabia and other key OPEC producers. According to IMF estimates, the fiscal breakeven oil price[17] for Saudi Arabia is around $80/bl.[18] Unlike many OPEC producers, Russia successfully implemented some economic reforms and demonstrated macro-economic prudence post the 2014 crisis. OPEC countries, particularly from the Middle East and North Africa, have announced bold reforms to reduce their exposure to oil price volatility but with limited success. Russia's flexible exchange rate and a well-developed domestic oil field services industry have better insulated it from the negative effects of a price crash. Russia's fiscal breakeven oil price dropped from almost $100/bl in 2014 to $50/bl in 2018.[19] The Russian government uses a conservative $42/bl oil price for its budgetary planning purposes. Extra oil revenues when oil prices were higher have been used to replenish the National Wealth Fund.

Reserves-to-Production Ratio, 2017
number of years

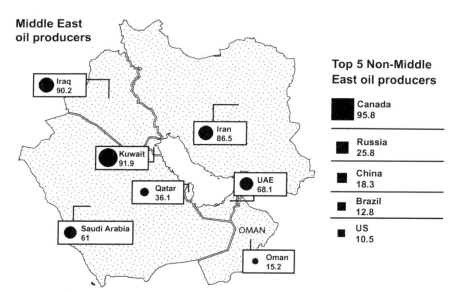

Figure 7.2 Reserves-to-production ratio, 2017.

Source: BP, 2018.

- Whereas all Saudi oil is produced by Saudi Aramco, the national oil company, Russian production comes from several independent companies that have to be coerced to fall in line with the authorities. While it is true that the largest Russian oil producers (e.g., Rosneft, GazpromNeft) are state-controlled and the remaining privately owned (e.g., Lukoil) are unlikely to challenge a direct government order, all of them have different strategies, shareholders, and creditors to respond to. The Russian tax code makes oil companies more exposed to higher oil prices as some instruments are imposed on a sliding scale varying with prices.

As a result, every production cut had to be imposed on the industry against the opposition of politically powerful CEOs. Igor Sechin, a former deputy prime minister, now the CEO of Rosneft and member of Putin's inner circle, has been openly expressing his dismay at agreement with other international producers. In 2014, he said that OPEC "practically stopped existing," only to confirm his unchanged stance six years later by calling the cooperation with OPEC "meaningless" and complaining that the deal allowed the United States to become the world's largest producer. According to Sechin, US exports to the Indian market rose tenfold and to European markets sixfold, from a low base but perceived as moving in the wrong direction. Russia's concerns about the expansion in US market share goes a long way in explaining its decision early March, though one can argue that they did not foresee the consequences.[20]

Overall, before COVID-19, based on market arguments alone, it was difficult to see how OPEC could keep Russia within the production agreements for much longer. The collapse in oil prices because of the pandemic gave OPEC+ a lifeline, after its brief fallout in March 2020. Challenges will reemerge once the crisis is over and prices recover.

Still, there are political reasons for Russia to decide to stick with its OPEC partners for longer. Collaboration with Saudi Arabia may be part of the Kremlin's broader political agenda in the Middle East. It is possible that Russia decides to maintain its OPEC+ partnership in exchange for support elsewhere in the region (e.g., in Syria). Riyadh's apparent interest in investing in Russia's Arctic Liquefied Natural Gas (LNG) project can be viewed through the lens of political relations as well.

Bilateral Deals

The Middle East and North Africa has provided a helping hand to Russia's economy thanks to the recycling of its petrodollars. Several Arab producers have accumulated substantial financial reserves in sovereign funds. Although the real value of the latter is not publicly known, according to the Sovereign Wealth Fund Institute there is nearly $3 trillion locked up in various sovereign and investment funds across the region, with their managers seeking lucrative options to invest in.[21] One such destination has been the Russian Direct Investment Fund (RDIF), a state-owned vehicle, designed to attract foreign funds to the country.

Founded in 2011, the RDIF has attracted $30 billion from abroad into the local economy, with the funds being directly invested in infrastructure and corporate equity. The fund has established partnerships with several from the investment bodies in the Gulf, for example, Abu Dhabi's Mubadala, Bahrain's Mumtalakat, the Kuwait Investment Authority (KIA), Qatar Holding, Saudi Arabia's Public Investment Fund (PIF), and DP World (United Arab Emirates—UAE). The KIA was the first Gulf-based sovereign wealth fund (SWF) to coinvest with the RDIF in 2012.[22]

Post-2014 and up until 2020, the inflow of funds from Arab Gulf states to Russia visibly surged. In 2015, during the visit of the then deputy Crown Prince Mohammed Bin Salman to Moscow, Saudi Arabia revealed that it would invest $10 billion in the RDIF. The figure was also stated in the Kingdom's "Public Investment Fund Program," as part of its Vision 2030.[23] According to the program, PIF and RDIF entered into a number of agreements for joint projects worth up to $10 billion over the period 2018–20, with $1 billion already invested in manufacturing, retail, infrastructure, and logistics.[24] There were also talks about Saudi Aramco acquiring a stake in the Arctic LNG-2 project led by Novatek, Russia's largest nonstate natural gas producer, which would start producing LNG in the next four to five years. In an act of solidarity, Russia announced that its banks and investors would be interested in taking part in Aramco's planned initial public offering (IPO), which enjoys the strong personal support of Crown Prince Mohammed bin Salman.

Such partnerships are at work with other Gulf states. In addition to the $2 billion committed to the RDIF in 2014, the Qatar Investment Authority, together with commodities trader Glencore, acquired a 19.5 percent stake in Russia's largest oil company, Rosneft, two years later, for a price tag of approximately $12 billion. The UAE and Russia created a joint investment fund of $7 billion to facilitate bilateral initiatives primarily for infrastructure projects in Russia. Other projects are expected to be covered in the field of aerospace, agriculture, and civil industries.[25] One note of caution: it is believed that many of the above deals have not fully materialized, if any. Following the collapse in oil prices because of the pandemic, it is likely that such investments will be further curtailed.

Rosneft and other Russian energy companies have pursued commercial opportunities across the region. They have invested directly in oil and gas projects, from Algeria, to Libya, Egypt, Lebanon, Bahrain, Iran, Iraq, and Oman, further building closer ties with various governments and local entities. For instance, in 2017, Rosneft signed a Cooperation Framework Agreement with the national oil corporation of Libya that "lays the ground work" for the company's investment in Libya's oil sector.[26] In Egypt, Rosneft acquired a 30 percent stake in the ENI-operated Zohr gas field.[27] The company also delivered 129,000 tons of LNG to Egypt under a contract signed in 2015 with Egyptian Natural Gas Holding (EGAS).[28] In Lebanon, Rosneft acquired the operational management of an oil storage facility in the northern part of the country, near the borders with Syria. The deal is for twenty years.[29] In Iraq, several Russian firms have invested in hydrocarbon assets. Lukoil, for instance, is a partner in the giant West Qurna-2 oil field. Meanwhile, Rosneft signed several controversial deals with the Kurdistan regional government to develop natural gas reserves and build a gas pipeline in addition to a $1.2 billion loan in prepayment for oil produced by companies other than Rosneft.[30] Although the deals angered the government of Baghdad, the latter's condemnations have had limited impact on Rosneft's strategy.

In Iran, Russian state-owned oil producer Zarubezhneft signed a contract for the development of West Paydar and Abadan fields. But the company pulled out as the United States reinstalled sanctions in November 2018. Rosneft followed the suit after it originally agreed, in November 2017, to work on several "strategic" contracts in Iran, which would bring up to $30 billion in investments.[31]

As put by Igor Sechin, CEO of Rosneft, "our interest in these projects is purely practical—this region features the largest resource base with low production cost and potential that is not fully disclosed yet ... if we include this region in the sphere of Eurasian business integration, we will contribute to solving general economic and social tasks—energy stability and advance in living standard."[32]

Nuclear Energy

In terms of producer–consumer energy diplomacy, Russia sees the Middle East and North Africa as an attractive opportunity thanks to the region's rapidly growing demand for electricity. Russia is one of the world's largest nuclear technology exporters. The Russian State Atomic Energy Corporation (Rosatom) is its main vehicle, describing itself as No. 1 in the world in terms of the number of simultaneously implemented nuclear reactor construction projects (six in Russia and thirty-five abroad).[33]

Russia helped Iran to build its first nuclear power plant (NPP) at Bushehr, which became operational in 2011. In 2016, Iran announced that it would build a second plant also with Russian help. Rosatom recently announced that it is in discussion with Saudi Arabia regarding the possibility of building some of the Kingdom's NPPs. In 2019, Russian energy minister, Alexander Novak, announced the opening of a Rosatom branch in Riyadh, as the two countries work on strengthening partnership in the peaceful use of nuclear technologies.[34] Saudi Arabia has an ambitious plan to build sixteen nuclear reactors by 2032. If the plan materializes, it will be the biggest commercial nuclear project in the region. Small wonder then that the world's leaders in nuclear power technology—American, Chinese, French, Korean, and Russian companies—are all courting the Saudis, seeking to benefit from a particularly lucrative commercial opportunity.

In 2014, Jordan signed a deal with Rosatom, after the company won the tender to build the country's first NPP. Russian state nuclear monopoly agreed to fund 49.9 percent of the $10 billion plant.[35] In 2017, Egypt also signed a deal with Rosatom to build four reactors over the next twelve years. Russia offered a long-term loan of $25 billion with a 3 percent annual interest rate to finance the construction of the El Debaa plant.[36] Although the Egyptian government claimed to have selected Rosatom out of three competitors in a tender, it is unclear who the other bidders were, or whether they actually existed. Given the strengthening diplomatic and military ties between Egypt and Russia (discussed by Alexey Khlebnikov in this volume), the outcome of the "bid" did not come as a surprise. Russia is also a key supplier of enriched uranium to Barakah, the UAE's (and the Arab world's) first NPP. Last but not least, Rosatom is behind the project to build Turkey's first NPP at Akkuyu, whose first unit is expected to come online in 2023.

The economic benefits of nuclear technology to the exporter are clear: as detailed in one study, the

> four-unit nuclear power plant construction by Rosatom keeps 24,000 people in work in various segments of the nuclear industry inside Russia, while each ruble of the nuclear loan brings 1.8 rubles into the economy by way of orders for Russian enterprises, including fuel supplies, staff training, decommissioning services, and so on. Each ruble also provides 0.54 ruble of direct income to the Russian budget.[37]

Furthermore, nuclear power deals rarely are stand-alone projects. They are usually negotiated between governments or companies with strong sovereign backing. And more often than not, they are part of a wider package of establishing cooperation with economic and political ties aimed at spanning decades to match the long life cycle of nuclear energy project. In this way, even if no power plant is built, civil nuclear cooperation oftentimes is the starting point for long-lasting economic cooperation. Commenting on the collaboration with Saudi Arabia on nuclear energy, Evgeny Pakermanov, president of Rosatom Overseas, stated, "We are working together with the Saudi side on a broad agenda that includes not only participation in the competitive procedure for large-capacity nuclear power plant construction project, but also an entire array of other promising areas."[38]

Conclusion

Russia's energy diplomacy in the Middle East and North Africa is proving to be successful. The growing energy ties with regional countries have, so far, resulted in mutual benefits. Russia and its partners have been able to respond to common challenges and maximize shared interests.

Before the COVID-19 pandemic, the OPEC+ deal exerted upward pressure on oil prices, providing much-needed support to these players. The influx of Middle Eastern petrodollars into Russia's coffers partly alleviated the impact of the Western sanctions against Russia. The investments by Russian oil and gas and nuclear companies in the sizable regional market are expected to have long-term positive repercussions for the Russian economy.

The Middle East and North Africa, however, is far from being a coherent bloc. On the contrary, bitter rivalries between and within countries are the norm. Russia has tried to maintain a positive relationship with countries across the region, mediating between the likes of Saudi Arabia and Iran, providing military aid to the Assad regime in Syria as it is fighting GCC-backed opposition factions, while at the same time signing lucrative commercial deals with the GCC.

As surprising as this may sound, it seems that Russia is skillfully maneuvering its way through the region's political maze to achieve its strategic goals. How long can this balancing act be sustained? Given the current trend toward diminished American and European engagement with the Middle East it seems likely that for now Russia will continue to pursue its strategy in the region, while avoiding becoming mired in local political wrangling.

Part III

Regional Partnerships

8

Russia and Iran: It's Complicated

Carol R. Saivetz

Even before US president Donald J. Trump withdrew the United States from the Joint Comprehensive Plan of Action (JCPOA)—designed to limit Iranian breakout to produce nuclear weapons—it was clear that Russia and Iran have been drawing closer. Their relationship is multifaceted and nuanced: They cooperate in Syria (discussed in Chapter 9), in the post-Soviet space, in the negotiations leading up to the JCPOA, and most recently as tensions between Teheran and Washington have increased in 2019.

This raises the question of whether Russia and Iran are strategic partners or whether there are limits to their mutual embrace. This chapter will answer those questions in the context of Moscow's strategic ambitions.

There seems to be general agreement that Vladimir Putin's and Russia's primary foreign policy objective is the restoration of Moscow's great power status. Andrey Kortunov, director of the Russian International Affairs Council, wrote: "Russia's geostrategic interests reflect the idea of the country's return to the world stage as a great power."[1] At the same time, Kortunov and others argue that the country's foreign policy behavior is constrained by its own weaknesses.[2] This sometimes tempts Russia into risky action.

Currently, the Middle East seems central to Russia's quest for great power status. If in the days of the Cold War, the Arab-Israeli conflict was the access point to the Middle East, today it is arguably Iran and Syria. Indeed, it seems that the Islamic Republic is becoming central to Russia's calculations in the region.[3] This chapter is comprised of three brief case studies. The first will analyze how Moscow and Teheran have cooperated in what the Russians call the post-Soviet space, including the 2018 agreement on the demarcation of the Caspian Sea. The second will look at the negotiations over the Iranian nuclear deal. The third will examine the current standoff in the Gulf. Taken together the case studies will provide a picture of Russia's Middle East policy and facilitate an assessment of the obstacles to Russia's foreign policy goals. The chapter will argue that despite the current congruence of interests between Teheran and Moscow, in the words of an observer, the two states are "not allies."[4] The divergence means that Russia's focus on Iran may yet prove to be risky.

The Post-Soviet Space

When the Soviet Union collapsed in 1991, both the Russian Federation and Iran had to adapt to new geopolitical realities. No longer were the two states contiguous and there emerged in their joint neighborhood six new Muslim-majority states. In the early 1990s, conflicts erupted within states, such as Tajikistan and Georgia, and between states, particularly Armenia and Azerbaijan. The Russian Federation reacted to—and in some cases, helped to foment—multiple crises. During the same period, Iran carved out a crucial role in the region. Even as Russia was wary of foreign interference in what it regarded as its backyard, it was ultimately able to work cooperatively with the Iranians to tamp down at least some of the conflicts.

For example, in the early 1990s, a civil war among rival clans and political factions erupted in Tajikistan. Russia sided with the self-proclaimed government in Dushanbe, while Iran at first seemingly backed what were seen as Islamist insurgents. Despite their mutual wariness, Iran and Russia cooperated to bring an end to the war. Teheran has invested heavily in infrastructure projects and has attempted to cultivate Tajik interest in rediscovering its Persian legacy.[5] Moscow, for its part, garnered permission for the deployment of forces along the Tajik-Afghan border. Together, the two powers thus reestablished stability in a strategically vital area.

Iran and Russia also pursued vital interests in the Caucasus. When war broke out between Armenia and neighboring Azerbaijan over Nagorno-Karabakh, both Moscow and Teheran backed Armenia—but for very different reasons. Iran, with its large Azeri population, was wary of the irredentist threat posed by now-independent Azerbaijan—not to mention the threat of waves of refugees—while Russia supported Armenia to gain a lever on Yerevan and deter Turkey from intervening in on the side of Azerbaijan. Despite sporadic fighting, a tenuous ceasefire basically maintained by both sides has largely held until 2020. Over the past few years, Russia shifted to a more neutral position and is currently selling arms to both. This is surprising in that Yerevan is a member of the Collective Security Treaty Organization (CSTO); and Russia, therefore, should not be selling arms to its enemy.[6] Iran, too, has not only deepened economic links to Yerevan but also begun to ameliorate ties with Baku. Most recently in 2019, the two neighbors signed an agreement to augment military cooperation.[7]

Central to the changed calculations is the emphasis on economics and trade rather than geopolitics. For its part, Iran has abandoned attempts to stir up Shi'a protests in Azerbaijan and instead sees Baku as an important link in the so-called North–South Corridor project.[8] For Russia, too, Azerbaijan is playing a major role in the energy sector, as well as in the North–South project. In an effort to promote the corridor, the presidents of Russia, Iran, and Azerbaijan met in Baku in August 2016 to discuss security and trade. News reports at the time noted that the three heads of state focused on the development of transportation and communication infrastructures in the region.[9] These trilateral summits have continued. Nonetheless, the project has largely remained aspirational. In early 2019, Iran sought a $5 billion credit from Russia to complete its piece of the infrastructure.[10] This potential Russian investment in Iran would further bind the two countries together.

Arguably, both the contradictions and the convergence of Iranian and Russian interests are most visible in the long-running discussions about the demarcation of the energy-rich Caspian Sea. Here, too, the collapse of the Soviet Union created new geopolitical realities: There were suddenly five littoral states asserting their jurisdiction over territorial waters and energy resources, estimated to be approximately 50 billion barrels of oil and nearly 9 trillion cubic meters of natural gas.[11] Export routing, including undersea pipelines, and naval operations were also contested. Baku took the initiative in attracting foreign investment in 1994, when it signed the so-called "deal of the century," opening up Azerbaijan's sector in the Caspian Sea for oil exploration and extractions. Around the same time, the Kazakh government signed a deal with Chevron to export oil via Russia and out to the port at Novorossiisk. Given these developments, the littoral states met repeatedly to discuss the demarcation question. Some progress was made in 2003, when Russia, Azerbaijan, and Kazakhstan agreed to demarcate the northern sectors of the Sea. But arguments remained: Azerbaijan and Turkmenistan continued to dispute fields in the center of the sea and Iran repeatedly objected to the multiple proposed delimitation schemes. In the most dramatic example, Iran went so far as to buzz a ship leased by British Petroleum and exploring for gas in the Azeri section of the sea.[12] Finally, in August 2018 a deal was agreed. Vladimir Putin praised the convention and stated that it "creates conditions for bringing cooperation between the countries to a qualitatively new level of partnership."[13] And then-Kazakh president, Nursultan Nazarbaev, claimed that "many years of thorough work" were put into the new agreement.[14]

As noted above, the Russian position has moved from blocking all development by other states through the 2003 tripartite agreement to this substantial arrangement among the five states. Moscow clearly understands reality and that it needs demarcation in order to exploit the resources in its region of the sea. Less evident is whether the new agreement unblocked the construction of the long-debated Trans-Caspian Gas Pipeline. Article 14 recognizes the right of any state to lay underwater pipes, subject only to the agreement of the states through whose territorial waters the pipeline traverses.[15] Yet, the same article states that any pipeline must comply with environmental standards. This leaves open the possibility that underwater pipelines could still be blocked by other littoral states. Indeed, Iranian president Hassan Rouhani explained that the delimitation of the seabed will require additional agreements.[16]

Significantly, the new convention sets limits both on the navies of the littoral states and, perhaps most importantly, prohibits any non-littoral military vessels from entering the sea. This mitigates Russian concerns about the potential for an increasing NATO presence in the sea. Nonetheless, the agreement does not override long-standing agreements by which Azerbaijan and Kazakhstan provide logistical support to US and NATO forces in Afghanistan.

Iran probably benefits least. After years of claiming an equal share of the coastline, Teheran received the smallest portion of the sea. Yet, some of Iran's concerns are mitigated by Article 1, which seems to offer compensation to those states disadvantaged by the drawing of lines.[17]

Iranian Nuclear Ambitions

In 2002, the National Council of Resistance of Iran announced the existence of nondeclared nuclear facilities near Natanz and Arak. The revelation began years of negotiations with the international community to curtail the Iranian program. At times, the Iranians, seeking to avoid sanctions, would acquiesce to inspections and would agree to voluntary suspensions of their nuclear program. But each step forward was followed by more evidence that Iran had pursued more clandestine activities.

In this period, Russia's immediate interest was the contract for the Bushehr reactor. Worth over $1 billion, the contract had initially been signed in 1995. At that point Boris Yeltsin, then Russian president, acceded to US objections and agreed to exclude gas centrifuges from the deal. At the time of the 2002–3 revelations and negotiations Russia announced that the reactor would be delayed until 2005 and that Moscow would not supply fuel for Bushehr unless the Iranians agreed to return all spent fuel rods to Russia. As international negotiations continued, Russia both tried to help Iran forestall sanctions and to maintain its standing in the international community. In 2005, for example, the head of the Russian atomic agency declared: "Iran is entitled to develop civilian nuclear energy; nonetheless, there are some issues that need to be elucidated via the International Atomic Energy Agency (IAEA)."[18]

Russian equivocation continued as Moscow tried both to protect its business interests and more generally its ties to Teheran and to look for ways to mediate between Iran and the other major powers. In particular, Russia proposed to Iran in 2009 that it send 1200 kilograms of Light Enriched Uranium to Russia for further enrichment. Ultimately, Iran demurred and the deal fell apart. Then again in 2011, Russian foreign minister, Sergei Lavrov, proposed a sequenced deal in which Iran would scale back its nuclear activities in return for the alleviation of sanctions. Iran initially accepted the proposal, but the Western powers did not. Analysts during this period noted that although Russia did not want Iran to acquire nuclear weapons, the Kremlin did not view such weapons as a direct threat to Moscow.[19] Despite the Russian equivocation, Moscow generally supported the international efforts to resolve the nuclear issue. Indeed, the Kremlin backed the increasing sanctions implemented against Iran and reneged on a deal to deliver S-300 missiles to Teheran (the Iranians even attempted to sue the Russians in international court), both the key part of the reset with the United States under Obama's administration.

Negotiations dragged on in fits and starts until 2015, when the so-called P5+1 and Iran finalized the JCPOA. Designed to limit Iran's breakout time to achieve a nuclear weapon, the deal signed in July 2015 also required quarterly IAEA inspections of its nuclear facilities. Russia was basically pleased with the JCPOA, expecting it to boost arms exports and pave the way for more dynamic economic exchanges with Iran. Moscow had already lifted its ban on the S-300s in April 2015, when Iran preliminarily agreed to the nuclear deal framework. Beginning in 2020, Moscow will be allowed to sell Teheran additional weapons. Russia has also begun to invest in the Iranian economy and generally to normalize ties with Iran. Yet, due to objections from the Congress, the United States was required to certify every ninety days that Iran was in compliance with the agreement. On October 13, 2017, President Donald Trump announced that his administration would no longer certify compliance and on May 8, 2018, he declared that the United States would cease implementing the JCPOA. Expressing "deep concern," the Kremlin proceeded to work with Iran and the other signatories of the agreement to maintain the deal.[20]

Tensions in the Persian Gulf

The US abrogation of the JCPOA was coupled with the reintroduction of major sanctions against Iran. At least initially, Washington permitted temporary waivers for the importation of Iranian oil, albeit at reduced amounts.[21] The US Administration also permitted waivers for nonproliferation projects at Arak, Bushehr, and Fordow. Concurrently, the other signatories are working to maintain the structure of the accord. On January 31, 2019, Germany, France, and the UK established a "special purpose vehicle," the Instrument in Support of Trade Exchanges (INSTEX).

Throughout spring 2019, the tit-for-tat cycle of escalation between the United States and Iran increased dramatically. At first, Washington ratcheted up pressure by adding other entities to the sanctions list including the Iranian Revolutionary Guard. In response, Iranian president Rouhani announced that Iran would install a cascade of twenty IR-6 centrifuges at Natanz. Then in early May, the United States further limited waivers, notably hurting Russian business interests by nixing the construction of a second reactor at Bushehr.

In mid-May, the US secretary of state, Mike Pompeo, traveled to Sochi to meet with Russian officials. Somewhat ironically, Pompeo's trip was designed ostensibly to improve bilateral relations with Russia. Within that context, it was understandable that Russia took a cautious tack. Putin stressed that he regretted the collapse of the JCPOA, but effectively warned Iran. First, he implicitly criticized Iran for breaching some of the terms of the agreement. He stated: "As soon as Iran takes its first reciprocal steps and says it is leaving, everyone will forget by tomorrow that the U.S. was the initiator of this collapse."[22] Second, he served notice that Russia would not be a "fire brigade."[23]

Also in May, John Bolton, then Trump's national security advisor, announced that the USS *Abraham Lincoln* Carrier Strike Group and additional troops would be moved to the region. A few days later, Iran retaliated by announcing that it would no longer be bound by the limitation on enriched uranium contained in the JCPOA and would restart work on the heavy water reactor at Arak. Worried that Iran might also withdraw from the Non-Proliferation Treaty, Russian deputy foreign minister Sergei Ryabov traveled to Teheran to urge Iranian authorities to remain in the deal.[24]

It should be noted that historically Russia has sought to use mediation as a way of establishing its presence and influence in the Middle East. One need only be reminded of the efforts of the late Yevgeny Primakov to persuade Iraq to withdraw from Kuwait in 1990. If Russia could calm tensions between the Trump Administration and Iran, it would be seen as a great success. Events overtook Russia's hoped-for role.

In mid-June, Japanese prime minister Shinzo Abe traveled to Iran in what turned out to be a vain mediation effort. Two days later, the United States accused Iran of attacking two tankers, one Japanese, in the Gulf of Oman. It is important to note that this was not the first attack on tankers ferrying oil from the Persian Gulf through the Strait of Hormuz. Again, Russia urged restraint. Ryabov furthermore voiced hope that the attacks wouldn't become a pretext for anti-Iranian actions.[25]

Then, on June 20, Iranian Revolutionary Guard forces downed a US drone. President Trump claimed that the UAV was operating in international airspace. However, in a signal that the Kremlin was losing patience with Washington, Nikolai Patrushev, the head of Russia's Security Council, stated unequivocally that the drone was in Iranian airspace.[26] Trump ordered a retaliatory strike but then called it back. Thus, as the United States hesitated, Russia was simultaneously shifting to a much more pro-Iranian position.

As of this writing, tensions in the Gulf remain high and the risks of stumbling into war loom. Iran and the United States both say they don't want war, but any miscalculation could precipitate a major escalatory crisis. Arguably, Russia benefits from the regional instability, short of war: Iran serves as a valuable geostrategic foil to US dominance in the Middle East.[27]

Looking Beyond

These three case studies come together in interesting ways. Russia's global ambitions can be seen as the underlying theme. Clearly, Moscow was and continues to be determined to get its way in the post-Soviet space. Reestablishing hegemony in the former Soviet Union is the first step in asserting Russia as a great power on the world stage. Iran, thus, played a critical, albeit secondary role: Teheran certainly aided Russia in Tajikistan and is currently a partner in the North–South Corridor. But the Caspian agreement illustrates how one-sided the relationship is. Iran was forced to balance its demand for a longer coastline and its hope to block undersea pipelines, with its goal of banning outside navies. Both Moscow and Teheran professed concern about a NATO naval presence in the Caspian Sea, yet the worry was undoubtedly more pressing for the Iranians. Concerned not only about a possible US deployment, Iran also feared deepening Azerbaijani-Israeli military relations. Indeed, Rouhani cheered the fact that, in his words, "The Caspian Sea only belongs to the Caspian states."[28]

Many observers note that Iran had little room for maneuver. Given renewed US sanctions coupled with Teheran's growing dependence on Russia, Teheran truly had to go along with the overall agreement. Yet if Iran in 2018 thought it would ease its isolation,[29] those hopes remain unfulfilled. In mid-June 2019, Iranian president Rouhani traveled to Bishkek, Kyrgyzstan, to attend the annual meeting of the Shanghai Cooperation Organization, where he hoped he would garner major backing. Although the member states voiced support for the JCPOA and the Iranian position and Vladimir

Putin criticized US actions, no offer of membership—which Iran had hoped for since 2008—was forthcoming.[30]

If the partnership is uneven within the post-Soviet space, it is more nuanced in the Gulf. If the two states, as noted at the outset, viewed each other warily, the heightened US pressure on Iran seems at the least to have forced Iran into a closer Russian embrace. When Iranian foreign minister Mohammad Javad Zarif traveled to Moscow in late May 2019, he emphasized that bilateral relations have never been closer. He also called for concrete measures from Moscow and Beijing to help salvage the JCPOA. Zarif clearly hoped that their cooperation in Syria would establish a base for more support vis-à-vis the United States.[31] From the Russian side, Alexei Pushkov, a member of the upper house of the Russian parliament, described the relationship as a "partnership which can evolve into a strategic relationship."[32]

At least initially, the US withdrawal was not a catastrophe for Moscow. First, the US abrogation actually boosted Iran's world image. After all, it was not Iranian violations that caused the deal to fall apart. This fact enhanced Iran's value to Moscow. Second, Trump's unilateralism deepens European distrust of the United States. If the separate trade mechanism, in which Russia has expressed interest, is actually implemented, it could potentially be a "prelude to the end of U.S. hegemony over the global financial system."[33] Third, tensions and uncertainty over the export of Iranian oil and gas helped to keep prices at a reasonable level for Russia (although COVID-19 drastically changed the situation). That, too, played to Moscow's advantage. In the view of Vladimir Yermakov, the director general of the Department for Non-Proliferation and Arms Control at the Foreign Ministry, the US pullout eases things for Moscow economically "because we won't have any limits on economic cooperation with Iran … energy, transportation, high tech, medicine."[34] Nonetheless Lukoil and Rosneft have already put any investment plans on hold in fear of US sanctions.[35]

It seems clear that as long as tensions simmer, Moscow benefits. Russia welcomes the US pressure on Iran, but only insofar as it pushes the current Islamic Republic's government to depend on Russian support.[36] Longer term, there are dangers for Moscow. On the one hand, it seems fair to assume that Vladimir Putin does not want military conflict in the Gulf. Indeed, when they met at the G-20 meeting in Osaka, Trump and Putin agreed that a diplomatic solution was desirable. By the same token, Russia has been unable to prevent the US pressure on Iran or resolve the crisis. Mark Katz (see his contribution to this volume in Chapter 14) noted that Russia's failure to alleviate US pressure "suggests that Russia can neither resolve nor even influence this crisis. This inability undercuts Putin's longstanding aim of reasserting Moscow's role as an influential great power."[37]

Looking ahead, Russia's ambitions are constrained by events on the ground and how Russia reacts could well determine the Kremlin's success or failure. The January 3, 2020, assassination of Iranian Major General Qassem Suleimani by the United States is a case in point on multiple levels. Suleimani was useful to Moscow: he coordinated the Iranian militias active in Syria and it was he, reportedly, who persuaded the Russians to intervene in 2015.[38] Not surprisingly, Russia criticized the killing and charged that it would escalate tensions in the region. In the immediate aftermath of the killing, Putin, in an effort to shore up Moscow's position in the Middle East and particularly in Syria, made a surprise trip to Damascus, followed by one to Ankara. Simultaneously, Putin must have worried that the assassination could unleash a war between Teheran and Washington. According to Konstantin von Eggert, such a war could have led either to a direct confrontation between Moscow and Washington or to a situation in which Iran would be badly beaten by the United States.[39] Ultimately, both the United States and Iran opted to de-escalate tensions following a relatively mild Iranian retaliatory strike on an airbase in Iraq. Russia heaved a sigh of relief that it didn't have to choose between unpalatable alternatives. Moreover, the Kremlin is now left to continue to support Teheran rhetorically and with weapons, while it positions itself as a mediator and power broker in the Middle East.

Within days of Suleimani's killing, Moscow found itself again buffeted by events beyond its control. On January 8, 2020, Iranian revolutionary guards accidentally shot down a Ukrainian jetliner shortly after its takeoff from Teheran airport. At first, Iran denied its involvement; authorities in Moscow hoped to deflect criticism of Teheran. Vladimir Dzhabarov, deputy chairman of the Foreign Affairs Committee of the Federation Council, stated, "The West has blamed Iran in advance for this tragedy. ... Anything is possible, but I don't see any proof thus far."[40] Even after Iranian authorities were ultimately forced to admit their guilt, Russia looked to explain the episode by blaming the United States. Russian foreign minister Sergei Lavrov, in his annual press conference, stated that the episode illustrated that tensions could easily get out of hand. He went on to claim that there were reports that "at least six F-35 fighters [were] in the air at the Iranian border" at the time.[41] Of course, the Kremlin would like to exculpate Iran and blame the United States. But, there are echoes in this case of the 2014 shoot down of the Malaysian jetliner by Russians during the war in Donbas. To this day, Russia denies its role in the earlier tragedy; in this 2020 case, it seems clear that Moscow is afraid of the parallels, which adds impetus to deflected Teheran's guilt.

Russia's inability to control events on the ground, whether the Suleimani killing or the downing of the Ukrainian jet, drives home Moscow's tenuous position. Therefore, we must question whether Russia could be tempted to overcompensate for its apparent weaknesses. In other words, is there a chance that Russia's desire to augment its role in the Gulf and the wider Middle East could lead it to take risks? Can Russia parlay its links to Iran to serve its own geopolitical interests? Or conversely, could Iranian provocations leave Russia in an awkward or even dangerous position? By its actions, it seems Moscow is desperate to avoid the latter.

The one constant in this complex picture—at least until the precipitous plunge in the price of oil—has been bilateral trade. Despite the vicissitudes of Iran's relations with the international community, Russia has maintained its trade relations with Iran, including a 100,000 barrel per month crude-for-services swap.[42] And at a June 2019 meeting of the Iranian-Russian Commission, Moscow announced its determination to continue expanding bilateral trade.[43] But, Iran and Russia are inherently competitors in international oil markets, even more so in conditions of its oversupply. Indeed, Russia has moved to make up for the Iranian oil that can no longer reach world markets because of US sanctions. Additionally, if Russia moves to fill the gaps for Iran's consumers when global economy starts to recover after COVID-19, Moscow will gain more market share and perhaps longer-term relationships that will outlive the current crisis.[44]

Clearly a war or threats to the Iranian regime's stability damage Russia's standing. Should the United States undertake regime change in Iran and install a pro-US government, that would obviously harm Russia's interests.

Perhaps to mitigate the dangers, the Russian government published in 2019 a new "Security Concept for the Gulf Area." Many of these proposals had been made previously, but they have been put together in a single document. At its heart, the proposal calls for creating a mechanism to combat terrorism and interstate conflict, and to provide humanitarian assistance to people and states in need. Specifically, it calls for abiding by international commitments, mutual obligations of military transparency, creation of demilitarized zones, and establishing a zone free of weapons of mass destruction.

But, it goes even further: "As more progress in the building of the security system is achieved, the discussion on downsizing the international military presence in the region and developing common confidence-building measures for regional and other states should be initiated."[45] Given that the US military presence in the region is much larger than the Russian deployments, this last is clearly a call for the United States to withdraw—or at the least significantly reduce its presence.

The Foreign Ministry proposal stands in stark contrast to US pitch for an Arab NATO. Instead, as Maxim Suchkov argues, this envisions a kind of Middle East Organization for Security and Cooperation in Europe.[46] To restate the obvious, although there is clearly a role for the OSCE, including a monitoring role in Ukraine, NATO is by comparison a major military force and one dominated by the United States. Might this new approach appeal more to the regional powers? Would this make Russia and the United States coequal in the Gulf context? Most importantly, should this proposal gain any traction, it will boost Russia's role as the mediator and power broker in the Gulf and beyond. As a commentator for the Valdai Club noted, Russia "is ready to provide a platform for negotiations between the nations of the Middle East."[47] Failing that, Russia risks looking impotent.

The bottom line seems to be that Iran is useful for Moscow—whether in Syria or beyond. By the same token, wholeheartedly backing Iran in its confrontation with the United States could conceivably lead to a war in the Gulf. Such an eventuality undermines Russia's goal to be a player in the region. Russian experts recognize the problem. As noted Middle East expert, Irina Zvyagelskaya, said: "Iran is important for us in Syria, but also in the Caucasus and Central Asia. ... But, that's not to say our relationship is free of friction and tension."[48]

9

Russia and the "Resistance Axis"

Julien Barnes-Dacey

Russia's deepening role across the Middle East is interwoven with its relationship with the Tehran-led "resistance axis" that now extends from Lebanon to Iran. This axis links Hezbollah, the powerful Lebanese Shiite paramilitary organization aligned with the Islamic Republic, the Syrian regime of Bashar al-Assad, as well as Iraqi militia forces and Iran itself. Russia's stepped-up Middle East position over recent years has in many ways been driven by partnership with these actors in the Syria conflict, where they have joined forces behind the now largely successful goal of ensuring the Assad regime's survival. But it is nonetheless a relationship tinged with uncertainty. Russia's goals in Syria are driven by wider ambitions, namely a desire to be seen as a great power and to thwart US-led designs at shaping the global order. Moscow's "resistance axis" partners in the Middle East are, by contrast, more immediately focused on securing regional security interests.

It has long been the aim of Western actors, and, increasingly, regional states, to drive a wedge between Iran and Russia in order to extract a more favorable settlement in Syria. Today, the United States and Israel, in particular, are intent on partnering with Moscow to force Iranian influence out of the country.[1]

This ambition is likely to be disappointed. While there are clearly divergences between Russia and the pro-Iran axis, relating to questions over the make-up and control of the state, the shared interests of preserving the Assad regime and opposing US-led efforts to shape the regional order trump these differences. They are likely to derail plans by Washington and its partners to secure Russia's support in curtailing Iranian influence. Moreover, Russia does not actually have the necessary leverage to chart an independent path and dislodge the Islamic Republic from Syria. Tehran remains the dominant external actor on the ground, and any move to exclude Iranian influence could result in severe challenges to the sustainability of Moscow's own position in Syria.

Ultimately, the Russian-Iranian regional relationship is largely focused on Syria. While the two share an anti-American worldview, the mutual utility of the relationship has been based on common goals in this conflict theatre. Moscow has not committed itself to a wider strategic relationship with Tehran. It is notable that Russia's close ties with Iran in Syria do not extend across other regional theatres, nor is Moscow strongly defending the nuclear deal, which the Trump administration has sought to end. Even as Moscow has strengthened ties with Tehran it has simultaneously nurtured relations with Iran's key regional foes, and if tensions do escalate between the Iranians and a US-led regional counter-alliance, Moscow is unlikely to come to Tehran's defense.

Convergence

The war in Syria represents ground zero for Russia's partnership with this "resistance axis," with both sides firmly committed to propping up Assad. The Russian military's 2015 intervention in Syria allegedly resulted from a visit to Moscow by the then head of Iran's Islamic Revolutionary Guard Corps (IRGC), Qassem Soleimani, where he pleaded the case for direct military support as Syrian opposition forces advanced toward Damascus, threatening Assad's very survival.[2]

Since 2015 the two countries have worked together—along with Syrian regime forces, those of the Lebanese militant group Hezbollah, and a broader array of Iranian-backed militias from Iraq and elsewhere—to shore up Assad's military position. Beginning in September 2015 Russia has provided critical aerial support to the pro-regime coalition, launching military strikes on Syrian opposition forces. Of noteworthy importance, it launched attacks from Iran's Hamedan airbase in 2016, the first time a foreign power has used the country as a military base since the 1979 revolution.[3] Russia, Iran, Iraq, and Syria also established a joint security and intelligence-sharing cooperation mechanism in October 2015, with operation rooms in Baghdad and Damascus.[4] This drew in Hezbollah and became known as the 4+1 group, though it does not appear to have emerged as a sustained mechanism. These combined efforts effectively ensured Assad's victory in the civil war, even if Damascus faces ongoing obstacles to gaining control of the entire country.[5] Moscow continues to provide military support to Assad's attempts to seize back control of the last opposition-held territories, namely Idlib province, as marked by a Russian and Iranian-backed offensive that began in December 2019, as well as the US-guaranteed Northeast. Moscow has simultaneously blocked Western-led measures in the United Nations Security Council (UNSC) aimed at sanctioning Assad or strengthening the prospects of a UN-mediated agreement.

The military track has been accompanied by Russian and Iranian participation, along with Turkey, in the Astana Process, which has sought agreement between the three key external actors on military dynamics. While Moscow has also used this track to cement its relationship with Ankara, seeking to draw it away from the Western alliance, it is notable that in Syria (as in Libya) Russia has nonetheless been willing to militarily oppose Turkish designs on the ground. The December 2019 Idlib offensive represented a Russian-backed push against Turkish forces on the ground. More often than not the Astana process has represented a venue for Russian-Iranian pressure on Turkey to rein in the Syrian opposition.

Fundamentally, Russia and Iran share a common interest in resisting the perceived US push for a regime change in Damascus, although they nonetheless view the conflict through different lenses.[6] For Russia, Syria is significant primarily within the context of the international order and Moscow's desire to block perceived hegemonic US attempts to engineer political change right across the globe. The conflict also offers Moscow an opportunity to reestablish itself at the top table of international power and diplomacy, an outcome that it views as having successfully achieved given Assad's military victory and its central role in ongoing diplomatic efforts to shape a Syrian settlement. This ambition also includes a desire to reassert a political and military role across the Middle East, an outcome that it has also secured. In the words of Arab government officials, Moscow is now the "new Mecca of the Middle East." The "resistance axis," the Gulf States and Israel, all look to Russia as one of the key external powers shaping regional developments, with its displays of hard power representing a more consistent approach than the perceived twists and turns of different US administrations.[7]

For Iran, by contrast, the conflict in Syria is centered on its position in the regional order. Tehran fears that regime change in Syria represents the first domino of a US-Israeli-Arab Gulf assault on Iran, with the ultimate goal of bringing about the collapse of the Islamic Republic.[8] The Trump administration's embrace of a maximum pressure campaign against Tehran cemented this fear. In this sense Iranians' commitment to the survival of the Assad order, which provides Tehran with strategic depth and allows it to project defensive power across the region, while also maintaining a deterrence capability against Israel and keeping the fight away from Iran's borders, is partly driven by perceived existential necessity. Here, Syria is one element of a broader regional battlefield that also includes Lebanon and Iraq.

While precise motives differ, the two countries share a firm commitment to ensuring that outside pressure does not dislodge Assad and that US regional designs are blocked. This extends to a shared understanding about the threat posed by Sunni extremism, which is seen as a tool that has been cynically mobilized by the United States and its regional allies against Tehran. Russia and Iran interpret "Sunni extremism" in the broadest possible sense as any group opposed to Assad and instrumentalized by the United States in its regime change agenda. While Iran sees Sunni militants as an immediate threat given geographical proximity, Russia also feels threatened by radicalization, particularly as it risks playing out among its own Muslim population.

Given Assad's continued struggles to wrest back control of the entire country and ongoing dependence on external support, this Syria-centric military relationship between Russia and Iran can be expected to endure. Indeed, Assad's failed attempts to seize back entire control of Idlib province in early 2020 are likely to cement the importance of the ensuring alliance. In part, Assad's Idlib failure highlights, anew, the fundamental weaknesses of the Syrian state and Assad's military capabilities. It reinforces the message that Russia will continue to need Iranian military support to guarantee Assad's ongoing position. At the same time, however, it also highlights that for Russia, Syria is one element of a broader geopolitical game. The other reason Assad's Idlib assault eventually halted was negotiations between Russia and Turkey to secure a ceasefire. This points to the fact that Russia's commitment to Assad will also be calibrated by wider ambitions, here marked by Moscow's desire to prevent Ankara turning back to the West.

Divergence

Even as this relationship has clearly delivered military success on the ground in Syria, it would be a mistake to overinterpret the strategic depth of the alliance. There are also clear differences between the two states.

Within Syria, these differences in many ways reflect the different motivations driving respective interventions. Russia remains focused on asserting itself as a major player on the international stage. Moscow has sought to use the conflict to secure a platform of international clout, including through high-level engagement with the United States, by presenting itself as the necessary pathway toward any solution to the Syrian crisis.

Toward this end Russia has, at times, invested in delivering the mirage of a political settlement that would give it international legitimacy (as well as providing an eventual exit strategy from ongoing conflict).[9] Despite being clear that it will not abandon Assad, Moscow has engaged with the ongoing UN process and recognized limited opposition aspirations in an attempt to jump-start a regime-favorable settlement. This has at times involved putting pressure on Assad to make minimal compromises by, for instance, accepting a Russian-drafted constitution advocating decentralization or by pushing for the creation of the UN-facilitated Constitutional Committee.[10]

But Assad has repeatedly rebuffed these efforts, playing off corresponding Iranian distrust. Iran's preoccupation with defending its regional security interests has pushed it, like Assad, to assume a zero-sum stance vis-à-vis the opposition. Both are fearful that any small compromise risks opening the door to wider change. Rather than work with Russia to exert pressure on the regime, Tehran has reinforced the Syrian leader's intransigence ensuring the continued failure of Russian diplomatic efforts.

Iran's position is partly shaped by ongoing unease over whether Moscow may eventually seek to dilute Iranian influence in the country.[11] This reflects some concern in Tehran that Russia might ultimately be willing to cut a transactional deal over their heads in exchange for wider international gains, such as Western concessions on Crimea and a loosening of broader international sanctions against Moscow. But it also reflects differences between the two over the desired end state in Syria, even under continued Assad rule. Russia is pressing for a strong central government and the institutionalization of non-state militias. Moscow has long seen the military as its central channel of influence in Syria and wants to curtail alternative sources of power. But it also appears to reflect a broader political and ideological position, extending beyond Syria, that power should lie with the central state. While Assad opposes Russian attempts to engineer a political track, he shares Moscow's desire to ensure central control over domestic security forces and has to contend with some internal pressures to ensure that Iran does not create a state within a state.[12]

Iran, which successfully deploys non-state actors right across the region, resists this approach. For Tehran, attempts to demobilize its militia forces in Syria, including by limiting the role of Hezbollah, threaten its ability to maintain influence and could make it vulnerable to wider pressures, particularly if Russia eventually turns against it. Moscow and Tehran have, on occasion, clashed on this issue including at meetings of the International Syria Support Group (ISSG) when Russia proposed the institutionalization of non-state forces.[13] Over the course of the conflict Moscow has also championed alternative military figures and networks to those supported by the Iranians, and internal reshuffles within Assad's military leadership, such as occurred in July 2019, have been attributed to ongoing palace intrigue between Iranian- and Russian-backed camps.[14]

These differences have manifested themselves with occasional displays of active rivalry on the ground. Tehran has repeatedly expressed concern that Russia's military and political initiatives, often accompanied by increased engagement with the United States, were taking place before Assad was sufficiently strengthened and at Iran's expense.[15] Tehran has at times played an active obstructionist role. In December 2016, for instance, Iranian-backed forces blocked an opposition withdrawal from Aleppo city negotiated by the Russians, forcing wider opposition compromises.[16] In June 2018, tensions arose between the Russian military and Iran's ally Hezbollah over respective deployments close to the Syrian-Lebanese border.[17] In 2020 there have been increasing tensions between Russian- and Iranian-backed military groups in southern Syria.

Russia, for its part, has occasionally hinted at retributory action. Some in Tehran, for instance, blamed Moscow for not providing air cover when thirteen IRGC fighters were killed in a Jabhat al-Nusra attack on the town of Khan Tuman near Aleppo.[18] Russia's control of Syrian air space has also allowed it to green light continued Israeli air strikes on Iranian-backed positions in Syria. Moscow also made no attempt to block US-led strikes on regime targets after its use of chemical weapons in April 2018. These have, in part, been interpreted as attempts by Russia to get Assad and Iran to fall into line with its ambitions. There were also reports that Moscow's unwillingness to step in and avert an acute energy crisis across the country in 2019—which resulted from heightened US restrictions on Iranian oil inflows into Syria—reflected a desire to exert leverage over Damascus and Tehran to be more constructive with Russian attempts to deliver a political track.

This rivalry has played out beyond the security sphere with intensifying competition between Moscow and Tehran for control of Syria's economic resources as the country now enters a postconflict phase.[19] Each sees control of economic resources and infrastructure as a way of establishing its longer-term influence in the country, but there is a degree of direct financial competition at play as well. Having invested significant economic resources in ensuring Assad's survival, Russia and Iran are both looking for payback through investment opportunities and profit schemes generated from access to Syria's resources and possible reconstruction plans.

Significant deals by both countries include securing leases on Mediterranean port facilities, Russia in Tartus and Iran in Latakia, and these have played out with increasing rivalry.[20] A 2018 agreement granting a fifty-year deal for the Russian company Stroytransgaz, controlled by Vladimir Putin's close associate Gennadyi Tymchenko, to develop phosphate mines near Palmyra reversed a contract that had previously gone to Iran. The change highlighted the nascent economic rivalry between the two, with Iranian media expressing concern that Russia is trying to edge Tehran out of postconflict financial rewards in Syria.[21]

In the Shadow of the Gulf States and Israel

Russia's alliance with Iran and the wider "resistance axis" needs to be placed in the context of Moscow's outreach to other regional actors, many of whom are Iranian foes. Even as Moscow has worked with Iran in Syria, it has continued to deepen ties with Arab Gulf states. Russian diplomacy has made a deliberate attempt to avoid the perception that it is siding with the Shia world in a sectarian regional conflict and has actively pitched itself as a security partner to Arab Gulf states.[22] Over recent years, and despite taking opposing views on the Syria conflict, there has been a significant intensification of engagement between the two sides, notably between Russia and Saudi Arabia. In October 2017 King Salman become the first sitting Saudi monarch to visit Moscow. Vladimir Putin, who in 2006 was the first Russian leader to visit Riyadh in eighty years, repeated the visit in October 2019. If the Iranian-led Shia regional axis is in many ways an exclusive alignment that pits it against Riyadh and its allies in a broader regional war, then Moscow has successfully managed to step back and maintain ties with all the players. Toward this end it also supports the position of the Gulf Arab States in Bahrain and Yemen, based on the proclaimed principles it applies in Syria regarding the importance of noninterference and the legitimacy of the central state. This essentially puts it at odds with the Iranian position in these other theatres.

The same is true for Israel, with whom Moscow has maintained extremely close ties despite working with Iran in Syria, including by permitting repeated Israeli air strikes against Iranian and Hezbollah military assets through Russian-controlled airspace (although this has occasionally led to antagonism, such as when Russia blamed Israel for provoking the Syrian army downing of a Russian military plane in September 2018).[23] It has also sought to limit Iranian influence in southern Syria to appease Israeli concerns. Russia has not been adverse to sending the message to both Israel and the Arab Gulf states that its presence in Syria—and a strengthening of the Assad-led state—should be welcomed as the best means of limiting Iranian influence. This sentiment has increasingly been embraced in Tel Aviv and Riyadh as military options to oust Assad and force Iran out of Syria have fallen by the wayside.[24] Somewhat ironically, Moscow has skillfully exploited this dynamic to position itself as an indispensable partner to those opposing the consequences of its military intervention and partnership with Iran in Syria.

However, Russia is careful to not overemphasize the point and simultaneously makes clear that its position is one of reducing the need for an ongoing Iranian presence in Syria rather than forcefully squeezing Iran out of Syria.[25] "[Iran] is playing a very, very important role in our common and joint effort to eliminate terrorists in Syria. That is why, for this period of time, we see as non-realistic any demands to expel any foreign troops from the entirety of the Syrian Arab Republic," said Moscow's ambassador to Israel in 2018, arguing that Russia "cannot" force Iran out of Syria.[26] Moscow also makes a visible demonstration of ongoing close outreach to Tehran to ensure that Iran is not alienated by Russian positioning. In July 2019 the Russian president's special envoy for Syria, Alexander Lavrentiev, traveled to Tehran in the immediate aftermath of a meeting between the United States, Israeli, and Russian national security advisors in Jerusalem that many read as a US-Israeli attempt to persuade Moscow to turn on Iran.[27] This balancing act reflects the core of Russian policy in the region over recent years.

In the backdrop of this Syria-centric landscape, Russia's ties with other core components of the "resistance axis" and the other regional states in which they are present, Lebanon and Iraq, are far less developed. This highlights the reality that the relationship with Iran and the "resistance axis" is not a profoundly strategic alliance cutting across the entire region.

For Moscow links to Hezbollah and Iraqi Shia militias are primarily viewed through the lens of the Syria conflict and appear to have largely been channeled via Damascus and Tehran. Russia does not maintain close bilateral ties with these individual groups. While Iran sees the value of a strong network of non-state regional allies that it can mobilize as conditions necessitate, Moscow's broader focus on strengthening central state actors means that the close alignment on Syria has not morphed into a broader regional front. Moscow's attempts to strengthen its role in these two countries, via the central governments rather than the groups making up the "resistance axis," were largely rebuffed. In Lebanon, a Russian attempt to initiate a $1 billion arms sales and cooperation package faltered, allegedly due to the opposition of then-prime minister Saad Hariri under US pressure.[28] A similar scenario unfolded in Iraq where a Russian offer of stepped-up military backing was turned down by then-prime minister Haider al-Abadi for fear of losing American support. Russia appears to now be looking to build up influence in both countries by deepening economic ties, but these do not equate to the deeper strategic relationships maintained by both Western actors, but also Iran, in these two states.

Meanwhile, Russia has not emerged as a strong defender of Iran's wider position and interests in the face of growing pressures from the Trump administration. While the US withdrawal from the Iranian nuclear agreement and imposition of crippling new sanctions on Tehran was not welcomed by Moscow, Russia has not taken serious steps to reverse this course of action or provide Tehran with the means of circumventing the emerging pressures. Equally Russia has not defended Iran's wider regional position in the face of growing escalation across 2019 and the increasingly real prospect of a regional conflict. While Moscow continues to navigate a careful balance between Israel and Iran over Syria, it has done little to suggest that it would play a more active role— let alone come to Tehran's defense—if a broader conflict was to break out. This reflects the reality that Moscow's broader ambitions and interests are not wholly aligned with those of Iran. Indeed, some might argue that Russian policymakers actually welcome intensifying tensions as a means of cementing Moscow's leverage and the importance of its position as the necessary mediator.

The Future of Russia and the Resistance Axis

Russia's ties to the "resistance axis" appear to be primarily driven by an alignment of interests focused on the immediate situation in Syria rather than a deeper strategic convergence. But there is a long way to go from this position to the prospect of a serious rupture between Russia and Iran, even if divergences could become more apparent over time. It is undeniably true that there is some Russian-Iranian rivalry for influence within the postconflict Syrian state. But it remains a mistake—one that has long bedeviled Western, and increasingly regional, policymakers—to imagine that the two countries can be significantly wedged apart, particularly over the question of Assad's fate. In many ways Russia is now stuck with Iran, whatever the message it is transmitting to Tel Aviv and Riyadh. On the one hand Moscow has often delegated the task of on-the-ground fighting in support of Assad to Iranian-backed forces. Even with Assad's strengthened hand, Damascus remains dependent on these forces. In the end any Russian attempt to seriously curtail the Iranian presence could threaten Assad's ability to consolidate his position, a risk Russia is unlikely to take.

At the same time, and perhaps more significantly, Russia does not actually have the leverage to drive Iran out of Syria. Tehran has autonomously cemented its position and Russia has neither the military nor the political appetite to mount a challenge. If anything, it is now Assad and Iran that wield the greater leverage. Both have on occasion succeeded in defying Putin's ambitions in Syria, to the extent that Moscow has often bent to their will rather than vice versa. In recognition of this dynamic, Russian officials continue to caution that the extent of their leverage over Assad or Iran should not be overstated and that Tehran will inevitably have been a necessary part of the end game in Syria, even if they state that they are willing to work with partners to try and see this influence diluted.

In some respects, Russia is now caught in a trap of its own making. Having so firmly tied its international credibility to defending the Syrian regime, it is unable to exert significant pressure on Assad or his Iranian backer when they act in defiance of its policy preferences. Ultimately, the tactical and ambiguous nature of Russia's relationship with Iran in Syria reflects the weakness of the Kremlin's position. It remains to be seen whether the internal contradictions of Russia's position in Syria will also extend to the regional level. Moscow's careful balancing act between multiple hostile regional actors has provided it with an unprecedented position of influence. But the darkening storm clouds of regional conflict risk exposing the fragility of this position.

10

Russia and Turkey: The Promise and the Limits of Partnership

Dimitar Bechev

Russia's relationship with Turkey is riddled with ambivalence. The two former empires are both partners and competitors: in the Middle East, the Southern Caucasus, as well as in the Balkans. Yet, historical memories and present-day divisions notwithstanding, Moscow and Ankara have managed to identify overlapping interests and build positive ties while containing conflicts. In less than a year, Presidents Vladimir Putin and Recep Tayyip Erdoğan went from tenuous cooperation, through outright confrontation after the downing of a Russian jet by a Turkish F-16 in November 2015, to a reinvigorated partnership. In the aftermath of the failed coup in Turkey on July 15, 2016, relations flourished anew. Moscow and Ankara are cosponsors of the Astana talks on Syria, while their militaries work side-by-side on the ground. Energy cooperation, dating back to the 1990s, is in full swing with the TurkStream natural gas pipeline complete and the Akkuyu nuclear power plant making headway. Trade flows freely and Russian tourists flock to Turkey's Mediterranean coast as they have done for years. Meanwhile, Russian-made S-400 surface-to-air missiles delivered to Ankara are sparking off a crisis in straining relations with the United States. Estranged from the West, the Turkish government has rebuffed the sanctions against Russia and opted for engagement instead. Putin and Erdoğan have turned into something of a double act in international politics, meeting frequently and taking up joint diplomatic initiatives. Western pundits and Turkish oppositionists alike draw a parallel between Erdoğan's authoritarian rule and Putin's firm grip on power in Russia (overlooking a number of differences, too).[1]

Relations between Turkey and Russia, though shaped by leaders' personalities, are a product of long-term forces such as the convergence of geopolitical interests and deepening economic interdependence. This chapter explores those structural factors at play and also maps out the implications for the Middle East and North Africa as well as for the West.

How It All Started: Russia and Turkey in the 1990s and Early 2000s

After the end of the Cold War, few would have ventured to predict that Russia and Turkey would befriend one another. Ankara was staking a claim to leadership in Central Asia, the Southern Caucasus, and even over the Turkic-speaking and Muslim communities within the Russian Federation itself. That was at odds with Moscow's own ambition to defend the integrity of the state, challenged by separatist movements like the one in Chechnya, and retain hegemony over the former Soviet Union. Turkey moreover positioned itself as an advance guard of the West in Eurasia, with initiatives such as the summits of the Turkic state presidents and Black Sea Economic Cooperation (BSEC). The Turkish security establishment regarded Russia with suspicion on account of its links to hostile states such as Greece, Syria, Armenia, and Iran. In 1997–8, the prospective delivery of Russian-made S-300 missiles to the Greek Cypriots triggered threats by Turkey's military that it would intercept the Russian Federation ships carrying the weapons.[2] By the late 1990s, however, Russia and Turkey had succeeded in improving ties. In December 1997, for instance, the two governments signed an agreement on building a natural gas pipeline under the Black Sea, the future Blue Stream. Turkish construction companies were already implementing projects worth millions of dollars in the Russian Federation, while "suitcase traders" imported large quantities of cheap textiles and consumer goods from Istanbul. The positive momentum gave shape to the Action Plan on Cooperation in Eurasia that foreign ministers İsmail Cem and Igor Ivanov adopted in November 2001. In the decade to follow, Putin and Erdoğan built on this inheritance. In 2004, Putin became the first Russian president to pay a state visit to Turkey.[3] Six years thereafter, High-Level Strategic Cooperation Council, a joint body bringing together the two governments, started regular meetings.

Drivers of the Russian-Turkish Partnership

Rapprochement over the past two decades reflects not only deepening economic links but also normative convergence, Turkey's geopolitical posture and domestic evolution. Russia's growing ambitions in the Middle East play a role as well.

Economic Interdependence

Thanks to natural gas, Russia (a major exporter) and Turkey (a consumer) have seen their energy systems increasingly intertwined. The Soviet Union started pumping gas over the so-called Trans-Balkan Pipeline in 1988. Two decades later, after Blue Stream came online in 2005, Turkey became Gazprom's second-largest market for Russian natural gas after Germany. TurkStream, which has now replaced the Trans-Balkan Pipeline, cements the relationship. Traditionally, Turkey takes around half of its gas imports from Russia. But despite new pipeline from Russia, Turkey would take under half of gas imports.[4]

After visas were abolished in 2011, Russians quickly became one of the largest groups of foreign visitors to the country, usually surpassed only by the Germans. Tens of thousands own vacation property along the Aegean and the Mediterranean coast. In 2018, a record 5.9 million Russian Federation citizens visited Turkey, an increase by 25 percent compared to the previous year.[5] The depreciation of the Turkish lira amidst economic turmoil over the past year or so has made the country even more attractive. At the same time, it has made energy imports from Russia, denominated in dollars, more expensive. That exacerbates the structural trade deficit that has been a sore spot in bilateral relations since the 1990s. Thanks to hydrocarbons, Russia is a top importer to Turkey, coming third after the EU and China. But Russia is far below in the list of Turkish export destinations, trailing behind the likes of Iraq, United Arab Emirates, Iran, Israel, and even Romania and Bulgaria. Of a total turnover of some $26.5 billion in 2019, imports from Russia stand at nearly $23.1 billion. The goal of reaching $100 billion, touted by Erdoğan for years, remains a bridge too far—especially given the poor growth rates in both countries and the likely recession ahead in the early 2020s.[6]

Converging Attitudes to State Power

Both Russia and Turkey share a political culture prioritizing the state's security and sovereignty over individual rights. In the 1990s, they started to accommodate one another over sensitive issues such as the Kurdish question and Chechnya. For instance, in early 1999, President Boris Yeltsin and Prime Minister Evgeny Primakov overruled the Duma with regard to the request by Abdullah Öcalan for political asylum. The leader of the Kurdistan Workers' Party (PKK) had sought refuge in Moscow, after his expulsion from Syria after Turkey threatened military action. A year later, Prime Minister Bülent Ecevit declared the second war in Chechnya was Russia's domestic business, after meeting Vladimir Putin, already anointed as successor to Yeltsin. Putin's strongman rule, defense of national interests against Western encroachment, and top-down modernization of society have always appealed to Turkish elites and society, transcending the secular/religious divide. "A Kemalist in the Kremlin," the Turkish press lauded the Russian president during his first visit to the country in 2004.[7] At that point, factions in the military and the bureaucracy, opposed to the EU-promoted liberal reforms and resentful of US foreign policy, embraced Eurasianism and argued for alliance with Russia. Originally at odds with the governing Justice and Development Party (*Adalet ve Kalkınma Partisi*, AKP) and Erdoğan, in the mid-2010s they shifted their loyalties to him. Soaring nationalism and anti-Western sentiments in Turkey facilitated the turn toward Russia.

Turkey's Geopolitical Posture

Turkey has always preferred engaging rather than picking fights with Russia. During the 2008 war in Georgia, for instance, it kept its allies at arm's length, eager not to antagonize Moscow. Policymakers in Ankara assessed that in case of an escalation Turkey would be left to fend for itself by the United States. Having invested in the Black Sea Naval Force (BLACKSEAFOR), a regional forum alternative to NATO, Ankara launched a Caucasus Stability and Cooperation Platform that aimed at reassuring Moscow and keeping Western powers at an arm's length from the area. Similarly, even if it decried the annexation of Crimea in 2014 and showed sympathy for the plight of fellow Tatars in the peninsula, Turkey rebuffed the Western sanctions. Since then, Ankara has been pursuing an intricate balancing act between the West and Moscow, seeing itself as a third pole rather than an extension of the Atlantic Alliance. With Russian military deployments in Syria, the South Caucasus and especially Crimea, Turkey finds itself encircled and vulnerable. Moscow's 2007 withdrawal from the Conventional Forces in Europe (CFE) agreement and, more recently, the Intermediate Nuclear Forces (INF) agreement adds to the Turkish predicament. Though Ankara contributes to NATO's "tailored forward presence" in the Black Sea and supports the pact's enlargement, it does that largely under the radar.

The Crisis in Relations with the West

Fourth, Turkey's authoritarian drift, culminating in the installation of a presidential regime through a constitutional change in 2017, has deepened the rift with the West. Ties to the United States and Europe have deteriorated and are now largely transactional. Russia's appeal is on the rise, as a consequence. Erdoğan has been the main protagonist in this story. He blamed foreign powers for the Gezi protests (a failed "colored revolution" of sorts), resented the Obama administration's failure to enforce its "red lines" after the Syrian regime used chemical weapons against civilians, and portrayed the Fethullah Gülen movement, linked to the coup attempt on July 15, 2016, as stooges of the United States and Israel. The collapse of the Kurdish peace process in Turkey in the summer of 2015 and the renewed fighting between the government and the PKK further poisoned relations. In 2014, the United States aligned with Syrian Kurds fighting the self-proclaimed Islamic State. Turkey sees the so-called Syrian Democratic Forces (SDF)—whose core is formed by the Kurdish People's Protection Units (YPG)—as a proxy of the PKK. Conversely, although it has its own links to the Syrian Kurds and unlike the West never listed either the PKK or its offshoots as a terrorist organization, Russia green lighted Turkey's incursions into northern Syria in 2016 and 2018 (operations "Euphrates Shield" and "Olive Branch").

Having clamped down on the Gülenists in the mid-2000s, the Russian authorities and Putin personally took credit for coming out firmly on Erdoğan's side during the 2016 coup attempt too.[8]

The United States meanwhile faces harsh criticism for its failure to hand over the exiled leader of the movement. Pro-AKP media and pundits hold America responsible for fomenting Erdoğan's overthrow, supporting Turkey's enemies, and even destabilizing the economy. At the same time, the Turkish president has been able to build a relationship with Donald Trump. In October 2019, Trump pulled out the bulk of US forces from northeast Syria and thus enabled the so-called Peace Spring operation Turkey mounted against the SDF/YPG. Despite that, Erdoğan continues to be a bête noire in the eyes of Congress and the US political establishment, with the procurement of S-400 from Russia triggering sanctions against Turkey.[9] For instance, Ankara has been excluded from the international consortium behind the F-35 jet fighter, state of the art in airpower.[10] In short, the Turkish government and its fellow travelers cast the West as an adversary. Russia, on the other hand, comes across as a geopolitical partner and supporter of regime stability in Turkey.[11]

Russia's Return to the Middle East

Last but not least, Turkey has proved an essential interlocutor for Russia in the Middle East. Ankara is critical to the Kremlin's bid to leverage military gains in Syria to secure a power-sharing agreement, cement Assad's rule, and underwrite Russia's long-term interests. Turkey is a bridge to various factions of the armed opposition and some of their backers across the region. The Russia–Turkey–Iran triangle cosponsoring Astana talks on Syria, ongoing since February 2017, has been one of Moscow's crown achievement. Ankara shares Moscow's view of Iran, otherwise its competitor, as an essential pillar of regional order. Turkey continues to support the nuclear deal and is critical of the Trump administration's sanctions against the Islamic Republic, even though it has reduced purchases of Iranian oil.[12]

Russian-Turkish Relations in Action

The following section looks at how Russia and Turkey interact across geographic domains and key policy issues: the war in Syria, the conflict in Libya, foreign fighters, energy, and security in the post-Soviet space.

Syria

In the initial stages of the Syrian conflict, Russia and Turkey simply agreed to disagree and compartmentalize their relationship. But during the "jet crisis" of 2015–16, Syria took a heavy toll on bilateral ties given the economic cost of the sanctions imposed by Russia. According to Deputy Prime Minister Mehmet Şimşek, Turkey lost more than $10 billion—over 1 percent of its GDP. Thanks to Russian airstrikes, Turkey's adversaries—the Assad regime and the Syrian Kurds—made territorial gains at the expense of its allies and clients, for example, the Salafist Ahrar al-Sham militia or the Free Syrian Army (FSA). But in August 2016, following the *rapprochement*, Russia gave the go-ahead to Turkey's incursion into the northern Aleppo governorate, as Turkey's own list of priorities gradually shifted from toppling the regime toward Kurdish militants and establishing a buffer zone along the border, while increasingly accepting the idea that Assad might remain in power in the end, thanks to Russia's intervention. With air support from Russia that targeted the ISIS, operation "Euphrates Shield" (August 2016–March 2017) created a buffer zone in the northern Aleppo province, and Ankara's intervention pushed out Daesh and stemmed the YPG's westward advance that, by mid-2016, was threatening to seal off the 900 kilometers of border between Turkey and Syria. In early 2018, Russia allowed Turkey to capture the Afrin enclave from SDF/YPG, by opening Syrian airspace and withdrawing its military police units that had been embedded with the Kurdish militia. By contrast, the two thousand–strong US contingent deployed in the Kurds-controlled areas prevented Turkey from taking the fight east of the Euphrates.

Yet Turkey's strategy of balancing between Moscow and Washington paid off. Trump's decision to pull out most of the troops in October 2019 from northeast Syria allowed the Turkish military and its Arab proxies to push out SDF/YPG from a buffer zone between the border towns of Ras al-Ayn and Tal Abyad (Operation "Peace Spring"). Russia adapted the shifting circumstances, having condemned the operation. Meeting in Sochi, Putin and Erdoğan hammered out a deal for joint Russian-Turkish patrols to separate Turkey's forces from the Kurds. In parallel, Moscow brokered an arrangement between the Kurds and Assad, which saw the regime move into parts of the northeast. Russian diplomacy talked up the prospect of a rapprochement between Damascus and Ankara too. In sum, both Turkey and Russia divided the spoils as the United States withdrew from the area.[13]

Friendship with Russia, as well as Iran, provides Turkey with a hedge to regional competitors such as Saudi Arabia. The fracture in Turkish-Saudi relations came into the open with the brazen murder of journalist Jamal Khashoggi in the Saudi consulate in Istanbul in October 2018. Yet tensions already ran high because of the diplomatic crisis between Riyadh and Qatar which broke out in 2017 (and was resolved only in 2021). Qatar, which now hosts a Turkish military base, has long been working with Ankara in cultivating the Syrian opposition as well as supporting the Muslim Brotherhood across the Middle East and North Africa. Thanks in no small part to Russia, the Turkish-Qatari bloc has been able to balance more effectively between the Iran-led alliance and Saudi Arabia and its friends in the Gulf.[14]

Russia has made a series of strategic gains through cooperation with Turkey too. Assad's army and Iran-backed militias conquered East Aleppo, vacated after a deal brokered by the Turks in December 2016. The talks in Astana, cosponsored with Turkey and Iran, enabled Russia to play the peacemaker and reach out to "the moderate opposition," that is, more or less anyone apart from Daesh and the al-Qaeda-linked Hayat Tahrir al-Sham (HTS). Moscow championed de-escalation zones across Syria, including the city and region of Idlib. With the failure of the Sochi conference (January 2018), however, Astana turned into a diplomatic fig leaf, allowing the regime and the Russians to push hard against the insurgent territories scattered across the country. Russia has furthermore been profiting from the tensions between Turkey and the United States. But it has been playing a double game all the same: never fully cutting its political and military links to the Syrian Kurds. (The latter were promised autonomy in a constitutional draft proposed by Russia.) Finally, though not insignificantly, the Kremlin sees Turkey as a contributor to the future postconflict reconstruction in Syria. In October 2018, Erdoğan welcomed German chancellor Angela Merkel and French president Emmanuel Macron along with Vladimir Putin to discuss the issue. The Turkish-held enclaves in the north, where the Turkish lira is now legal tender, have seen the influx of funds from Ankara at a time when the Syrian economy is in free fall.[15] The areas in question have turned into a smuggling channel badly needing foreign currency into regime-controlled parts of the country.[16]

Turkey's vulnerability vis-à-vis Russia has been on display in the case of Idlib. In September 2018, Putin and Erdoğan brokered a deal under whose terms the Turks would demilitarize the area, meaning neutralization of HTS, in exchange for a ceasefire and halt of all regime offensives. Home to some 3 million, including internally displaced civilians and antigovernment militias transferred from other parts of Syria following agreements with the regime, the northwestern enclave poses the threat of a massive refugee flow to neighboring Turkey. Turkish society, initially welcoming Syrians, have been turning hostile to the new arrivals.[17] The Russian-Turkish deal floundered from the outset, as HTS seized the greatest portion of the enclave, routing out or cannibalizing other factions. That in turn provided an excuse for repeated regime offensives in 2018–19, with Russian air support. Russians' inability or unwillingness to restrain Assad has prompted Turkey to scale up the transfer of arms to its allies on the ground.[18]

The situation around Idlib came to a head in late 2019 and the early months of 2020. Russia's air force gave full backing to a regime offensive aimed at recapturing the entire area. Fighting pushed Moscow and Ankara dangerously close to the brink, as Turkey ramped up its military presence and took on Assad's forces. On February 27, 2020, thirty-three Turkish soldiers were killed in an air strike that may have been carried out by the Russians. However, Ankara lay the blame on the regime and sought to engage Moscow. Russia meanwhile stood in the sidelines as Turkish drones took heavy toll on Assad. It also guaranteed the security of Turkish observation points that had remained behind front lines and were surrounded by the regime. At the end, yet another summit by Putin and Erdoğan (March 5) produced a ceasefire, which in effect partitioned the Idlib area, and launched joint patrols along the critically important M4 highway linking Latakia and Aleppo. Turkey was spared from a major influx of refugees. Russia meanwhile obtained Ankara's tacit agreement for transferring strategically located chunks of the enclave to Assad. This most recent deal on Idlib could unravel, for example, because of Turkey's inability to disband HTS. But it testifies to the resilience of Russian-Turkish relations.[19]

Libya

Russia and Turkey found themselves at odds in the conflict in Libya as well. While Erdoğan threw his weight behind the Government of National Accord (GNA) in Tripoli, Russia has rendered tentative support to General Khalifa Haftar based in the country's east.

Remarkably, Ankara seems to be applying lessons from the Russian mission in Syria. It dispatched military support in the form of heavy equipment and UAVs,[20] instructors, mercenaries (including a reported seven thousand Syrian militiamen), deployed its navy off the coast of Libya, and has been using intelligence gathering capabilities to back Tripoli. At the same time, Russian mercenaries from the Wagner Group, likely backed by operatives from Russia's military intelligence (GRU), have been fighting alongside Haftar's Libyan National Army (LNA).[21] Yet unlike in Syria, Russia was not initially at the forefront of the conflict, with its influence growing only lately. It is part of a broader coalition supporting Haftar, which includes the United Arab Emirates, Egypt, Saudi Arabia, as well as some Western governments. Moscow keeps channels open to Tripoli too. Erdoğan and Putin tried to find common ground. In January 2020, they called for a ceasefire in Libya and also took part in an international conference in Berlin.

The failure of the conference led to Turkey's doubling down on its political and military support for GNA.[22] GNA repelled Haftar from Tripoli and moved the front line to Sirte, the gateway to the eastern oilfields, and Jufrah air base, LNA's operational hub in central Libya. That induced Moscow to beef up its support to Haftar, deploying warplanes to both Jufrah and Khadima and possibly advanced-level air defense systems.[23] Together with UAE and Egypt, the Kremlin drew a red line before Turkey. Fighting de-escalated and UN-led negotiations gathered momentum. Eventually, GNA's head Fayez al-Sarraj and the speaker of the rival, Benghazi-based parliament Aguila Saleh (who bypassed Haftar) eventually agreed on a ceasefire in October 2020. But in contrast to the Berlin conference, Russia and Turkey—which insisted on LNA withdrawal from Sirte—were not at the forefront of the diplomatic effort to reach a settlement to the civil war.[24]

Foreign Fighters

A less visible but equally important aspect involves foreign fighters from Russia and the former Soviet Union residing in Turkey or passing through Turkey en route to Syria and Iraq. Initially, Turkey tolerated the "jihadi highway" as it furthered the fight against the Assad regime. Russia, too, reportedly gave radicals free passage in 2012–13—to counter potential risks during the Sochi Winter Olympics.[25] However, from 2014 onward, Turkey itself became the target of Daesh attacks as, after much foot-dragging, it joined the international coalition. Some of the perpetrators have come from post-Soviet Central Asia. Still, Russia and Turkey find it hard to cooperate at the level of intelligence and law enforcement services. True, the two militaries fought side by side against Daesh in 2016–17. At the same time, Turkish authorities typically turn down requests for extradition of Russian nationals suspected of terrorist links. Immigrants from the North Caucasus, adhering to Salafism (whether of the militant variety or not), are staunch supporters of Erdoğan and the AKP. The Turkish authorities also resent the assassinations of Chechen activists on Turkish soil, with Russia's Federal Security Service (FSB) under suspicion.[26] It is worth mentioning that Russian Muslims and Central Asians fight in the ranks of not only Daesh but also Salafist militias such as Ahrar al-Sham and Jaish al-Islam (which the Russian military has been negotiating with but also fighting against).[27]

Energy

Apart from the Syrian conflict, energy is an area where Russian and Turkish strategic interests intersect. Poor in indigenous resources but with a growing economy and a rising population, Turkey is dependent on imported hydrocarbons. Russia has been a top source of natural gas (covering around 60 percent of Turkey's consumption) and, to a lesser degree, crude oil. Once the nuclear power plant at Akkuyu is completed in the mid-2020s,[28] Rosatom, the Russian state nuclear corporation, will have a stake in the domestic electricity market as well. With 1,114 MW, Akkuyu's first (out of four in total) unit corresponds to roughly 1.6 percent of the country's current generation capacity. Turkey hopes to partly replace Ukraine as a transit country for Russian gas. The TurkStream pipeline consists of two parallel strings with a combined capacity of 31.5 bcm, one catering for the Turkish market and the other bound for the EU. Putin and Erdoğan jointly launched the first string at a ceremony in Istanbul on January 8, 2020. Russia is currently working with Bulgaria, Serbia, and Hungary with regard to the second string. However, regulatory hurdles related to the EU legislation, the uncertainty concerning the volumes of Russian gas available for the new pipeline, and potential US sanctions put the construction of TurkStream 2 (or Balkan Stream) on hold and the transit of Russian gas through Turkey is therefore still work in progress.

At the same time, Turkish policymakers and experts regard dependence on Russia as a challenge. The priority has been to diversify energy imports and transform from a consumer to a transit country or even a trading hub. The much-discussed Southern Gas Corridor, tapping into deposits off Azerbaijan's Caspian coast, is becoming a reality with the Transanatolian Pipeline (TANAP) and its extension into the EU, the Transadriatic Pipeline (TAP). TANAP was unveiled in June 2018, while TAP (started in 2016 with an initial capacity of 10 bcm) came onstream in November 2020. The Southern Gas Corridor is now shipping natural gas from South Caucasus, northern Iraq, Central Asia, and, potentially, the newly expanded offshore deposits in the Eastern Mediterranean.[29] It is noteworthy that Turkey has expanded its purchases of liquefied natural gas (LNG) from suppliers such as Algeria, Qatar, Nigeria, too. Thanks to advantageous prices, LNG outpaces pipeline gas in certain months.[30] As a result, gas imports from Russia shrank by more than a third in 2019.[31] The bulk of long-term contacts with Gazprom are set to expire by 2025 and Ankara will no doubt use LNG and Caspian gas as a bargaining chip to extract better terms.[32]

This development suggests that in the future Russia's footprint on the Turkish market may shrink further. In a similar vein, the growth of renewables as well as Turkey's economic woes could also limit the demand for electricity and put in question the adding of new units to the Akkuyu nuclear plant.[33] Recession in the wake of the COVID-19 pandemic is sure to drive down energy demand on the Turkish market and harm Russian firms.

Security in Wider Europe

Like Russia, Turkey is a country with connections to multiple regions. Apart from the Middle East, the focus of its foreign policy since the outbreak of the Arab Spring if not before, it has strong historical, sociopolitical, and economic ties to the Caucasus and the Balkans too. In the Southern Caucasus, Turkey has been cultivating a three-way alliance with Georgia and Azerbaijan, which has diplomatic, defense, and economic dimensions. A case in point is the Baku–Tbilisi–Kars railway inaugurated in 2017 as well as the Baku–Tbilisi–Erzurum gas pipeline and the Baku–Tbilisi–Ceyhan oil pipeline. The grouping is a form of soft balancing against Russia as well as Armenia, Russia's closest partner in the region.[34] The same goes for Turkey's thriving partnership with Ukraine that has both trade and security dimensions (e.g., delivery of drones to Kyiv). Turnover stands at around $4 billion and a free-trade deal is near conclusion, as the one Turks have with Georgia and Moldova. Relations are steered by a High-Level Strategic Cooperation Council, as is the case with Russia.

Another flashpoint is Nagorno-Karabakh where tensions between Azeris and Armenians remain high, after the conflict's escalation in the spring of 2016—coinciding with the standoff between Putin and Erdoğan over the Su-24 shoot down at the Syrian border. Then, Russia and Turkey avoided being dragged in another local military conflict. But then in September 2020, even more vicious fighting started, with Turkey—unprecedentedly—dispatching Syrian mercenaries, military instructors, UAVs, and, according to allegations, its own air force to the frontlines. The war wrong-footed Russia as it exposed its waning influence in its own backyard, inability to restrain Armenia and Azerbaijan, as well as the limited relevance of the defense alliance with Yerevan. A ceasefire brokered by Putin on 9 November led to the insertion of a two thousand-strong Russian peacekeeping force. Turkey set up jointly with Russia military monitoring point—floating plans for own permanent bases in Azerbaijan. Erdoğan attended the victory parade in Baku, a testament to the reinforced Turkish-Azeri security relationship. Turkey, at the same time, scored points at Russia's expense thanks to the territorial gains made by the Azeris. Still, Nagorno-Karabakh does not overrule the fact that overall Ankara holds less influence than Moscow in the Black Sea area.[35]

There are clear limits to the extent to which Turkey could use connections to post-Soviet states to even the playing field with Russia. Given the Russian military buildup in occupied Crimea post-2014, the upgrade of bases in Armenia (a stone's throw away from the Turkish border) and presence in Syria, and poisoned relationship with the United States, Turkey has much less wiggle room than in the past. At the end of the day, NATO remains the best insurance policy for Ankara.[36]

Conclusion

History and geography puts Turkey in an altogether different category from the bulk of countries in the Middle East, when it comes to Russia. Not only do memories reach back centuries but also today's Turkish Republic is a direct neighbor of Russia in the Black Sea as well as, in a sense, in the Caucasus. Moscow is no new arrival; it has always loomed large, even during the period of decline and retrenchment in the 1990s. Geopolitics dictates that this relationship is to be managed with caution, especially in light of Turkey's ambivalent ties to the West. Russia in turn has correctly identified Turkey as a weak link in the Western alliance, a profitable market, and flexible interlocutor with the Middle East.

One should nonetheless not forget that Turkish foreign policy is fundamentally driven by unilateralist impulse and seeks to balance between Moscow, Western powers, and Middle Eastern neighbors. Ankara is thus unlikely to leave NATO, even if it comes under harder US sanctions. In Syria and surrounding region, it will seek to leverage its ties to both the Kremlin and the West to what it considers its vital interests. The deal struck between Erdoğan and Trump over northeast Syria is a case in point. Turkey has likewise tried to involve its Western allies into Idlib, even using the threat to unleash a wave of refugees into the EU. Turkey works with but also hedges against Russia. This is why it is premature to proclaim the birth of a Turkish-Russian-Iranian triangle capable of replacing US hegemony in the Middle East. Internal discord dividing the trio as well as the influence other regional actors have rule out such an outcome.

For what it is worth, the marriage of convenience with Turkey is not necessarily a bad outcome from a Russian perspective. Flawed as it may be, such partnership is an impressive geopolitical win for Moscow. By co-opting Turkey and exploiting its quarrels with allies, Russia has consolidated its position in the Middle East and gained advantage in its rivalry with the West.

11

Understanding Russia–GCC Relations

Dmitriy Frolovskiy

Relations between Russia and the Gulf Cooperation Council (GCC)[1] have undergone significant changes over the past two decades. In the early 2000s they were frequently strained and occasionally fractious, due in large part to Moscow's suspicions that the Gulf monarchies were lending support to the Islamist insurgency in the Northern Caucasus. In the mid-2000s, ties gradually improved, with economic issues coming to the fore, only to be challenged again in 2011 by the events of the Arab Spring. The Kremlin's recent power play in Syria and Libya, as well as the diplomatic and economic initiatives launched across the Middle East, has complicated the picture, while altering previous patterns of interaction. The downfall of the OPEC+ deal and oil price that ensued, however, revealed that Russia and GCC relations lack strong institutionalization. Tumbling prices threaten to undermine the diplomatic achievements of the past years.

The Evolution of Russia's Policy toward the GCC

Following Russia's military campaign in the Northern Caucasus in the 1990s, Russia–GCC relations were marked by controversy. The Russian authorities accused the Gulf monarchies of funding Islamic terrorism in the region.[2] After Russia regained control of the situation in Chechnya and following the economic rebound of the mid-2000s, relations began to improve. The Kremlin stopped viewing Saudi Arabia as the chief sponsor of international terrorism, with Crown Prince Abdullah visiting Moscow in September 2003.[3] However, the scope of relations remained confined to shared concerns about economic cooperation in global energy markets.

The Arab Spring emerged as another challenge to Russia–GCC relations. The Kremlin perceived the 2011 uprisings and the change of Arab regime as harmful to its long-standing alliances and partnerships in the region as well as to its geopolitical influence.[4] The prospect of Bashar al-Assad being toppled put Russia at the risk of losing its only strategic foothold in the Middle East. Moscow also grew alarmed about the possible spread of antigovernment sentiment and political Islam across the Central Asian states and at home. By contrast, Qatar and the United Arab Emirates (UAE) advocated for a no-fly zone over Libya, and Doha emerged as a vocal opponent of the Assad regime, pouring in tens of millions of dollars to arm the Syrian rebels.[5]

Russia's military deployment in Syria in 2015 opened a new chapter in Russia–GCC relations. The campaign allowed Moscow to expand its presence in the Middle East and secure access to the corridors of power across the region unseen since before the expulsion of the Soviets from Egypt by Anwar Sadat. Despite the new agreement in April, the collapse of the OPEC+ deal in March and renewed tough competition on the oil markets revealed the fragility of relations. Against this background, however, it is important to understand what drives Russia–GCC relations and, in particular, what are the ultimate political and economic goals pursued by both parties.

Russia–GCC: A Look at the Region

The Kremlin's approach toward the GCC reflects its grand vision of the Middle East. The rise of radical non-state actors such as Daesh—or the so-called Islamic State of Iraq and Syria (ISIS)—and other militant groups posed a direct threat to Russia's own southern borders. While the ISIS menace is currently at its lowest level, it has not gone away completely. In addition, the unpredictability of the Trump administration allowed Moscow to fill a vacuum and expand its influence in the region. What is also at play is Russia's well-established relations with major regional powers, including Egypt, Israel, Iran, and Turkey. The decision by the Assad regime to extend lease of military facilities in Tartus and the Khmeimim air base by a further forty-nine years could help Russia to shape geopolitical dynamics in the Middle East for many decades.[6] Iran's growing influence across the Levant and formation of the so-called axis of resistance highlight Russia's status as a power broker amidst persisting Sunni and Shi'a rift.

Russia perceives the GCC as divided into three.[7] Saudi Arabia, the major power, and its closest allies, Bahrain and the UAE, constitute the first subgroup. While Manama and Abu Dhabi take a moderate line that is occasionally at odds with Riyadh, both are overwhelmingly dependent on the Saudis. The second subgrouping is made of Kuwait and Oman who subscribe to a neutral policy. Both have worked in tandem to promote diplomatic solutions to the war in Yemen and the rift between Saudi Arabia and Qatar, and serve as back channels between Riyadh and Tehran.[8] Qatar, the small but wealthy peninsular nation in the Gulf, constitutes the third entity in this subdivision. Blessed with enormous hydrocarbon wealth, its leadership pursues an independent foreign policy and wields soft power to project external influence.

Russia's approach toward the GCC reflects its own strategic considerations and exploits, covertly, the existing divisions within the entity. On the one hand, Kremlin has expressed commitment to deepen ties with Riyadh, with King Salman bin Abdulaziz's historic visit to Moscow in October 2017 and Crown Prince Mohammed bin Salman's, the country's de facto ruler, follow-up trips. On the other hand, Moscow seeks to maintain good working relations with the Saudis' regional adversary, Qatar.[9] This was demonstrated by the visit to Moscow of Emir Sheikh Tamim bin Hamad Al Thani in March 2018 and deepening diplomatic exchange.[10]

By engaging with both sides, Moscow is keen to gain recognition as an "honest broker" by the GCC.[11] The Kremlin notably tried to play this role during the GCC conflict over Qatar (ultimately resolved in 2021), when it refrained from taking sides and urged the opposing parties to resolve the impasse through dialogue, highlighting shared concerns for regional stability.[12] When the crisis erupted, Foreign Minister Sergei Lavrov remarked that Moscow's intention was to remain uninvolved: "These are bilateral relations of the states. We do not interfere in these decisions."[13]

The Kremlin's major priority is to reduce the GCC countries' alleged support for militant Islamist groups across the region and opposition to the Assad regime. Even though Saudi Arabia, the UAE, and Qatar reject the request of Damascus to join the Arab League (though the position of the former is softening), Moscow is still hoping for financial support in the postconflict reconstruction. This goal dictates the need to engage with the most intransigent players as Qatar and Saudi Arabia. Moscow hopes that in the light of the reconstruction and division of Syria into spheres of influence dominated by the major powers involved in the conflict—Russia, Iran, and Turkey— the Kremlin's interests and claims will receive additional weight. Its strategy to attain that goal prioritizes the application of coercive diplomacy vis-à-vis the GCC nations.

Moscow is also preoccupied with the trends toward radicalization within its own rapidly growing Muslim population.[14] Russia links the rise of nontraditional Islam to foreign funding, including from the GCC, which threatens to spark religious extremism and insurgency. Sluggish economic growth and the thorny path to recovery after the end of COVID-19 restrictive policies might catalyze radicalization and antigovernment sentiments. This concern likewise motivates Russia to seek cooperative and friendly relations with major Islamic hubs across the Middle East, including those in the GCC, to build trust with the Sunni Arab states.

Russia's efforts have been partially successful. The Zogby research poll shows that Russia has witnessed a significant rise in its favorability since 2016, with an average 13 percent higher in 2018. In the Gulf, however, the success is mixed; Russia's popularity rose by 30 percent in Saudi Arabia, but tanked by 20 percent in UAE.[15] Nonetheless, looking at the next tier of choices for dependable partners over the next ten years, Russia is ranked second in Saudi Arabia with 29 percent.[16] According to another survey conducted in 2018, the largest sample of public opinion among young people in the Middle East, Russia is increasingly regarded as the top non-Arab ally, with 20 percent seeing it as the region's best friend. Still, the majority of young Arabs do not view Russia as a role model to follow; it's the wealthy and developed Western states (Canada, United States, and Germany) that appeal the most.[17] According to the Zogby poll, Russia is ranked as the least important international player for the Arabs to improve relations with over the next decade.[18]

Russia's weaker economic clout bears on its strategy toward the GCC too. Moscow's struggling economy and lack of foreign investment add motivation to seek new sources of funding. In effect, Russia is willing to exert hard power and exploit possible security risks to the GCC to obtain economic benefits in return.[19] Decline in oil incomes, limited ability to borrow abroad due to Western sanctions coupled with COVID-19 effects might exacerbate economic hardships in Russia and trigger political repercussions. Although, on the one hand, growing fiscal conservatism in the Gulf might dramatically decrease levels of foreign investments, including to Russia, on the other hand, Moscow could be eager to engage into foreign ventures in the Middle East in order to boost oil prices and attract financial flows from the Gulf.

The Gulf nations, while troubled by continuing internal dissensions and most recently declining oil revenues, see Moscow's strategy as coherent. They perceive Russia as a declining power that strives to preserve and protect its hydrocarbon market share, and that therefore it relies on hard power to secure its objectives. The monarchies keep geopolitical options open, in light of a broader regional competition with Iran that might grow more acute because of the US pressure and Tehran's poor state of affairs. For them, Moscow is both a rival and an intermediary. Therefore, the GCC countries consider that stable diplomatic exchange and engagements are more preferable and these so far served their needs well. Furthermore, they are pragmatically acknowledging that Russia will not dramatically change its strategy in Syria and across the Middle East, unless heavy economic damages inflicted by COVID-19 trigger a full-fledged political crisis.

Russia and Saudi Arabia: Drivers of Rapprochement

Within the GCC, the Kremlin places a higher premium on relations with Saudi Arabia. Back in 1926, Bolshevik Russia was among the first to recognize the would-be Saudi Arabia, after the House of Saud unified the Kingdom of Hejaz with the Sultanate of Nejd. In the 1920s, the Soviets tried to open the local market for oil and agricultural products. Politically, they strived to outmaneuver the British Empire and create a diplomatic bridgehead in order to spread their influence across the Middle East.[20] Today, Moscow perceives Riyadh as a major regional player thanks to the holy sites on its soil and, most importantly, hydrocarbon reserves and influence over energy markets worldwide. Riyadh, too, acknowledges Russia as a leading player in security and energy.[21] It seeks to engage and utilize its energy wealth and investment muscle as powerful bargaining chips.

The Saudis look at Russia's close relations with Tehran and Bashar al-Assad as a threat to national interest. They also believe that Moscow lacks the potential to prevent Iran from entrenching itself in the Levant. Russia therefore can only serve as an effective backchannel when Sunni–Shia tensions rise. Russia, in contrast, acknowledges that Saudi Arabia remains one of the major US allies in the region. It reckons that the regime has enough resilience to withstand economic and political disruptions at least for the next decade. The mismatch of perceptions underscores the limitations of rapprochement, on the one hand. On the other, it also sets the scene for limited but quite fruitful engagement in areas where interests converge, without excluding occasional bickering.

The upcoming accession to the throne of the presumably reform-oriented Crown Prince Mohammed bin Salman indicates that changes might be in the offing. Given high youth unemployment (currently running at 32.6%), rampant corruption, sectarian tensions in the oil-rich Eastern Province, and more, it is clear that changes are badly needed for the survival of the regime. Riyadh's oil reserves are likely to run dry in seventy years' time, which poses a long-term challenge.[22] Increased repression, arrests of the members of the royal family, and the absence of serious economic or social improvements, however, reveal that the Crown Prince has been more interested in consolidating his power, as well as inciting local nationalism. This means that the regime would become even more centralized and repressive in the near future, with foreign policy bearing directly on domestic affairs.

Saudi Arabia's domestic concerns drive its rapprochement with Russia. The success of the so-called Saudi Vision 2030 reform initiative and domestic stability depend on security and peace in the short term.[23] That implies cooperation with Russia as the self-proclaimed regional powerbroker and an aggressive declining power. It also seems that Putin and Mohammed bin Salman developed good chemistry, adding to cooperation at state-to-state level. However, the collapse of the OPEC+ deal in March 2020 might have affected this relationship. With diplomatic partnership largely a function of positive personal ties, both leaders, as versatile bazaar traders, could continue to pursue pragmatic engagement and minimize frictions. The resurrection of OPEC+ deal in April 2020 signals exactly that. Still, it is difficult to predict how relations between the two leaders would evolve as patterns of bilateral exchange lack institutionalization and are very vulnerable to disruptions.

Russia–Saudi Arabia relations are also marred by controversies. Both countries hold different views on Yemen and the blockade imposed on Qatar. Differences, however, do not stop from limited cooperation between their leaders. The Kremlin's proactive diplomacy amidst the strategy of nonalignment with both Qatar and Yemen asserts own interests and sends a powerful signal of acknowledgment of Riyadh's foreign policy. The same works for Saudi Arabia.

Riyadh policymakers see Russia as a regional partner of Iran. Saudi Arabia is losing ground to pro-Iranian actors across the Levant and finds itself bogged down in Yemen. For the Saudis, it is important to woo Moscow away from Tehran.[24] At the same time, both Russia and Saudi Arabia have good relations with Egypt and support President Abdel Fatah al-Sisi's claim that he is fighting terrorism. Both countries also share largely similar views on Libya where they are aligned with General Khalifa Haftar.

Better relations might help Moscow in softening Saudi Arabia's opposition to Assad. With the scramble for Syrian territory coming to an end and Moscow actually seeking to freeze the conflict, the postconflict reconstruction phase is also looming on the horizon.[25] Russia needs to secure Riyadh's neutrality in order to avoid the anti-Assad factions disrupting the process. It is likewise hoping for support in the future with its version of the political settlement, but so far it is unclear how and at which price Moscow can obtain such support from Riyadh.

Both nations have becoming involved in public diplomacy. Riyadh increased the quota of Russian citizens traveling to the country for hajj to 20,500 in 2018 and kept it on the same level in 2019.[26] The number of pilgrims to Mecca is the highest in Russia's history. Saudi Arabia contributes to these exchanges as well. The St. Petersburg International Economic Forums (SPIEF) in 2018 and 2019 were attended by the largest Saudi delegations in its twenty-three-year history.[27]

Saudi Arabia has been resorting to economic diplomacy in order to smoothen relations with Russia. During King Salman's visit to Moscow in October 2017, Russian officials reported about Riyadh's plans to invest in more than twenty-five different projects in the country.[28] Special attention should be given to evolving partnership between two sovereign funds: the Russian Direct Investment Fund (RDIF) and the Public Investment

Fund of Saudi Arabia (PIF). Announced in the wake of the Saudi monarch's visit to Russia, its aim is to establish a new vehicle for investment in the energy sector.[29] Two years prior to King Salman's trip, a deal was agreed between the PIF and the RDIF for the joint investment of $10 billion in infrastructure and other projects.[30] Russia's intention was to use RDIF as a means to take part in Saudi Aramco's (SA) initial public offering (IPO),[31] which Saudi authorities ultimately conducted in December 2019. In February 2019, RDIF and SA agreed on the main terms of investment in Novomet Group, one of Russia's largest developers and producers of submersible equipment for the oil industry.[32] According to the Russian side, between 2015 and 2019 under PIF and RDIF deal over $2.5 billion have been invested in joint projects.[33] In 2018, Novatek PJSC and SA agreed to team up on the former's $20 billion liquefied natural gas (LNG)-2 project in the Arctic. Despite reports that the negotiations have failed, Aramco reiterated its interest and confirmed extension of its offer to the Russian side.[34] Riyadh's interest in reducing its domestic power sector's dependence on crude oil and Russia's quest to boost its LNG exports could deepen cooperation further.

In October 2019, Putin received a lavish reception in Riyadh, complete with sixteen Arabian horses accompanying his motorcade from the airport. He oversaw the signing of some twenty bilateral agreements, including between RDIF and PIF, worth more than $2 billion. The collapse of the OPEC+ deal in March 2020 and the new agreement in April thanks to Trump's mediation, however, might cancel all the previous achievements and halt or change the format of further economic cooperation.

Russia and Qatar: Getting Slightly Closer

Russia–Qatar relations have seen ups and downs. Doha and Moscow treat each other as major competitors on the global gas market and have serious differences with regard to Bashar al-Assad's regime in Syria.[35] Moscow values the wealthy emirate's independence from the Saudis and its pragmatic foreign policy. The Qatari leadership appreciates Russia's growing geopolitical ambitions and yet also perceives it as a declining power and a rogue authoritarian regime. Pragmatism and to a certain degree like-mindedness bring the two countries together.

The relatively recent past has not been problems-free. Qatar remains convinced that Russia was behind the 2004 assassination of Zelimkhan Yandarbiyev, a former president of the breakaway Chechen Republic who was killed in Doha.[36] Qatari law enforcement apprehended the culprits, Russian Federation citizens, but then extradited them to Moscow to avoid conflict. Bilateral relations came under strain again following an incident involving the Russian ambassador Vladimir Titorenko at Doha airport in 2011. He was assaulted after allegedly refusing to show to security officials diplomatic mail that he was carrying. In response, Russia temporarily downgraded diplomatic relations. The ambassador had previously made public statements in support of the Syrian regime.[37]

Doha has various assets to protect itself and project regional influence. The country hosts the Al Udeid Air Base, which is one of the largest US military facilities overseas.

Hydrocarbon and the pan-Arab Al Jazeera television network add to Qatar's clout too.[38] In addition, Doha backs Muslim Brotherhood and other Islamist groups. Yet Russia's military campaign in Syria has frustrated Doha's regional ambitions and stimulated more active diplomatic and economic engagement with Moscow.

Although Moscow remained impartial in the GCC rift over Qatar, Russian officials expressed readiness to increase supplies of food to Doha to relieve the blockade imposed by Saudi Arabia and its allies.[39] The Qatari leadership appreciated Russia's offer. Two official visits to Moscow by the new emir, Sheikh Tamim bin Hamad Al Thani, in 2016 and 2018, and regular communication by phone with Vladimir Putin sent bilateral relations on an upward trajectory. In March 2019, Russian foreign minister Sergey Lavrov also visited Qatar. He ignored the ongoing blockade by flying directly from Doha on to Riyadh.[40] In effect, Russia distanced itself from the rival camps within the GCC and signaled its readiness to talk to all sides, tacitly acknowledging Qatar's predicament.

As Russia is looking to attract foreign funds to bolster its struggling economy, it might well turn to Qatar.[41] As the Qatari ambassador to Moscow Fahad bin Mohamed Al-Attiyah put it to Bloomberg in March 2019: "[w]e see Russia's economy to be stable and the potential for growth is huge."[42] Despite this upbeat declaration and Doha's announced readiness to acquire a stake of up to 25 percent in Moscow's Vnukovo International Airport, Russia's third-largest hub, Qatar's investments stock in Russia is relatively modest. The Qatar Investment Authority's overall assets in the country are valued at more than $2.5 billion.[43] But this volume of investment is rather low compared to Qatar's trading partners from Western Europe, North America, and East Asia; in the case of Russia, Doha appears to be using investment as an add-on or a tool in the service of diplomacy.

Russia and Qatar are the world's largest LNG exporters and since recently started to cooperate more within the framework of the Gas Exporting Countries Forum (GECF). However, the forum still plays a largely symbolic role. There were more positive outcomes in the oil field. Doha became the owner of a 19.5 percent stake in Rosneft PJSC after the troubled Chinese CEFC Energy Co announced that it would not proceed with the original deal.[44] In 2019, leaks revealed hidden political rationale behind the deal: sources claimed that a large share of the acquisition was financed by VTB, a Russian state-owned bank, via complicated loan scheme to QIA.[45] Nonetheless, cooperation in energy gradually spills over to other domains. During the visit of the emir of Qatar to Russia in March 2018, Rosneft and the Qatar Foundation signed a cooperation agreement in the area of science and education.[46] Economic and political exchange is meanwhile growing. Qatar was set to attend the SPIEF in 2020 as the main guest nation.[47] The cancellation of the event due to the coronavirus pandemic postponed its participation for 2021.

Doha waived entry visa requirements for Russian citizens in 2017 in the hope of boosting tourist numbers.[48] Early in 2018 Doha opened a representative office of Qatar Tourism Authority in Moscow; 2018 was also declared the Qatar–Russia year of culture.[49] Yet levels of cultural exchange and tourism remain insufficient to influence bilateral relations and will most likely stay on the same level.

Russia and the UAE: Economic Diplomacy

Russia does not pose a security threat to the UAE and disagreements are kept under control. Moscow sees the emirate as a development-oriented oasis of peace pursuing moderate foreign policy. Abu Dhabi perceives economic opportunities too. Thus Russia–UAE relations are mostly confined to diplomatic and trade exchanges.

Nominally, Russia and UAE back opposing sides across the Middle East. Yet Abu Dhabi became receptive to Moscow's involvement in the region, long before Doha or Riyadh did so. The Emiratis refrained to call out Russia for its actions in Syria. Russia, in turn, maintained links to the UAE leadership and expressed support in the long-standing territorial dispute with Iran over the islands of Abu Musa, Greater Tunb, and Lesser Tunb.

Both Russia and the UAE have been vocal advocates of religious moderation and the fight against extremism. In 2016, the Abu Dhabi-based Tabah Foundation co-organized the Grozny Conference bringing together Sunni Islam's most influential leaders. Notably, the event excluded Salafism and Wahhabism from its definition of Sunni Islam.[50]

Both were united in supporting Egyptian president Abdel Fatah al-Sisi as well as Libyan strongman Haftar. To Russia, Libya presents both a valuable opportunity to project its geopolitical influence within the region and beyond, including abilities to influence southern European nations such as Italy, and also utilize its relations with Haftar to boost its stance throughout oil markets. To UAE, Haftar appears as the only alternative to the Islamists and the major figure capable of bringing the fragmented nation together. Thus, Abu Dhabi so far has been generally receptive to Russia's engagement.

Moscow is keen on boosting economic, energy, and defense industry links with the UAE, hoping to attract investment in infrastructure as well as tourism. Abu Dhabi is interested in Russia's agricultural exports, especially given its own food security concerns, and is likewise eager to have more Russian visitors.[51]

In October 2019, Putin was greeted with decorated cars resembling a Russian police vehicle and the white–blue–red tricolor painted in the sky of Abu Dhabi. The visit that included talks with Sheikh Mohammen Bin Zayed, the crown prince, yielded deals worth $1.3 billion. They included sectors such as mining, financial services, logistics, and retail, yet energy was the main highlight. Lukoil acquired a 5 percent stake in the Ghasha sour gas field, the first time ever a Russian energy firm was allowed to participate in exploration projects in the UAE.[52] But just like in case with Saudi Arabia, collapse of the OPEC+ deal and growing fiscal conservatism pushed Emirati leadership to have some distance in relations with the Kremlin.

With both nations sharing concerns about the political settlement in Syria and recognizing the need for a wider security framework across the GCC, political goodwill has greased the wheels for new exchanges. It is, however, hard to tell how much difference Russia's power play in the region has made. Economic cooperation between Russia and the UAE had been building up for years before the aerial campaign in Syria started in 2015, but it still remains marginal for both countries' trade balance.

During the past five years the value of non-oil trade between UAE and Russia reached $14 billion, exceeding $3 billion of the annual turnout for the first time in 2019. The UAE hosts over three thousand Russian companies, the largest number of all the Middle East, and accounts for some 7.7 percent of the entire Russian foreign trade with the Arab world. In 2013, Abu Dhabi agreed on a $3 billion endowment with RDIF to develop Russia's agricultural sector. Russia and the UAE also formed a consortium to acquire a stake in Russian Helicopters. In 2019, FlyDubai announced a new flight to Sochi, whereas Russia's low-cost carrier Pobeda is mulling a line to Dubai.[53] The Abu Dhabi Investment Authority (ADIA) has committed to multibillion-dollar infrastructure deals in cooperation with RDIF.[54] Mubadala Investment Company has also committed up to $6 billion for infrastructure and transport projects.[55] But as with all pledges originating from the Gulf monarchies, it remains to be seen how much of those promises will materialize. A potential rift between Russia and Saudi Arabia as well as plunging oil prices might likewise undercut achieved progress in diplomatic and economic ties.

Conclusion

Relations between Russia and the GCC countries were previously characterized by distrust and tensions. But the pattern has changed within the span of just a few years. Change is attributable to GCC nations' ability to skillfully adapt to new geopolitical realities and Russia's rising geopolitical profile backed by aggressive hard power and resilient diplomacy. Moscow, meanwhile, carefully navigates a path between the GCC actors, trying to maintain open communication channels to all the parties in the area. It is committed to the self-assigned role of an "honest broker," an extension of its overall strategy in the Middle East. As a result, a more balanced and cooperative relationship emerged between Russia and GCC over the last decade. Nonetheless, due to weak institutionalization and overreliance on personal chemistry between leaders, this is prone in the future to disruptions, volatility, and backsliding.

12

Russia and Egypt: A Precarious Honeymoon

Alexey Khlebnikov

Egypt is arguably one of Russia's closest partners in the Middle East. Since seizing power through a coup in 2013, Abdel Fateh al-Sisi has regularly been in the company of President Vladimir Putin. Cooperation has flourished across various areas: defense, energy, agriculture, high-tech, education, and culture. Egypt has bought large volumes of Russian-made advanced weapons. Humanitarian ties are strong as well. Around thirty-five thousand Russian Federation citizens[1] reside in Egypt. Moscow takes interest and values Cairo as a pivotal power in the Middle East. Egypt, in turn, considers Russia as a key global and regional player.

At the same time, bilateral relations, going far back in history, can be described as complex. Since the Second World War, the two countries went through phases of close collaboration followed by alienation, stagnation, rethinking, and revival. The current upsurge has a lot to do with Middle East dynamics and the opportunities created by the US policy. However, structural factors and realities within Egypt's domestic setting and in the region impose limits to the burgeoning Russian-Egyptian partnership.

The Pendulum Effect

Tsarist and Soviet Russia occasionally engaged with Egypt when it formed part of the Ottoman Empire and later under British protectorate. In the 1760s, Russia sent arms to Egypt, when Mamluk leader Ali Bey Al-Kabir declared independence from the Porte. Although the Bolshevik government reportedly made attempts to reach out to weak local Communist forces in the 1920s and 1930s,[2] they never had much enthusiasm for either Egypt or its neighbors in the Levant.[3] Moscow's disinterest stemmed from the perception that there was little potential for a communist movement to take root.[4] The Soviets started to treat Egypt more seriously after the 1952 revolution carried out by Mohammed Naguib and Gamal Abdel Nasser and Stalin's death the following year. The USSR started to cultivate relations with neutral, non-aligned countries, some not necessarily (pro-)communist. Nasser, initially an anti-communist, reached out to Moscow only after 1955–6.[5] It was only then that relations were formalized and put on a permanent footing.

The relationship between Moscow and Cairo went through four phases. In the 1950s–1970, under Nasser, the Soviet Union and Egypt became close partners and nurtured strong links. Soviet aid helped build ninety-seven big industrial enterprises, including the famous Aswan dam, the iron and steel plants in Helwan and Nag-Hammadi, hundreds of kilometers of high-voltage electricity transmission lines, among others.[6] The USSR educated tens of thousands of Egyptian engineers and industrial specialists as well as army officers. In addition, Moscow provided modern military equipment and dispatched thousands of military advisors to train the Arab republic's forces.[7]

The second period started with Anwar Sadat's coming to power in 1970 and lasted until the mid-1990s. Egypt's reorientation to the West resulted in the expulsion of Soviet advisors and progressive evacuation of the Soviet navy and air force, accompanied by rapid shift toward the United States. During that time, Sadat put on halt joint projects and downgraded diplomatic ties with Moscow. The third period, from the mid-1990s till the end of the 2000s, brought in new forms of cooperation. The Russian Federation and Egypt sought ways to restart relations and adapt them to the changing world. The 1997 and 2001 visits of Hosni Mubarak to Russia produced a set of agreements institutionalizing the rejuvenated partnership. Putin's trips to Egypt in 2005 and 2007 gave the relationship a further boost, laying the groundwork for the current *rapprochement*. In the 2010s, the fourth phase, Egypt and Russia intensified cooperation even further for reasons that will be explored in the following section.

What's Behind the Intensified Partnership?

Russia and Egypt have deepened ties owing to a confluence of global and region-specific factors.

Moscow exploits Egyptian elites' growing distrust of the United States. Traditionally, America has focused on security relations with Israel, Egypt, and Saudi Arabia. But when in 2011 the Egyptian president Hosni Mubarak had to resign under pressure from mass protests, views of the United States in Cairo changed. The Egyptian secular establishment felt betrayed by the United States. First, Washington did nothing to save its ally Mubarak in 2011. Second, it suspended its annual financial transfers of $1.3 billion in response to the 2013 military coup organized to topple President Mohammad Morsi and oust the Muslim Brotherhood. As a result, Egypt began to diversify its international partnerships and moved to upgrade its relations with Russia.

The shift in Cairo's posture offered Moscow a valuable opening. Russia had demonstrated unemotional and pragmatic attitude toward Egypt in the aftermath of the 2011 revolution. President Putin met Morsi on the sidelines of the BRICS[8] summit in Durban, South Africa, in March 2013 and rolled the red carpet for him in Moscow the following month. But when Morsi was deposed by the Egyptian military, Moscow swiftly embraced the country's new leader, Abdel Fateh al-Sisi. Overall, starting from 2013, cooperation intensified. Since Sisi seized power, he has met with Vladimir Putin eleven times. The initial meetings were of great help to the Egyptian strongman in gaining international legitimacy. The summits injected life into the hitherto dormant commission for trade and economic cooperation. In parallel, the two countries' ministers of defense and foreign affairs initiated regular meetings in "2+2" format. That in itself signals the high degree of convergence and the importance Russia and Egypt assign to one another.

It also should be highlighted that Egypt traditionally avoids putting all eggs in one basket. Even under Sadat and Mubarak, although relations were drastically scaled back, Cairo maintained political and economic ties to Moscow. In 1982, for instance, Egypt solicited Soviet Union to resume supplies of the spare parts for Aswan Dam hydroelectric station and send civilian experts. Two years later, consultations on foreign policy issues resumed on lower level too.[9] Reengagement allowed Egypt to set the door ajar and keep the option of a renewed relationship with the Soviets on the table. The same holds true today: despite being a strategic partner of the United States, Cairo is consistently deepening relations with Moscow across the board, in the field of defense first and foremost. In March 2015, Moscow and Cairo set up the commission on military and technical cooperation and soon Cairo got the license to assemble Russian T-90S tanks.[10]

At the same time, Russian leadership clearly understands that, irrespective of its fading appetite to intervene militarily in the regional affairs hidden behind belligerent rhetoric (e.g., Iran), the United States stays as the key player in the Middle East and the partner of choice for Egypt. Russia's increased foothold in the region (military presence in Syria, growing ties with Saudi Arabia, UAE, Qatar, Egypt) over the last years also makes it important for Moscow to coordinate with the United States, beyond pursuing unilateral initiatives aimed at exploiting opportunities.

Opportunities

Moscow's policy toward Cairo is largely driven by security and economic interests. Russia views Egypt as an important regional partner in the fight against terrorism and for consolidating its position in the Mediterranean.[11] In the economic domain, the Russians are interested in Egypt as a buyer of agricultural products, weapons, and nuclear and industrial technologies.

Security

In October 2015, when a Russian jet crashed over the Sinai Peninsula and killed 224 people, Russia singled out Egypt as a battlefield in the struggle against jihadi terrorists, including ISIS that claimed responsibility. In response, Moscow banned direct flights to Egypt, which brought tourist industry damages to the tune of $3 billion.[12] Before 2015, around 3 million Russian tourists were visiting Egyptian resorts annually. In 2018 and 2019, 145,000 and 150,000 Russians, respectively, came to the country, according to the Egyptian tourism ministry and Russian tour operators, a mere 5 percent of the pre-2015 figure.[13] The 2017 resumption of flights by Aeroflot and Egypt Air to Moscow and Cairo has not made a difference. Russia has not reopened direct flights to Egyptian sea resorts, arguing that security requirements have not been fully fulfilled.[14] More importantly, the halfway normalization of transport connections hands Moscow effective leverage over Egypt. Thanks to the ban, Moscow is in a position to exert political pressure and defend its interests.

In late November 2017 Russia and Egypt drafted an agreement on joint use of the airspace and air bases by the two militaries.[15] The deal has not been finalized yet, but once it reaches implementation stage it will establish legal grounds for Russia's access to Egyptian infrastructure and vice versa. The agreement will also allow Moscow to broaden its footprint in North Africa and to project more influence in regional conflicts. As an example, Russia might use Egyptian military airfields for refueling or for emergency landings, as well as for reconnaissance flights in the broader region. Potentially, it might also open the door for talks on similar agreement regarding naval facilities, which will allow Moscow to enhance its naval outreach in the Mediterranean. Moreover, Egypt is looking at the intervention in Syria and sees opportunities for working with Russia in the campaign against ISIS in the Sinai.

As active fighting in Syria is abating (bar the Idlib Province), Russia is in a position to divert potential resources to elsewhere in the Middle East. Egypt could be a place to start with. Moreover, during 2017 Russia had reportedly deployed a small contingent of special forces and military advisors to Sidi Barrani, a Mediterranean town (formerly host of a Soviet naval facility) close to the Libyan border.[16] Though refuted by Russian and Egyptian authorities,[17] reports suggested that talks were underway regarding the lease of an Egyptian airbase in the area. Such negotiations are likely to continue with the Russian military obtaining access to Egyptian defense infrastructure. In addition, Egypt is a springboard to Libya where Moscow hopes to contribute to a political settlement in the war-torn country and restore lost business contracts.[18]

Russia and Egypt have already made headway in counterterror cooperation. Paratroopers from the two countries held their first ever joint drills in the Egyptian desert in October 2016.[19] Navies exercised in the Mediterranean near Alexandria in June 2015.[20] Exercises have become regular, with Russia hosting in 2017 and 2019, and Egypt in 2018.[21] Growing military-to-military links signaled new level of the relations and demonstrate that Russia is ready to assist Cairo in its fight against terrorism originating from Libya and Sinai. Moscow and Cairo have created a working platform for sharing experience on countering terrorism.

Intense security cooperation with Egypt testifies to Russia's interest in establishing a foothold in North Africa allowing it to project force in Libya. Cairo along with Saudi Arabia and the UAE support General Khalifa Haftar and his Libyan National Army (LNA). Haftar's forces operate from the city of Tobruk close to the Egyptian border and control nearly the entire eastern Libya. Cairo is naturally interested in keeping tight control over the border and prevent the infiltration of any terrorist elements. Moscow can help on this account, not least because it is well-informed about dynamics on the ground in the volatile North African country. According to the head of Russia's contact group on Libya Lev Dengov, Russia "can monitor the situation and affect it from all sides."[22] Russia maintains working contacts with all parties in Libya, including the LNA, Government of National Accord (GNA), Misrata, and southern tribes—trying to remain equidistant from everyone.[23] This is not to say that Russia is interested in getting involved directly in another conflict militarily but to indicate its willingness to be in the club of international power brokers who could bring warring factions to the negotiating table. Noteworthy, in 2019 Moscow received both General Haftar and foreign minister of the Libyan unity government Mohamed Taher Siala. Russia threw its weight behind the organization of Berlin conference and also coauthored (with Turkey) a ceasefire proposal for the parties of Libyan conflict. Evidently, Kremlin tries to increase its diplomatic role and influence in the settlement of the Libyan crisis. In addition, Moscow seems to believe that its experience in Syria, especially the work of its Reconciliation Centers, which focused among other things on facilitating negotiation process between the opposition groups and the Syrian government, on delivery of humanitarian aid to civilian population and on temporary ceasefires, may be applicable.

Egypt also assisted Russia to negotiate deals on de-escalation zones in Syria. In 2016–17 Egypt hosted several rounds of talks between Russian defense officials and different Syrian opposition groups, which resulted in establishing two de-escalation zones in Syria (Eastern Ghouta and Homs).[24] The so-called "Cairo group" of the Syrian opposition enjoys good relations with Russia and is more inclined toward compromise, in contrast to the Higher Negotiations Committee based in Riyadh, Saudi Arabia. It also has its military wing that operates on the ground in several provinces (al-Hasakah, Deir ez-Zor, and Raqqa) and also cooperates with SDF.[25] Thus, Egypt proved to be a platform that can unite different opposition groups in Syria as well as an extra communication channel to the Saudi-led GCC.

Economic Cooperation

Trade between Egypt and Russia grew significantly, from $3 billion in 2013 to $7.6 billion in 2018,[26] which made Moscow the third most significant partner after the EU and China.

Agricultural products, energy, and arms dominate exchanges. In recent years about 30 percent of Russia's export to Egypt is agricultural products.[27] Russia is the biggest exporter of grain to Egypt covering about 65 percent of its demand.[28] Thanks to the food embargo introduced in response to the EU sanctions on Russia, it has become the major importer of Egyptian vegetables and subtropical fruits. Almost 80 percent of Egypt's exports to Russia are made up of vegetable products.[29] Agricultural imports are cheaper due to Egyptian pound's devaluation. Beneficial exchange rates create incentives for Russian companies to localize production to Egypt.

Since 2001 the Russian oil company Lukoil has been extracting oil near the Red Sea port of Hurgada. In October 2017, Rosneft acquired a 30 percent stake from the Italian energy firm ENI in the concession agreement for the development of Egyptian Zohr field, the largest gas field in the Mediterranean Sea.[30]

In May 2018 Russia and Egypt signed a deal to establish a Russian Industrial Zone in East Port Said,[31] which is expected to increase the number of Russian companies and investments. In the coming years, Russia plans to invest about $6.9 billion in creating its industrial zone in Egypt. In 2018 the total number of the Russian companies in Egypt was 451.[32] Moscow aims at establishing a diversified industrial production and a logistics hub in Egypt, which will also help it to get access to other countries in the Middle East and Africa.

Egypt is also expected to sign a free-trade agreement with Russia-led Eurasian Economic Union (EEU), which will ease the exchange between the two countries.[33] Egypt will obtain access to a large market, while Russia will benefit from its regional integration project gaining greater international legitimacy.

Arms contracts feature prominently in economic relations. In 2014 Russia and Egypt signed several deals worth over $3.5 billion[34] for the delivery of new fighter jets (MiG-29M/M2), helicopters (Mi-35M), S-300VM missile complexes, coastal defense systems, and so on. Later, in 2015 Egypt purchased 50 Ka-52[35] helicopters for its two Mistral helicopter carriers (which were initially ordered by Russia in France but were not delivered because of Crimea-related sanctions on Russia in 2014).[36] In the end of 2018 the two countries struck another arms deal worth at least $2 billion for deliveries of a couple of dozen of Su-35 fighter jets (Flanker-E).[37]

All those big arms contracts became possible largely thanks to the US decision to suspend some military aid and to block delivery of hardware to Egypt after the 2013 coup. Russia effectively exploited the opportunity and struck lucrative arms deals on a scale unseen from the 1960s.

Moreover, Russia is aiming to build Egypt's first nuclear power plant (NPP) in el-Dabaa. Russia plans to open $25 billion loan line to Egypt for this project, repayable in thirty-five years. In effect Moscow will create an entire new industry in the country and train a generation of specialists. As of now, the NPP has received a permit of site approval from the Egyptian Nuclear Regulation and Radiological Authority (ENRRA) and works on site might begin in 2021.[38]

The upturn in economic ties has already made Egypt Russia's second most significant partner in the Middle East and North Africa after Turkey. There is even further potential, especially in energy and manufacturing. Moscow has managed to monetize historical links, changing regional environment and profit from the cracks in Egypt's relationship with the United States. Still, trade and investment cooperation have limits. Russia's trouble-ridden economy, targeted by Western sanctions, has little chances to compete in the long run with the United States and the EU. Both of them have more to offer, especially in terms of technologies and FDI.

Limits

Russia and Egypt do not see each other eye to eye on many regional dossiers: the role of Hezbollah and Iran in the region, the war in Yemen, to name just a few of them. Still differences on various regional affairs have existed before. Soviet intervention in Afghanistan has not derailed the slow but steady normalization of bilateral relations under President Mubarak in the 1980s.[39] Opposing views on regional issues have not yet hindered thriving ties in the 2010s. What could put constrains on the relationship in the short to mid-term are structural factors: the US–Egypt strategic partnership, financial dependence on the Arab Gulf states, and America's sanctions policy.

The Egypt–US Strategic Partnership

It is important to remember that overwhelming majority of Egypt's principal economic partners—with the exception of China and Russia—are also US allies. That includes UAE, Saudi Arabia, Canada, and the EU, which tops the list. America provides $1.3 billion in financial assistance to Egypt. Besides, since 2011 Cairo is dependent on funding from the Saudi-led GCC, which helps Egypt to keep its economy afloat and to a certain extent restrains Cairo from public criticism of the Kingdom's policies in the region. Over the last four years, GCC transfers—financial aid, grants, direct investments, zero-interest loans—are worth more than $35 billion.[40] Since the 2011 uprising the Gulf countries have supported Egypt with nearly $92 billion.[41] Egypt also significantly relies on the IMF and the World Bank. This is a solid argument against those who question Egypt's strategic priorities.

However, this is not to say that Cairo shares an identical approach with Saudi Arabia and UAE to critical regional issues such as Iran, Yemen, Syria, or Libya. Thus, Egypt's staunchly held views and effort to assert autonomy, in combination with its alignment with the United States and the Gulf, make it a valuable partner for Russia. Its heavyweight status as it is the most populous (over 95 million) Arab country and impact on public opinion across the Middle East should be taken into account as well. In the end, Egypt matters thanks both to its size and its willingness to chart a foreign policy of its own, despite links to the United States and the Gulf.

No doubt, Egypt looks at Russia as a counterweight to American influence and source of leverage. However, with the Biden administration and assumingly its more or less traditional approach to the region (continued lack of will to be involved more), Cairo might easily tilt back to Washington as in the pre-Obama period. Moreover, if Biden's Middle East policy demonstrates commitment to Egypt, or indeed pressure Cairo to decrease its cooperation with Moscow, the likelihood of such a scenario will definitely grow. In the end, the United States has more to offer to Egypt than Russia does.

The US Policy on Sanctions

The US sanctions can become an additional roadblock to Russia–Egypt military–technical cooperation. In August 2017, President Donald Trump signed the Countering America's Adversaries through Sanctions Act (CAATSA). Under this legislation, countries trading with Russia's defense and intelligence sectors can face secondary sanctions. It means that the United States is in a position to sanction Egypt for cooperation with Russia in the military–technical field.

Egypt's new contract with Russia for the purchase of Su-35 fighters is potentially at risk. Egypt is among the most important US partners in the region and its continuous interest in Russian military technologies and weapons is an irritant for the United States.

Washington has already imposed secondary sanctions on Beijing over its purchase of Russian Su-35 fighter jets and S-400 anti-aircraft systems[42] and Turkey over its further batch of surface-to-air missiles. This established a precedent and sent a clear signal to Russian partners that the United States might sanction them as well. The United States already warned Cairo that it would face sanctions if it goes through with the procurement of Russia's Su-35 fighter jets.[43] In fact, it puts many countries at risk, including Moscow's long-time partners, not only Egypt.

However, given Egypt's shaky economy, it is unlikely that America will impose harsh punishments on its partner. Such a move can generate risks and would certainly undermine President Abdel Fattah el-Sisi. Both Egypt and the United States are interested in forging a compromise.

Overreliance on GCC Financial Aid

As already noted, Egypt remains highly dependent on its GCC partners that provide it with necessary financial and economic aid. Overreliance on grants and loans puts Egypt in a delicate position and constrains its external behavior. At the same time, it is thanks to this funding that Egypt is able to pay Moscow for its goods, including grain and arms. Thus, if GCC states decrease or stop helping Egypt or decide to condition their aid, this can have a direct influence on Moscow's economic ties with Egypt. Although Russia's export to Egypt is relatively hard to replace given the attractive cost–benefit ratio of Russia's arms and wheat, there is still a risk that cooperation with Cairo might be spoiled by external factors.

Conclusion

It is patently clear that both Russia and Egypt are interested in developing and profiting from closer bilateral ties. The Egyptian leadership wants to diversify its international partnerships in order to expand its strategic autonomy and maximize geopolitical and economic returns. At the same time, Moscow would like to ensure that no major power shift occurs in Egypt, or the wider region, while simultaneously reaping security and commercial benefits from cooperation. Turmoil in Libya along with Russia's ambitions to play a constructive role there as well as to increase its visibility in North Africa reinforce Russian reliance on Cairo, too.

That said, it is important to keep an eye on what policy the United States is going to conduct vis-à-vis Cairo in the following years. The Biden presidency and changing international environment may have serious impact on US approach to Egypt and to the broader region. It is going to show whether Egypt is going to keep Russia at its disposal or deviate from traditional approach and rather put all eggs in one basket. For now, it is clear that Washington is unwilling to increase its military involvement in the region or to drastically change its approach that was relatively consistent over the last twelve years.

Russia's policy toward Egypt will likely remain to be a reflection of security and economic interests. As long as regional dynamics in the Middle East allow Moscow to extract greater benefits from Cairo, it will continue to do so. But if the situation turns against Russia, it would see its influence declining. Moscow has neither the capacity nor the requisite leverage to counter the United States or EU if they reach out to Egypt.

No doubt, Russia is gradually building up links with the Egyptians, marketing itself as an indispensable partner in all spheres. At the same time, it has learnt its lessons from past experience and will not overinvest in a relationship that could shift overnight.

Intensified Russia–Egypt relations and Russia's increased regional footprint not only challenge but also offer opportunities to Europe. First of all, it is an opportunity for deepening counterterrorism cooperation and agreeing on joint measures to stabilize Libya. Moscow's wide network of contacts with all conflicting parties in Libya could be a basis for EU and Russia to cooperate. Turkey's intervention in early 2020 and the importance of Libya's stability to Europe's southern flank make a case for cooperation stronger.

Likewise, Russia's growing naval presence in the Mediterranean through Tartus in Syria and, possibly, future access to Egyptian military infrastructure presents a challenge to Europe. Yet, it also makes improved coordination with Moscow on maritime matters a priority. The parties need to learn how to live and act together in a shared environment. Third, the competition between Russian and European arms producers for the North African arms market will intensify, with Egypt playing not the last role in this contest.

13

The "Comrades" in the Maghreb

Dalia Ghanem

Back in its day, USSR had a stable relationship with the countries of the Maghreb, drawing on political affinities. Moscow's influence faded in the 1990s with the collapse of the Soviet state. Since the early 2000s, Russia has been working toward regaining its status, making use of its economic resources. Russia has actively sought to capitalize on opportunities, relying on its energy diplomacy and sales of military equipment to attract Maghrebi states. Russia reacted with caution to the Arab uprisings in early 2011. It first called[1] to outside powers to not intervene and then voiced its concern about potential rise of radical Islamists.[2] In Tunisia, Egypt, and Libya, despite its initial reluctance, Russia aligned with the West and accepted a more democratic political system. The decline of US influence in the region, Putin's return to the presidency in 2012, and the political dynamics in the Arab world offered Russia the chance to demonstrate its clout, boost its international visibility, and restore its lost influence. Later, the Kremlin would capitalize on its military success in Syria as well.

This chapter looks at relations with three states in the Maghreb: Morocco, Algeria, and Tunisia. It addresses two main questions. First, what are Russia's goals in North Africa, and what are the means to achieve them? What are the prospects for Moscow's engagement with the region?[3] Ties with those countries have allowed Russia to make inroads into a region that has traditionally fallen into the Western sphere of influence. Moscow is rebuilding its presence through energy deals, humanitarian contacts, trade, and security and defense links. In short, what drives Russian policy is the competition with the West, the pursuit of status in world affairs, and the search for economic benefits.

Russia–Algeria: More Than Just Weapons?

Algeria is a crucial country for Russia's policy in the Middle East, the Maghreb, as well as in the Mediterranean and Africa. Bilateral ties have deep historical roots. During the war of independence (1954–62), the Soviet Union and its Eastern European satellites supported the National Liberation Front (FLN) and sent military aid to its armed branch, the National Liberation Army (ALN). The USSR established diplomatic relations with the Provisional Government of the Algerian Republic (GPRA) as early as March 23, 1962. In the following years and decades, oiled by Soviet loans, cooperation in the fields of trade, energy, and defense thrived. Besides, dozens of Russian volunteers, military advisers, and technicians (e.g., oil industry) stayed in Algeria for extended periods.[4] Thousands of Algerians were educated in Moscow and Leningrad (now Saint Petersburg).

A long-standing ally, Algeria was also a loyal customer of the Soviet weapons and defense systems. Between 1962 and 1989, Moscow is believed to have supplied $11 billion in military equipment, up to 80 percent of Algeria's stock of armaments.[5] These weapons were paid for through Soviet loans. The USSR provided affordable financing for the construction of Algerian heavy industry (e.g., steel) and the production of equipment. In the 1990s, the relationship came to a halt as both countries faced domestic challenges. Between 1991 and 2002 ("the black decade"), Algeria plunged into civil war. Russia had to deal with the aftermath of the Soviet Union's dissolution and the overhaul of its economic and political system. Both states were inward-looking and spent the main bulk of resources on domestic challenges.

Since the start of the new millennium, Russia has tried to recover its position in this formerly lucrative market. With an increase in arms imports of 277 percent between 2012 and 2016, Algeria is now the world's fifth-largest importer of weapons.[6] Russia played a leading role in the acquisition surge. In 2006, Moscow announced the settlement of Algeria's $4.7 billion debt dating back to the Soviet era.[7] As elsewhere in the Middle East and North Africa, the write-off paved the way for improving relations. The same year, Algeria ordered $7.5 billion in Russian battle tanks, missile system, jet fighters, and training aircraft.[8]

This and other deals that followed made Russia a leading arms supplier to Algeria, accounting for 90 percent of imports between 2009 and 2013.[9] As a result, the overall trade between Algeria and Russia went from $700 million in 2007 to near $5.4 billion in 2018, with weapons accounting for two-thirds of the turnover.[10] The North African country ranks among the top three customers of Russian armaments. In the period 2014–18, almost 14 percent of all Russian arms exports went to Algeria, which equals the share of sales to China. In consequence, Algeria has been trying to diversify its imports—for example, by turning to suppliers from China, Italy, and Sweden. Russia's share for the 2014–18 period declined to 66 percent of Algeria's weapon imports.[11] Despite these fluctuations, Algeria is poised to remain Russia's primary arms export market in the region, even if it faces fierce competition. Cooperation might spread to other fields: for example, the digital technology sector as well as in cybersecurity.[12]

Although trade between Russia and Algeria recovered in the 2000s, it is still of little significance for either side. Algeria accounted for almost 0.8 percent of Russia's overall trade turnover in 2018. The relationship is highly asymmetric. It is not only that Russia runs a comfortable surplus of more than $5 billion, but the turnover is in favor of Moscow's industrial products. The strategic partnership of 2001 intended to give relations a "fresh start" has been to Russia's benefit. Algeria supplies to the Russian food market, affected by the ban on EU agricultural imports, with fresh vegetables and fruits. Agriculture represented 86 percent of the Algerian exports in 2018, worth $10.5 million.[13] This is insignificant even in comparison to other North African countries. For instance, Tunisia's overall exports to Russia amounted to $136 million and Egypt's $526 million in the same year.[14]

Moscow might improve its position in case Russian wheat exporters elbow their way into Algeria's market. Indeed, Algeria is attractive as it is the third-largest importer of wheat worldwide, with a yearly national consumption of 10 million tons. Since Algeria's independence, France has remained the leading supplier, with 55 percent of its grain exports going to its former territory. Algeria imported no less than 4.6 million tons of French wheat at the end of April 2018. However, this situation might change. In October 2018, Algerian authorities decided to look for other, cheaper sources and declared its intention to import grain from Russia. A delegation visited Moscow to take a sample for analysis, before the conclusion of a formal agreement.[15] Following the visit, Russia first sent a trial cargo of wheat in spring 2019.[16] Russia is well-positioned to compete for the Algerian market. In 2017, it produced 135 million tons of grain, beating the Soviet Union's 1978 record of 127.4 million tons.[17] The share volume of wheat available on short calls makes Russia a price-flexible trader too.

Russia tried to launch cooperation in energy. In 2006, Gazprom and Algeria's government-owned oil and gas corporation Sonatrach signed a Memorandum of Understanding (MoU) and later in 2008 set up a joint venture to explore the El Assel onshore field.[18] However, energy ties remain limited. Algeria is Africa's largest natural gas producer and second-largest oil producer after Nigeria. It is also Europe's third-largest gas supplier after Norway and Russia and therefore competing with both for the same market. Still, greater coordination between the two gas producers remains a possibility, highlighting Europe's dependency on external supplies.

Russia has also been active in the civilian nuclear technology sector. An agreement signed in 2014 led to an MoU between the Algerian Atomic Energy Commission (COMENA) and the Russian State Atomic Energy Corporation (Rosatom) three years later. Algeria was planning a nuclear power station with a pressurized water reactor for 2025.[19] It allows Moscow to showcase its technology across the region.

Domestic developments in Algeria injected uncertainty as to relations with Russia. That is why the Kremlin has been watching the mass protests closely in the country since 2019. Peaceful protests broke in Algeria on February 22, 2019, refusing Bouteflika's candidacy for a fifth term in office.[20] In response, the Russian foreign minister, Sergey Lavrov, announced in March 2019, before the departure of Bouteflika, that Russia is "very concerned" about the events in Algeria and the "ongoing attempts to destabilize the country." Later, Russia showed more precaution. Through the spokeswoman of the Ministry of Foreign Affairs, Maria Zakharova, Russia hoped that "the problems that arise will continue to be resolved constructively and responsibly" and insisted that "it was an internal affair of a friendly country of Russia."[21]

Russia was cautious because, at that stage, it was hard to foresee the outcome of the protests, and the country needed to maintain its long-term influence in the North African state and its valuable weapon deals. For Russia, it was crucial to preserve these contracts no matter who would succeed Bouteflika. The latter eventually stepped down and was replaced by interim president Abdelkader Bensalah. However, the peaceful protests have not stopped despite the election of a new president, Abdelmadjid Tebboune, in December 2019.[22] Since then, Russia welcomed the vote, and shortly,

President Putin extended an official invitation to Tebboune to visit Moscow. Due to the COVID-19 outbreak, the visit had to be pushed for a later date. However, one thing remains certain: for Russia, Tebboune is good news as the old regime showed it was able to regenerate itself. Russia is likely to continue to support the Algerian system, or its remnants, to maintain its political and economic influence in the Maghreb's pivotal state.

Russia Flirts with Morocco

Close ties with Algiers have not stopped Russia from reaching out to Morocco, Algeria's neighbor and rival with whom relations have been hostile because of the decades-old conflict in Western Sahara. In the spirit of Soviet diplomatic tradition Moscow aims at developing links with all North African countries, without forming an exclusive alliance with any one of them.[23] In 2016, Russia signed a "deep strategic partnership" with Morocco, as it had done with Algeria in 2001. A year later, the two countries signed eleven cooperation agreements, one of which focused on arms exports.[24]

Russia is applying "positive neutrality" regarding the Western Sahara issue, in contrast to the Soviet Union, which sympathized with and rendered clandestine support to the Algerians.[25] The 2016 "deep strategic partnership" declared that "the Russian Federation [took] due account of the position of the Kingdom of Morocco for the settlement of this problem and [took] note of the socio-economic projects launched by Morocco in the southern provinces to develop the region and improve the living conditions of its population."[26] At the same time, the Kremlin enjoys warm relations with the Polisario Front, whose representatives visit Moscow regularly.[27] Russia demonstrates to Moroccans that it holds leverage, which could be brought to bear if need be.

Morocco's trade with Russia has been growing steadily since mid-2000. Volumes reached almost $1.5 billion in 2018 against $200 million in 2001.[28] Moscow and Rabat also signed several cooperation agreements in sectors such as education, air traffic, marine fishery, environment, military, energy, as well as agriculture.[29] The latter industry accounts for 64 percent of Moroccan exports to Russia: 33 percent of all its citrus fruits and 15 percent of Morocco's tomatoes are exported to the Russian market.[30] Morocco is also Russia's largest supplier of frozen sardines. Russia's exports to Morocco are dominated by mineral and chemical products (84 percent of the export).[31] Although the trade has been growing, it remains highly asymmetric and more favorable to Russia. Morocco runs a deficit, having imported $929 million worth of goods from Russia and exported $546 million.[32] Still, Morocco's trade deficit with Russia is significantly smaller than that of Algeria. The absence of significant arms imports from Russia explains a more balanced trade relationship.

Cooperation between the two countries has been extended to nuclear energy with an MoU signed in 2017 by the Moroccan Ministry of Energy, Mines, and Sustainable Development and Rosatom. Though there are no plans yet for a nuclear power plant, the documents testify to Russia's interest. There are cooperation prospects about religious affairs. Russia needs more educated moderate imams to counter the spread of Salafism among the young and growing cohort of Russian Muslims. Moscow looks to Rabat to close this gap. In 2016, the Ministry of Endowments and Islamic Affairs in Morocco and the Central Religious Organization in Russia adopted a memorandum for the training of Russian imams by the Kingdom.[33]

Russian Inroads in Tunisia

Tunisia is Russia's least significant partner in North Africa, yet ties are in good shape. The presence of the two Russian Orthodox parishes (in Tunis and Bizerte) and the housing of the Tunisian Embassy in Moscow in the former mansion of Stalin's henchman Lavrenty Beria hint at that. However, symbolism prevails over substance. Presidents Habib Bourguiba and Zine El Abidine Ben Ali chose to align with Europe and the United States rather than with the Soviet Union. Following the changes in 2011, Russia was ready to develop relations either with the Ennahda Party-led coalition "Troika" government[34] (2011–14) or with Beji Caid Essebsi, who came from the party of the "old" Tunisian elite led by Nidaa Tounes. Essebsi's associates visited Moscow during the Troika reign in 2012 and 2013, as well as members of the Ennahda Party leadership in 2017 and 2018. Since then, several meetings at the level of officials have discussed strengthening cooperation in trade, economy, science, technology, and security. The two sides have been exploring the perspective of setting a free-trade zone.[35] However, the 2019 electoral cycle in Tunisia and the deadlock in forming the coalition government (until February 2020) put the critical contacts between Moscow and Tunis on ice.

In the economic field, the Russian market holds significant potential for Tunisian exporters. Russia is the world's second-largest importer of fruits and a fourth of vegetables. Tunisian agro exporters have not been particularly successful; however, their share in the Russian market remains almost constant, in the range of 13–14 percent. On the positive side, unlike neighboring Algeria and Morocco, Tunisia sends more higher-value industrial products to the Russian Federation. Textiles, machinery, and vehicles represent 78 percent of the export volume. Yet, just like with Tunisia's neighbors, Russia runs a large trade surplus of $500 million.[36] Russian investments in Tunisia are insignificant as they amounted in 2017 at $6.8 million and created 780 jobs. Nine Russian companies are operating in Tunisia in the sectors of industry, agriculture, and services.[37]

Cultural exchanges are well established between the two countries. Russian citizens participate in the national and international festivals that take place in Tunisia each year. Tunisian youth continue to study in Russia as well. Their numbers are on the increase as several universities, such as Sfax University and El Manar, have partnership agreements with institutions in Russia.[38] Besides, the Russian language is taught at the Higher Institute of Languages at the University of Carthage and in several other Tunisian institutes.

Russian-Tunisian economic relations are above all focused on tourism, which accounts for 8 percent of Tunisia's GDP. Though there is an agreement dating to 1998, Tunisia has never been among the most popular destinations for Russian holidaymakers. In 2014, only 250,000 traveled to Tunisia, compared to 4 million in Turkey and more than 2.2 million in Egypt.[39] The 2015 terrorist attacks in the Bardo Museum and Sousse resort hit the tourist sector hard in Tunisia. Visits dropped across the board, with the number of visitors from Russia going down to just fifty thousand.[40] However, in 2016, Russians came back to make the third-largest group of tourists in Tunisia after Algerians and Libyans.[41] That was due to a ban on direct flights to Egypt because of concern over the downing of a passenger plane on October 31, 2015, that led to the death of 224 Russians. In 2017, 520,000 Russian tourists, out of 6.7 million in total, visited Tunisia. The number reached six hundred thousand in 2018[42] and eight hundred thousand in 2019.[43] Due to the COVID-19 outbreak, the number of Russian visitors to Tunisia might significantly drop just like in 2015. Regardless of potential fluctuations, tourism has become the cornerstone of bilateral economic cooperation and provides Moscow with political leverage in Tunisia.

Russia in the Region: What's Next?

Since the beginning of the 2000s and especially after the 2011 Arab revolutions, Russia has made a comeback in the Middle East and North Africa (MENA). Moscow has shown skill in developing ties with mutually antagonistic actors both in the Middle East and the Maghreb. It has made inroads in North Africa thanks to its flexibility and appreciation for the fluidity of local political and security context.

The Maghreb is likely to remain on the agenda of the Kremlin for the upcoming years; Foreign Minister Sergei Lavrov chose the region for his first foreign trip in 2019. Moscow will continue to explore political and economic opportunities. Military cooperation is likely to endure as the Maghrebi countries' defense budget soar and Russia offers its weapon system at a comparatively reasonable price. Prospects for nuclear energy are less bright because of the high cost of the projects and local economies' modest growth.

Influence in North Africa is an asset for Russia's foreign policy at the global level. In working with the EU's southern neighbors, Russia is gaining an advantage in Europe and burnishes its image internationally. The Maghreb is also a stepping-stone to sub-Saharan Africa that is both a market and potential economic partner, as demonstrated by the Chinese expansion. And the first Russia–Africa Summit in 2019 cochaired by President Putin and Al-Sisi speak Kremlin's ambitions.

At the same time, Russia's influence should not be overestimated. North Africa is not central to Russia's geopolitical agenda, unlike the post-Soviet space, the West, or Asia-Pacific. However, it is still safe to say that in the years ahead, both the EU and the United States will have to come to terms with the Kremlin's increased presence in the Maghreb.

14

Russia and Israel: An Improbable Friendship

Mark N. Katz

Israel is closely allied with the United States—the country which Vladimir Putin regards as Russia's greatest adversary. Russia cooperates closely with Iran—the country which Israeli prime minister Benjamin Netanyahu regards as an existential threat to the Jewish state. Simple logic would suggest, therefore, that Russia and Israel must be seriously at odds since each works closely with the other's main adversary. But this is not the case. Especially since the rise of Putin at the turn of the century, the two states have developed close, friendly relations. They cooperate extensively in the economic, military, and intelligence spheres. In addition to their government-to-government relationship, there is also a strong societal connection between the two countries as a result of over a million Russian speakers having emigrated to Israel from the former Soviet Union and of large numbers of Russian tourists visiting every year (including over 550,000 in 2016) before the outbreak of the coronavirus in 2020. There are, of course, some serious differences between Russia and Israel—including over Moscow's relations with Tehran. However, they have pursued good relations with each other despite these differences. The Russian-Israeli relationship, then, defies simple logic because it is the result of a more complicated equation based on a common fear of radical Sunni Muslims, personal chemistry between Putin and conservative Israeli leaders, and a willingness to continue bilateral cooperation despite divergences on certain issues (especially Iran).

A Counterintuitive Partnership

The Putin era has not been the only time when Russia has enjoyed cooperative relations with Israel. Under Stalin, the Soviet Union was one of the very first countries to recognize the Jewish state after it declared independence. After Khrushchev came to power, however, Moscow became aligned with Arab nationalist governments that were both anti-Western and anti-Israeli. Moscow, though, maintained diplomatic relations with Israel during the early part of the Cold War until it severed them at the time of the June 1967 Arab-Israeli War in which the Jewish state defeated the forces of Egypt, Jordan, and Syria. Yet while the Soviet Union was a vocal supporter of the Palestinian cause, it did not call for the destruction of Israel as certain Arab governments and

Palestinian groups did at that time.[1] And despite the severance of diplomatic ties, Soviet-Israeli contacts continued via the Russian Orthodox Church's representation in Jerusalem.

Relations were restored at the very end of the Gorbachev era in October 1991 and improved under Yeltsin in the 1990s during the high point of Jewish emigration from the former Soviet Union to Israel. But under the direction of long-time Soviet Middle East expert Yevgeny Primakov (who served as foreign minister and then prime minister under Yeltsin), Moscow was more focused on strengthening links with anti-American regimes in Iran and Iraq and therefore became more critical of Israel.[2]

After Putin came to power at the end of 1999, Israeli prime minister Ariel Sharon began courting him in the early 2000s. While most Western leaders either criticized or remained silent about Putin's reintervention in Chechnya, Sharon actually praised it. His argument that Russia and Israel were both threatened by Muslim terrorists (whether Chechen or Palestinian) apparently resonated with Putin—especially when Russian-Israeli intelligence cooperation deepened in the wake of the 2004 Beslan incident. When Putin made his first visit to Israel in 2005 (a trip which also included Egypt, but not Syria), he expressed his strong support for the security of the Jewish state.[3]

There are other factors that have made good relations with Israel valuable to Russia. One is that Russian arms sales to certain countries are enhanced with the addition of Israeli technology. Another is that Israel has become one of the only sources of Western military technology for Russia (including for unmanned aerial vehicles or "drones")—especially after France canceled the sale of Mistral aircraft carriers to Russia in 2015. Furthermore, Israel did not join Western governments in criticizing Russia for the 2008 war in Georgia (indeed, Israel halted its budding military cooperation with Tbilisi during this war),[4] annexation of Crimea in 2014, and intervention in eastern Ukraine afterward.[5] Beyond government-to-government ties, the Russian-Israeli relationship has been strengthened by extensive trade and cultural links; the million-strong Russian-speaking diaspora in Israel (including many Jews who, like Natan Sharansky, left the USSR or Russia because they did not like how they were treated there, but then became advocates of close Russian-Israeli relations later after moving to Israel); the hundreds of thousands of Russian tourists visiting Israel every year; and Israeli accommodation of Russian Orthodox Church interests in the Holy Land.[6]

Converging Interests in Syria and Beyond

While Barack Obama and some other Western leaders sought to embrace the political change represented by the Arab Spring, Putin and Netanyahu both preferred the preservation of the status quo and feared that the overthrow of ruling regimes would unleash forces hostile to both Russia and Israel.[7] While it had long objected to the Assad regime's cooperation with Iran in aiding the highly anti-Israeli Lebanese Shia movement, Hezbollah, the government in Israel did appreciate that Damascus had maintained peace on the Syrian-Israeli armistice line established after the 1973 war.[8] Israeli fears that this border would no longer remain calm if the Assad regime was weakened or replaced have made the Netanyahu government more sympathetic to Russian arguments that the Assad regime remaining in power is the least bad alternative for Syria.[9]

What has been disturbing for Israel about Syria, though, is the role played there by Iran and Hezbollah. It does not want to see these two actors gain predominant influence across the Syrian border and thus be in a better position to mount attacks.[10] But that being the case, the Russian intervention in Syria that began in 2015, which was so upsetting to the West, was actually somewhat reassuring to Israel since Iran and Hezbollah could be more easily restrained by the Russians if they are present in Syria than if they are not. Indeed, as Samuel Ramani noted, "Putin's March 14 [2016] announcement of a partial Russian military drawdown from Syria surprised the Israeli political establishment, and increased fears of Iranian belligerence."[11] While it is not clear whether or what sort of agreement Israel and Russia may have reached regarding Syria, what is known is that Netanyahu and Putin have consulted extensively about it and Moscow has not stopped Israel from attacking Iranian and Hezbollah targets in territories controlled by the regime.[12] Indeed, now that Assad's internal opponents have suffered near defeat, not only has competition heated up between Moscow and Tehran for influence in Damascus, but Russia has indicated support for calls made by Israel for Iranian forces to depart from southern Syria.[13]

There are other areas besides Syria in which Russian and Israeli interests either coincide or do not clash. Both welcomed the overthrow by Abdel Fattah al-Sisi, the Egyptian military leader, of the elected Muslim Brotherhood president Mohammed Morsi in 2013. Neither Russia nor Israel has shown much concern about the al-Sisi government's subsequent suppression of the opposition and crackdown on democracy.[14] Russia and Israel both cooperate with Saudi Arabia and the United Arab Emirates (UAE).[15] And both have likewise sought cooperation with Turkey, although the Turkish president Erdoğan has not been an easy interlocutor to deal with for either of them.[16] Moscow does continue to criticize Israel for its treatment of the Palestinians, but Putin does not give the Palestinians any material support that would allow them to seriously challenge Israel either.[17]

Thus, despite the fact that they each cooperate closely with the other's greatest adversary, Russia and Israel have established a strong reciprocal relationship on the basis of the common interests that they share and a mutual willingness to pursue them notwithstanding their differences.

What Can Ruin the Partnership?

There are, however, several possible scenarios that could undermine this state of affairs.

One relates to the most important difference between them: Iran. If it turns out that Moscow proves unwilling or unable to prevent Iran from becoming more powerful in Syria and increasing its support for Hezbollah there, Israel is highly likely to take matters into its own hands and act forcefully against both adversaries. Indeed, just such an episode in September 2018 created serious strains in Russian-Israeli relations. In response to an Israeli air attack, Syrian forces fired an S-200 missile that missed the retreating Israeli F-16 but hit a Russian warplane in the vicinity, killing all personnel aboard. Although it was Syrian forces that fired the missile that downed the Russian naval patrol aircraft,[18] the Defense Ministry in Moscow blamed Israel for its loss. Russian officials specifically accused the Israeli military of failing to give adequate notice of the attack to their Russian counterparts in Syria as per their de-confliction agreement, and that the Israeli jets used the presence of the Russian aircraft as "cover" in their escape.[19] Putin himself seemed unwilling to allow tensions to escalate, but Moscow did agree to transfer the more powerful S-300 air defense missile system to Syrian forces. But if this move was a Russian attempt to deter similar such Israeli attacks, it has failed—and the Syrian military has reportedly criticized the S-300 air defense system as being ineffective.[20]

If tensions with Iran and its Shia allies escalate further, Israel is likely to receive American assistance. Should Russia side with Iran and Hezbollah, it will alienate Israel and collaboration between them will rapidly diminish. But even if Moscow seeks to avoid taking Iran's side, American-supported Israeli action against Iran and Hezbollah in Syria (and perhaps elsewhere) will make Russia look like a bystander in Syria and not a great power—something that Putin will clearly not appreciate. Indeed, he can be expected to strongly resist behavior on the part of any state making Russia look less than the great power. Putin has worked hard to rebuild his country's international status and will sacrifice the benefits it derives from cooperating with Israel if this is necessary to pursue this more important goal.

Whether or not this scenario arises, of course, depends on how Iran behaves in Syria now that the Assad regime is no longer seriously threatened by its opponents. It also hinges on whether Moscow can actually keep its reported assurances to Israel that its presence in Syria serves to restrain Iranian behavior. According to *The Economist*, "Israel's security chiefs are coming to realize that the Kremlin will not exert itself to limit Iran's role in Syria."[21] It is possible, of course, that worsening conditions inside Iran due to heightened US sanctions as well as the ravages of the coronavirus may serve to limit the Islamic Republic's ability to project power in the region.

Another possible threat to continued Russian-Israeli cooperation is that US–Russian relations deteriorate so much that Washington is no longer willing to tolerate Israeli collaboration with Moscow, or at least not to the extent that it has so far. While Israel is well known for being able to go its own way in defiance of Washington's advice and requests, an end to security cooperation with Russia might well be a demand to which Israel may have to acquiesce to if America really insists on it. But without Russian-Israeli cooperation continuing, Moscow will have much less incentive to take Israeli interests into account in its relations with Tehran. Moreover, if these two scenarios (both heightened Israel–Iran conflict and increased US–Russian tensions) play out simultaneously, the Russian-Israeli relationship is even more likely to be negatively affected.

While there is a significant possibility that either or both of these first two scenarios might occur in the short term, there is a third, long-term scenario that might well arise independently of them. Putin does hold in high regard and pursues Russian-Israeli cooperation. According to Dmitri Trenin, the Russian military and security services, along with ordinary Russian citizens, also value Moscow's ties to the Jewish state.[22] But if Putin's successor does not share this positive view of Israel, it is not at all certain that the present level of cooperation can continue. Some Russian sectors and institutions that currently benefit from close bilateral links, such as the arms export industry and certain elements of the security services, may seek its continuation, but a new leader with a different perspective on Israel may change policy. Recent constitutional amendments now allow Putin to remain in office until 2036. At some point, though, there will be a successor in the Kremlin. Whether there is sufficient Russian interest to continue working with Israel or whether this was something idiosyncratic to Putin will then become clear.

Yet while the scenarios that could lead to its diminution or even termination are real, Russian-Israeli cooperation is quite strong at present. Because of the benefits it provides for both sides, both Putin on the one hand and Netanyahu (or any other Israeli prime minister) on the other are likely to work hard to prevent outside factors from derailing it. This was demonstrated on April 13, 2019, when Israeli F-16s flying over Lebanon launched missile attacks on targets in Syria. While Syrian forces launched less capable weapons at these aircraft which did not hit them, they did not fire any of their new S-300 air defense missiles which could have. According to one analyst, this was because Russian approval is needed for Syria to fire these, and Russian officials did not grant such approval since Israeli forces provided the requisite fifteen minutes advance notice of an Israeli attack to Moscow that Israel reportedly agreed to provide.[23]

But just as Russian-Israeli relations might deteriorate under certain circumstances in the future, they could also improve further. It has long been observed that if Israel does not accept a two-state solution for the conflict with the Palestinians and stays determined to retain control over all of Palestine and its inhabitants, it will confront a trade-off between remaining a democratic state and a predominantly Jewish one. The hard line policies toward the Palestinians pursued by Netanyahu and conservative politicians like him suggest that they will prioritize being a Jewish over a democratic state. But while a more authoritarian Israel may antagonize the Western democracies, this is not something that Putin's Russia is likely to find especially discomfiting. Indeed, Israel may find a Russia seeking to preserve authoritarian stability throughout the region a more congenial partner than Western states which (whether via their governments, media, or nongovernmental organizations) criticize it for its democratic and human rights deficits. Of course, Western democratic governments have long histories of supporting autocratic Arab governments and so might adjust to supporting an authoritarian Israeli one as well. But just as Arab authoritarian regimes cooperate with both Russia and the West, a more authoritarian one in Israel could also do so.

Can Moscow Mediate?

Whatever impact on Russian-Israeli relations that may result from eventual leadership change in Russia and political trends in Israel, the more immediate question is whether the current level of Russian-Israeli cooperation can survive increased Israeli-Iranian, US-Iranian, and US-Russian tensions. One possibility for this would be if Russia could serve as a mediator between Israel and Iran. While negotiating a rapprochement or friendly relations between these two Middle Eastern antagonists is unlikely to be accomplished by the Russian or any other government, Moscow might be able to help them avoid conflict or even reduce tensions. Indeed, Russia has reportedly offered to serve as this sort of mediator between Iran and Israel (as well as between Iran and Saudi Arabia).[24]

Russia certainly stands to increase its influence with both sides, as well as its worldwide standing, if it could succeed in just reducing tensions between Israel and Iran. And Russia seems far better placed to do this than the United States as a result of Iranian-American relations having grown increasingly hostile since the outset of the Trump Administration, especially after its withdrawal from the Iranian nuclear accord (also known as the Joint Comprehensive Plan of Action, or JCPOA). Russia, by contrast, enjoys good ties with both Israel and Iran, and so can talk to both. Indeed, Moscow now seems to be in a similar position to America in the 1970s when it was able to broker the Camp David peace agreement between Israel and Egypt. Back then, Washington had good relations with both sides while Moscow did not.

There are, however, two important differences between the two situations. First, by the time of the Camp David negotiations, Egypt and Israel had already fought three wars and did not want to fight another. Both were ready for a peace agreement but could not reach one on their own. Second, the United States was willing and able to provide military and economic assistance to both sides in order to achieve and maintain the peace agreement between them.

By contrast, neither Israel nor Iran seems ready to reduce their mutual tensions, much less reach a peace agreement. Indeed, there appear to be key players on both sides who are eager for a conflict because they each think that their side can prevail. Further, Russia seems neither willing nor able to provide indefinite assistance to Israel and Iran as the United States has done for decades vis-à-vis Israel and Egypt as an inducement to peace.

The problem that Moscow faces is that it is impossible to persuade opposing parties to peacefully resolve their conflict when neither wants to do so. Nor does Moscow appear to have the ability to coerce them into mediation either. Increased US support for Israel would surely follow if Russia tried to pressure Israel. Nor does Putin seem willing to apply serious pressure on Iran and risk undermining their joint effort to support Assad.[25] Finally, despite the hostility toward Iran displayed both by Trump and his advisers, the president's statements calling upon Iranian leaders to "call me"[26] suggest that he too had hopes for bringing about a rapprochement between Iran on the one hand and the United States along with its Middle Eastern allies on the other. Trump's ham-fisted efforts did not succeed. Yet his statements signal that Moscow cannot count on the United States allowing Russia to always have the advantage of claiming to be a better mediator by virtue of being able to talk to all sides. Perhaps if the United States and Russia worked together, they might be able to reduce tensions between not just Iran and Israel but between themselves. Achieving this desirable state of affairs, though, may require a different leadership mindset in all four countries, which might not occur any time soon.

Conclusion

It was noted at the beginning of this chapter that Russia and Israel have managed to build a remarkably friendly relationship despite the fact that each has close ties to the state that the other considers to be its most hostile adversary (Israel with the United States and Russia with Iran). With this situation unlikely to change, it is doubtful that Russian-Israeli relations will be able to grow closer than they are now. On the other hand, the fact that Russia and Israel have managed to cooperate for as long and as much as they have despite each being closely linked to the other's main adversary suggests that the Russian-Israeli relationship is a durable one and that it is likely to continue.

15

Russia in the Middle East and North Africa:
A Balance Sheet

Dimitar Bechev, Nicu Popescu, and Stanislav Secrieru

Russia is firmly anchored in the Middle East and North Africa and its footprint in the region's politics, diplomacy, military affairs, and the economy has expanded beyond recognition. Achievements speak for themselves. However, Russian foreign policy has incurred liabilities and is faced with obstacles and constraints. The balance sheet is therefore mixed.

The Achievements

Thanks to the intervention in Syria, Russia has put "boots on the ground" in a war zone outside the post-Soviet region. It controls the Khmeimim airbase and has transformed Tartus into a permanent naval base. Russian military police units now are patrolling jointly with UN peacekeepers the Golan Heights region on the Israeli-Syrian border.[1] In Libya, Russia has trained the forces of strongman Khalifa Haftar and dispatched mercenaries from Wagner Group as well as warplanes, while keeping the door open to UN-recognized government in Tripoli.[2] RSB Group, a Russian private contractor, conducted demining operations in Benghazi.[3] Russia negotiates with Egypt the use of airspace and airbases.[4] The Iranian base of Hamadan, from which the Russian air force launched strikes in Syria, is reportedly in the Kremlin's focus too.[5]

Moscow has benefited from an uptick of arm sales to both traditional partners such as Syria and to US allies and customers such as Egypt and Turkey, a member of NATO. Algeria and Egypt have obtained licenses for the production of T-90 tanks. Russia is eying the Gulf market as well. There is even an ambitious project to develop a next-generation fighter with the UAE.

Russian diplomacy is in full swing too, with initiatives in Syria and Libya and even a proposal on security in the Gulf. The words of the long-time Soviet foreign minister Andrey Gromyko, "as long there are rivalries in the Middles East, there is a need for us," ring true again.[6] Stepping into the fray to save the Assad regime has driven up its geopolitical stock and prestige. As this volume demonstrates, regional players, from Saudi Arabia to Turkey, to Israel to Iran, have adjusted to Russian presence. Moscow has done a good job to navigate and avoid being caught in the crossfire in local conflicts and, thanks to the Astana Process, lead the effort to negotiate a settlement in Syria; although not always fruitful Russia's measured behavior in the Middle East is in vivid contrast with its volatile and often bullying approach to post-Soviet neighbors. As a result, even potential adversaries such as the Gulf monarchies welcome Moscow's involvement. In addition, the Kremlin is scoring points against the United States at a moment America seeks a way out from the region.

Assertive policy in the Middle East has delivered economic gains. In the late 2010s, wheat exports shot up thanks to harvests beating Soviet records from forty years beforehand. Nearly three-quarters of Egypt's grain imports in 2018 came from the Russian Federation.[7] Russian tourists are all over the region, whether it is the Turkish or Tunisian beaches or Dubai's shopping malls. Nuclear power, oil and gas drive cooperation with Iran, Turkey, Egypt, and the UAE. And even Russian banks explore—cautiously—opportunities in the region.[8] In the past, Russia often acted as a free rider in global oil markets, undercutting OPEC in pursuit of greater sales. Now it works together with Saudi Arabia and other producers to shore up prices through coordinated curbs on output, with variable success. The war in Syria is turning into a profitable venture as well. Close associates of President Putin have put hands on phosphate production business in the country and seaport in Tartus.[9] More infrastructure contracts involving Russian companies, such as the renovation of Damascus airport, might be in the pipeline.[10]

Russia's success is a product of its own effort as well as favorable geopolitics.

Upgraded military capabilities have been key to Russian strategic gains. Despite still many limitations, Russian army managed to project and sustain power overseas for the first time in three decades. The post-2008 military reform is paying off and providing Russian diplomacy with a credible hard power clout it lacked through the 1990s and the 2000s. Russia is also more self-confident in the wake of its swift annexation of Crimea in 2014 and the subsequent war in Eastern Ukraine. Russia's threshold for the use of military force is much lower compared to a decade ago. And as domestic politics often become closely intertwined with external politics, from the Kremlin's point of view, as long as casualties are kept to a minimum, a small war can be useful for the purpose of mobilizing domestic opinion and feeding society's great power pride. According to a 2017 Levada poll, Russians singled out intervention in Syria as the most important event that year. Authorities are trying to capitalize on foreign achievements, even if, understandably, Russian society's priorities lie closer to home.

International and regional factors have given Russia an advantage too. America's progressive withdrawal from the Middle East after 2010 opened space for Russia to insert itself. Local actors, while not thrilled by the prospect of Russian dominance, are comfortable with Moscow's presence. That includes partners of the West that are frustrated about the United States and Europe. In contrast to Western powers, Russia is seen as credible. While Washington turned its back on Egypt's Mubarak in 2011 and failed to enforce its red lines on the use of chemical weapons in Syria two years later, Putin came to Bashar al-Assad's rescue. "*Svoikh ne sdaem*" (we won't give up on our people), as the Russian expression goes. As a result, Russia has become indispensable to the regional balance of power. Israel wants the Russian troops to remain in Syria as a counterbalance to Iran. Turkey hedges between Moscow and Washington to maximize its strategic position. Saudi Arabia, despite brief bitter dispute in March 2020, needs the Russians to keep oil prices stable. Russia is doing well in the Middle East's geopolitical bazaar because it is not constrained by commitment to values and principles, however superficial that might be. With its own lackluster human rights record, it is an easier and more flexible interlocutor than the United States or the European powers.

The Liabilities

Achievements have come at a cost, however. At closer reading, Russia's return to the Middle East and North Africa is far from an unqualified success.

To begin with, Russia may have had a "good" war in Syria, but to what end? Beyond saving Assad and fighting ISIS or other radical groups however, initial goals included resetting relations with the West, diluting the sanctions regime, and winning concessions over Ukraine. Most of those broader geopolitical objectives have now been abandoned. Instead, Moscow's attention is now fixated on reaping dividends form relations with Syria, Iran, Turkey, Israel, and other local players. Russian effort to achieve a political settlement to end the Syrian conflict is faltering and there is no grand plan for the Middle East coming from the Kremlin. In a television interview President Putin confirmed the open-ended character of Russian military presence in Syria, reiterating that troops "will be there as long as it benefits Russia."[11] It seems that the leadership in Moscow keeps reinventing the mission and moving the goalpost, according to dynamics on the ground, in order to legitimize the intervention. No exit strategy is in sight. But it is easy to enter the Middle East sands, than to leave them unscathed. Notably, since Russia last declared victory, in December 2017, its troop deployment went up.[12] But, from the Syrian regime perspective, these forces are of diminishing value. In early 2020, Russia stood on the sidelines as the Turkish military inflicted a heavy blow to Assad's army in Idlib, only for Putin and Erdoğan to strike a diplomatic deal at the end.

Russia's "Afghanistan syndrome" constrains its actions as well. The scars left by intervention in Afghanistan and the two Chechen wars maintain Russian society's sensitivity to massive combat casualties. While the deployment in Syria, far from Russian borders, has partly mended fears of overextension and domestic blowback, the imperative to keep troops out of harm's way still reigns supreme. Russia relies on "contactless warfare" through its air force and the use of mercenaries in the battlefield[13] alongside Hezbollah and the Iranian Revolutionary Guards Corps (IRGC). A large-scale operation replicating the Soviet overseas deployments during the Cold War is not in the cards.

Russia's economy is similarly a weak spot. With a GDP roughly the size of Spain's, the Russian Federation can offer little to its clients by way of postconflict reconstruction and development assistance. Bankrolling a small war is a different matter from funding rehabilitation after the fighting ends. Russia has been insistently calling on the West to pull out its checkbook and help Syria rebuild, stabilize, and take back more than 5 million refugees. Echoing the Russians, Bashar al-Assad has quoted the sum of $400 billion.[14] Irrespective of whether this figure is realistic or not, the regime would need to look elsewhere than Moscow and Tehran to foot the bill. Reconstruction shifts the focus to the Arab Gulf states with deep pockets and better local networks.

Scarce resources put a strain on defense spending. The country's expeditionary warfare capabilities, a sine qua non for continued presence in the Middle East, have come under pressure. The State Armaments Program for 2018–27 deprioritized the construction of a blue-water navy (apart from submarines) for reasons of cost. Smarting from the effects of Soviet collapse, the Russian defense industry has not made up for the loss of skills needed to build large war vessels with a wide radius of operation.[15] The operation in Syria has diverted funds away from modernization of the military, not to mention badly needed investment into education, infrastructure, and human capital.

Russia's economic diplomacy also oftentime look more promising on paper than in reality. Usually, the Russian state underwrites Rosatom nuclear projects abroad with loans. However, in negotiations with Jordan regarding installing two reactors by 2022, Moscow requested that the customers should raise funds through commercial lenders. As a result, Rosatom's plans for expansion into the country fell apart. In the same vein, Russia's courtship of the Gulf states in relation to joint investment projects seeks to compensate for the dwindling stream of Western credits and loans as a result of the Western sanctions. The success in stabilizing oil markets though cooperation with OPEC has helped the government balance the budget. Yet it has also disincentivized it from carrying out structural reforms in the interest of long-term growth. Some achievements have proven short-lived too. The collapse of oil prices in early 2020 is a case in point.

Intervening in Syria has generated political costs too. Russian actions have only hardened the resolve of certain states not to grant Moscow sanctions relief or even emboldened them to slap new restrictions. Polls indicate Middle Eastern populations have not become enamored of Russia either.[16] The diplomatic shield that Putin provided for the Assad regime at the UN following the chemical attacks has alienated public opinion in the region. Popular discontent and pressure on leaders from the proverbial Arab street might force a change of tack on relations with Russia. At the first sign of weakness, Moscow may find itself pushed by the wayside, as happened during the Cold War. Even cozy ties with Israel might not last beyond Putin's tenure, given the extent of his personal investment in the relationship.

Last but not least, Russia's surge in the region is leading to pushback from the West. The Kremlin launched the military operation in Syria with the ambition to launch anti-terrorist coalition with the United States, not unlike in the aftermath of 9/11. Despite the friendly response by Donald Trump, as presidential candidate and later occupant of the Oval Office, these hopes have been dashed. For the first time since the Cold War ended, Russia and the United States found themselves facing off in a direct military confrontation when Russian mercenaries directly attacked American marines near Deir-ez-Zor in February 2018. Instead of rebooting relations with Western powers, Moscow's intervention inflamed new tension. Russia is certainly more respected now, but the United States and its European allies continue to hold geopolitical cards.

What Comes Next?

The Cold War demonstrated how fickle the balance of power in the Middle East could be. Political shifts have hurt in the past both the United States and Russia. As Mark Twain reputedly said, even if history never repeats itself entirely, it often rhymes.

Observers should take Russia's rise in the region with seriousness. The Kremlin has demonstrated agility and skill to gain influence at relatively modest cost. Until the perception of success is proven wrong, Moscow will stick to the approach combining diplomacy and military muscle. And apparently a never-ending sequence of crises and local wars will keep presenting Russia with opportunities to further cement its position. Though Russia might not be able to deploy ground troops on a grand scale in the Middle East, its arms acquisition program till 2027 reveals efforts to boost air power projection capabilities (e.g., transportation and air-refueling planes, heavy attack drones, airborne warning system aircrafts). In the next decade there might be more Russia in the Middle Eastern skies. And should Russia's air force fail to impress or intimidate rivals, its "mosquito fleet" armed with long-distance cruise missiles will be able to deliver the message in the most remote corner of the region. Overall, Russia will have higher capacity to raise the costs for regional or great powers whose actions could prove to be at odds with Moscow's interests. Therefore, Russia's surge needs to be factored and constantly reassessed.

At the same time, overestimating Russia's capacity to sustain its presence and project influence over local politics, however, would be the wrong call. Russia has shown aversion to regime change. It has also helped extend Assad's political life. But to extrapolate that Russia will enforce this same principle across the region would be grossly misleading. Kremlin does not have either the will or the means to play the local cop in the Middle East. Russia has shown disquiet with 2019 mass protests in Algeria (a major arms customer) and the resignation of the country's long-standing ruler Abdelaziz Bouteflika, but it acted with restraint realizing quickly its inability to stamp off a peaceful democratic transition. Luckily for Russia, the political regime in Algeria has been able to self-reproduce, endowing Moscow with chance to preserve influence in this country. But it was a warning call; a repeat of the 2011 Arab Spring, with activists applying lessons learned during the last unsuccessful push for political transition, will limit Russia's chances to convert crises into regional influence.

Popular discontent brewing inside Russia, potentially reinforced by COVID-19 effects on the national economy, could also undercut its foreign policy ambitions. While a radical transformation echoing the 1990s is not in the offing, public opinion has rallied on multiple issues: pension reform, green spaces, garbage dumps, abusive arrests, respect of electoral rights. And these have direct implications on Russians' views of international affairs. According to one opinion poll, the share of those believing that government spends too much time on foreign policy went up from 25 percent to 33 percent between 2017 and 2019. At the same time, the percentage of Russians according to whom the country is successful abroad fell from 60 percent to 48 percent.[17] A majority (55 percent) thinks that the operation in Syria will be terminated, as compared to 49 percent in 2017.[18] In other words, foreign policy is gradually but steadily turning into a liability, rather than a source of legitimacy for the government as in the recent past. To be fair, the Kremlin has an admirable track record in manipulating public preferences. It might be successful in this case, too. However, as displays of public discontent multiply and the end of Putin's term in 2024 draws near, the leadership will come under pressure to dedicate more time and resources on issues closer to home, rather than managing the enmity between Iran and Israel, rebuilding Syria, or intervening in Libya. As a result, Russia might take away temporarily its eyes from the Middle East and North Africa—or even quietly pull out.

Notes

1 Introduction

1. Department of Defense, "Soviet Military Power," Washington, DC, 1984. http://www.dtic.mil/dtic/tr/fulltext/u2/a152445.pdf.
2. Soviet arms flowed to the Iranians too, through Syria. Policymakers in Moscow turned a blind eye. In the early stages of the war, in 1980–2, USSR had offered to send weapons to Iran but received a refusal. See Alexey Podtserob, *Rossia i Arabskii Mir* [Russia and Arab World] (Moscow: MGIMO Universitet, 2015), 295–6.
3. See R. Craig Nation, "The Sources of Soviet Involvement in the Middle East: Threat or Opportunity?" in *The Soviet Union and the Middle East in the 1980s*, ed. Mark V. Kauppi and R. Craig Nation (Lexington: Lexington Books, 1983), 59–60.
4. Nicu Popescu and Stanislav Secrieru (eds.), "Russia's Return to the Middle East: Building Sandcastles?," Chaillot Paper no. 146, July 2018. Editors are grateful to the EUISS for permission to reproduce major parts of the paper in this volume.
5. For more on Primakov's thinking: Yevgeny Primakov, *Russia and the Arabs: Behind the Scenes in the Middle East from the Cold War to the Present* (New York: Basic Books, 2009).
6. Just like Soviet Union from time to time relied on top communist officials from Muslim republics to build bridges with leaders of the Muslim world (e.g., trip of Salikh Batyiev, first secretary of the Communist Party of the Tatar Republic, to Libya in 1970), Russia relied on Kadyrov for important outreach missions in the Middle East. For more on Kadyrov's foreign policy profile: Pavel Luzhin, "Ramzan Kadyrov: Russia's Top Diplomat," *Riddle*, April 19, 2018. https://www.ridl.io/en/ramzan-kadyrov-russias-top-diplomat/.
7. Podtserob, *Rossia i Arabskii Mir*, 340–1.
8. "Speech and the Following Discussion at the Munich Conference on Security Policy," Kremlin.ru, February 10, 2007. http://en.kremlin.ru/events/president/transcripts/24034.
9. See Talal Nizammedin, *Putin's New Order in the Middle East* (London: Hurst, 2013), 153–97.
10. Michael McFaul, *From Cold War to Hot Peace* (New York: Houghton, Miffin, Harcourt, 2018), 158–75.
11. Gleb Bryanski, "Putin Likens U.N. Libya Resolution to Crusades," *Reuters*, March 21, 2011. https://www.reuters.com/article/us-libya-russia-idUSTRE72K3JR20110321.
12. Alexandra Kuimova, "Russia's Arms Exports to the MENA Region: Trends and Drivers," *EuroMeSco Policy Brief*, no. 95, 2019. https://www.euromesco.net/wp-content/uploads/2019/03/Brief95-Russia-Arms-transfer-to-the-MENA-region.pdf. See also Borisov's chapter in this volume.

13. Christopher Philips, *The Battle for Syria: International Rivalry in the New Middle East* (New Haven: Yale University Press, 2016).

14. Steve Holland and Jeff Mason, "Obama, in Dig at Putin, Calls Russia 'Regional Power'," *Reuters*, March 25, 2014. https://www.reuters.com/article/us-ukraine-crisis-russia-weakness-idUSBREA2O19J20140325.

15. "Global Arms Trade: USA Increases Dominance; Arms Flows to the Middle East Surge," Stockholm International Peace Research Institute (SIPRI), March 11, 2019. https://www.sipri.org/media/press-release/2019/global-arms-trade-usa-increases-dominance-arms-flows-middle-east-surge-says-sipri.

16. Alec Nove and J. A. Newth, *The Soviet Middle East: A Model for Development?* (London: Allen & Unwin, 1967).

17. Elena Milashina, "Halifat? Primanka dlya Durakov! [Caliphate? Trap for Fools!]," *Novaya Gazeta*, July 25, 2015. https://www.novayagazeta.ru/articles/2015/07/29/65056-171-halifat-primanka-dlya-durakov-187.

18. "Obama: Russia Heading for 'Quagmire' in Syria," *CNN*, October 2, 2015. https://edition.cnn.com/2015/10/02/politics/president-obama-syria-russia-assad/index.html; "Obama Says Russian Strategy in Syria is 'Recipe for Disaster'," *The Guardian*, October 2015. https://www.theguardian.com/world/2015/oct/02/us-coalition-warns-russia-putin-extremism-syria-isis.

19. "News Conference Following Talks with Austrian Federal President Alexander Der Bellen," *Kremlin.ru*, May 15, 2019. http://en.kremlin.ru/events/president/news/60527.

2 The Soviet Union in the Middle East: An Overview

1. Yezid Sayigh and Avi Shlaim, "Introduction," in *The Cold War and the Middle East*, ed. Yezid Sayigh and Avi Shlaim (Oxford: Clarendon Press, 1997), 3.

2. Rami Ginat, "The Soviet Union and Egypt, 1947–1955" (Ph.D. Thesis, London School of Economics, 1991), 24.

3. Joel Gordon, *Nasser's Blessed Movement: Egypt's Free Officers and the July Revolution* (Oxford: Oxford University Press, 1992), 121; Stella Margold, "Agrarian Land Reform in Egypt," *American Journal of Economics and Sociology* 17, no. 1 (October 1957): 9–19.

4. Syria had procured a small consignment of tanks from Czechoslovakia the year prior. The Soviets' aim was, in part, to deter Turkey, a NATO ally, which was mounting pressure on the neighboring Syrians.

5. "Letter from Prime Minister Eden to President Eisenhower: 1 October 1956," in *Britain and Suez: The Lion's Last Roar*, Scott Lucas (Manchester: Manchester University Press, 1996), 69.

6. John W. Copp, "Egypt and the Soviet Union, 1953–1970" (Master's Thesis, Portland State University, 1986), 121. https://pdxscholar.library.pdx.edu/cgi/viewcontent.cgi?article=4806&context=open_access_etds.

7. Vladimir Zolotarev, *Rossia (SSSR) v Lokalnyh Voinah* [Russia (USSR) in Local Wars], (Moscow: Kuchkovo Pole, 2000).

8. Mohamed Heikal, *The Sphinx and the Commissar: The Rise and Fall of Soviet Influence in the Middle East* (New York: Harper and Row, 1978), 65.

9. In fairness, the Soviet Union bore part of the responsibility for the Six-Day War as it advised Nasser that an Israeli offensive against Syria was imminent, quoting its own intelligence. That was not necessarily the case. In any case, brinkmanship went over

the brink. Yacov Ro'I and Boris Morozov, *The Soviet Union and the 1967 Six Day War* (Palo Alto: Stanford University Press, 2008).

10. Galia Golan, *Soviet Policies in the Middle East: From World War II to Gorbachev* (Cambridge: Cambridge University Press, 1990), 96.
11. Heikal, *The Sphinx and the Commissar*, 191.
12. Patrick Seale, "Syria," in *The Cold War and the Middle East*, 38–77.
13. Zolotarev, *Rossia (SSSR) v Lokalnyh Voinah*.
14. Arkadii Vinogradov, *Nepridumannaya Siria* [Syria in Real Life], (Moscow: Mezhdunarodnye Otnoshenia, 2017), 46.
15. Ronen Bergman, *Rise and Kill First: The Secret History of Israel's Targeted Assassinations* (London: John Murray, 2018), 606.
16. "Middle East: Top Assad Aide Assassinated at Syrian Resort," *The Guardian*, August 5, 2008. https://www.theguardian.com/world/2008/aug/05/syria. lebanon; Wikileaks; "The Global Intelligence Files." https://wikileaks.org/gifiles/docs/24/2436109_-os-syria-lebanon-security-wikileaks-france-said-syrian.html; "Wikileaks: France Said Syrian General Killed in Regime Feud," *Naharnet*, August 25, 2011. http://www.naharnet.com/stories/en/13646-wikileaks-france-said-syrian-general-killed-in-regime-feud.
17. Anatolii Chernayev, "Iz Vospominanii: Brezhnev i Gorbachev" [From Memoirs: Brezhnev and Gorbachev], *Polis*, no. 3 (2012): 165.
18. Heikal, *The Sphinx and the Commissar*, 195.
19. Seale, "Syria."
20. Habib Bourguiba, "Nationalism: Antidote to Communism," *Foreign Affairs* 35, no. 4 (July 1957): 646–53.
21. "From the Archive, 8 September 1973: Gaddafi and Castro Clash over Soviet Union," *The Guardian*, September 8, 2015. https://www.theguardian.com/world/2015/sep/08/gaddafi-castro-soviet-union-communism-1973.
22. "Libya-Soviet Ties Reported Strained," *New York Times*, May 6, 1986.
23. Heikal, *The Sphinx and the Commissar*, 275.

3 What Drives Russia's Policy in the Middle East?

1. See Dmitri Trenin, *What Is Russia Up to in the Middle East?* (Cambridge: Polity, 2018).
2. The Fact-Finding Mission of the Organization for the Prohibition of Chemical Weapons conducted on-site investigation of the incident regarding alleged use of chemical weapons in Douma in April 2018. Almost one year later it produced its final report: OPCW, *Fact-Finding Mission Report*, April 2018. https://www.opcw.org/sites/default/files/documents/2019/03/s-1731-2019%28e%29.pdf.
3. Neil Hauer, "Russia's Failure at Sochi Means More War for Syria in 2018," *Middle East Eye*, February 7, 2018. https://www.middleeasteye.net/opinion/russias-failure-sochi-means-more-war-syria-2018.
4. " 'Guarantor of Peace': Russia Inserts Itself between Israel, Syria in the Golan Heights," *National Post*, August 14, 2018. https://nationalpost.com/news/world/russia-to-help-un-with-patrols-along-syria-israel-frontier.
5. "Russian Delegation to Syria Proposes Kurdish Autonomy," *Moscow Times*, June 26, 2017. https://www.themoscowtimes.com/2017/01/26/russian-delegation-proposes-autonomy-for-syrian-kurds-a56934.

6. There are still no confirmed numbers of dead and wounded. Estimates range from a few fatalities, which is probably too low, to several hundred, which appears exaggerated. However, the fact that casualties occurred, and the way in which they were inflicted, is more important than their actual number.
7. "President Putin's Remarks during the Direct Line Phone-in Session," *Kremlin.ru*, June 20, 2019. http://en.kremlin.ru/events/president/news/60795.

4 Russia in Syria: A Military Analysis

1. "Foreign Fighters in Syria and Iraq," The Soufan Group, December 2015. http://soufangroup. com/wp-content/uploads/2015/12/TSG_ForeignFightersUpdate3.pdf.
2. "Vyhodtsy s Kavkaza v Ryadah IG (IGIL) [Peoples from the Caucasus in the Ranks of the IS (ISIS)]," *Kavkazski Uzel*, March 1, 2018. http://www.kavkaz-uzel.eu/articles/251513/.
3. "Official: Russia 'Deliberately Targeting' US-Backed Forces in Syria," *Fox News*, October 14, 2018. http://www.foxnews. com/politics/2015/10/14/official-russia-deliberately-targeting-us-backed-forces-in-syria-dozens-killed.html.
4. "Four-Fifths of Russia's Syria Strikes Don't Target Islamic State: Reuters Analysis," *Reuters*, October 21, 2015. https://www.reuters.com/article/us-mideast-crisis-syria-russia-strikes/four-fifths-of-russias-syria-strikes-dont-target-islamic-state-reuters-analysis-idUSKCN0SF24L20151021.
5. "Interview to American TV Channel CBS and PBS," *Kremlin.ru*, September 29, 2015. http://en.kremlin.ru/events/president/news/50380.
6. "Latvian President: Russia Using Syria to Divert Attention from Ukraine," *Baltic Times*, December 3, 2015. https://www.baltictimes.com/latvian_president__russia_using_syria_to_divert_attention_from_ukraine/.
7. "Sergey Lavrov's Press Conference Following Russia's Presidency of the UN Security Council, New York," *MID.ru*, October 1, 2015. http://www.mid.ru/en/foreign_policy/news/-/asset_publisher/cKNonkJE02Bw/content/id/1825252.
8. "Obama: U.S. Working to 'Isolate Russia'," *Time*, March 3, 2014. http://time.com/11900/obama-u-s-working-to-isolate-russia/.
9. "Vladimir Putin of Russia Calls for Coalition to Fight ISIS," *New York Times*, September 27, 2015. https://www.nytimes.com/2015/09/29/world/europe/russia-vladimir-putin-united-nations-general-assembly.html.
10. "DOD Puts Military-to-Military Activities with Russia on Hold," *U.S. Department of Defense*, March 3, 2014. http://archive.defense.gov/news/newsarticle.aspx?id=121759.
11. "Obama and Putin's First Formal Meeting in Two Years Described as 'Businesslike' Despite Tensions," *ABC News*, September 28, 2015. http://abcnews.go.com/US/obama-putin-set-rare-sit-meeting-amid-tensions/story?id=34094684.
12. "Putin Is Filling the Middle East Power Vacuum," *Bloomberg*, October 3, 2017. https://www.bloomberg. com/news/articles/2017-10-03/putin-is-now-mr-middle-east-a-job-no-one-ever-succeeds-at.
13. "Interview with Alexey Pushkov," *Europe1*, October 2, 2015. http://www.europe1.fr/emissions/l-interview-politique/la-coalition-americaine-a-fait-semblant-de-bombarder-daech-pendant-une-annee-2523383.
14. "Bogdanov: Operatsiya VKS v Sirii Dolzhna Byla Prodlitsya Neskoliko Mesyatsev [Bogdanov: The Operation of the VKS in Syria Was Expected

to Last Several Months]," *RIA Novosti*, September 26, 2016. https://ria.ru/syria/20160926/1477859123.html.

15. "Interview with Chief of Russian General Staff," *Komsomolskaya Pravda*, December 27, 2017. https://www.kp.ru/daily/26775/3808693/.

16. Mark Galeotti, "Not-So-Soft Power: Russia's Military Police in Syria," *War on the Rocks*, October 2, 2017. https://warontherocks.com/2017/10/not-so-soft-power-russias-military-police-in-syria/.

17. "More Russian Military Police Arrive in Syria after Moscow-Ankara Deal," *RFL*, October 25, 2019. https://www.rferl.org/a/more-russian-military-police-arrive-in-syria-after-moscow-ankara-deal/30236285.html.

18. "Breaking of Idlib Siege Leaves Three Russian Servicemen Wounded," *ITAR-Tass*, September 20, 2017. https://tass.com/defense/966624.

19. "Russian Military Police Deployed to Saraqeb," *ITAR-Tass*, March 2, 2020. https://tass.com/defense/1125825.

20. Official Data by the Central Election Commission of the Russian Federation, March 2018. http://www.foreign-countries.vybory.izbirkom.ru/region/foreign-countries?action=show&global=true&root=994001256&tvd=499400168175&vrn=100100084849062&prver=0&pronetvd=null&region=99&sub_region=99&type=226&vibid=499400168175.

21. "Chto Izvestno o Pogibshih v Sirii Rossiiskih Voennyh [What Is Known about Russian Military Personnel Killed in Syria]," *Kommersant*, May 27, 2018. https://www.kommersant.ru/doc/3460282.

22. Calculated by the author based on media reports.

23. "Turkey's Downing of Russian Warplane—What We Know," *BBC News*, December 1, 2015. http://www.bbc.com/news/world-middle-east-34912581.

24. "Isis 'Destroys' Syrian Airbase and Four Russian Helicopters," *Independent*, May 24, 2016. https://www.independent.co.uk/news/world/middle-east/isis-destroys-syrian-airbase-and-four-russian-helicopters-a7046646.html.

25. "Zhertvoi Fugasa Stal Rossiiskii General [The Russian General Fell Victim of IED]," *Kommersant*, March 6, 2017. https://www.kommersant.ru/doc/3235107.

26. "Proekt 'Myasorubka'. Rasskazyvaiut Tri Komandira 'ChVK Vagnera' [Project 'Meat Mincer'. Three Commanders of 'PMC Wagner' Speak Out]," *Radio Svoboda*, March 7, 2018. https://www.svoboda.org/a/29084090.html.

27. "Russian Mercenaries: Vagner Commanders Describe Life Inside the 'Meat Grinder'," *Radio Free Europe*, March 14, 2018. https://www.rferl.org/a/russian-mercenaries-vagner-commanders-syria/29100402.html.

28. Ibid.

29. "Bolishoe Interviu Chlenov ChVK Vagnera [A Big Interview with Wagner's PMC Members]," *Onpress.info*, November 2017. https://onpress.info/bolshoe-yntervyu-chlenov-chvk-vagnera-112488.

30. "No Sign of Obama's Predicted 'Guagmire' as Russia's Engagement in Syria Escalates," *Washington Post*, September 30, 2016. https://www.washingtonpost.com/world/no-sign-of-obamas-predicted-quagmire-as-russias-engagement-in-syria-escalates/2016/09/30/5b3e4d18-8723-11e6-ac72-a29979381495_story.html.

31. "Opposition Party's Report on Russia's Syria Campaign Costs Dismissed by Government," *The Jamestown Foundation*, July 31, 2017. https://jamestown.org/program/opposition-partys-report-on-russias-syria-campaign-costs-dismissed-by-government/.

32. "Syrian Government Loses 5/6th of Territory, IHS Says," *IHS Market*, August 22, 2015. http://news.ihsmarkit.com/press-release/aerospace-defense-security/syrian-government-loses-56th-territory-ihs-says.
33. "Syria Death Toll 384,000 after Nine Years of War: Monitor," *RFI*, March 14, 2020. http://www.rfi.fr/en/wires/202000314-syria-death-toll-384000-after-nine-years-war-monitor.
34. "Map of Control and Influence in Syria: February 16, 2018," *Omran Center for Strategic Studies*. https://omranstudies.org/publications/reports/map-of-control-and-influence-syria-16-february-2018.html.
35. Ibid.
36. "Russia Stance on Assad Suggests Divergence with Iran," *Reuters*, November 3, 2015. https://www.reuters.com/article/us-mideast-crisis-syria-russia/russia-stance-on-assad-suggests-divergence-with-iran-idUSKCN0SS0TY20151103.
37. "Rossiya Protestirovala v Sirii Yeshche 43 Obraztsa Novogo Oruzhiya [Russia Tested 43 More Types of New Weapons in Syria]," *RIA Novosti*, December 24, 2019. https://ria.ru/20191224/1562776515.html.
38. "Over Half of Russian Military Police Have Syrian War Experience—Official," *Moscow Times*, February 18, 2019. https://www.themoscowtimes.com/2019/02/18/over-half-of-russian-military-police-have-syrian-war-experience-official-a64532.
39. "V Minoborone Raskryli Chislo Uchastnikov Voennoi Operatsii VS RF v Sirii [The Defense Ministry Revealed the Number of Participants in the Military Operation in Syria]," *Zvezda*, January 3, 2019. https://tvzvezda.ru/news/forces/content/201901031142-b4d1.htm.
40. "Rossiiskie Bespilotniki Vedut Kruglosutochnyi Kontroli v Sirii, Zayavil Shoigu [Russian Drones Are Conducting Round-the-Clock Observation in Syria, Shoigu Said,]," *RIA Novosti*, October 27, 2017. https://ria.ru/syria/20171027/1507669571.html.
41. "Rossiiskie MI-28 Osnastili Provalinoi Elektronikoi [Russian Mi-28 Equipped with Subpar Electronics]," *Lenta.ru*, November 30, 2017. https://lenta.ru/news/2017/11/30/mi28/.
42. "Russia Steps up Military Presence in Syria, Despite Putin Promise," *Fox News*, January 11, 2017. http://www.foxnews.com/world/2017/01/11/russia-steps-up-military-presence-in-syria-despite-putin-promise.html.
43. "Operatsiya v Sirii Pokazala Silu Rossii [Operation in Syria Showed the Strength of Russia]," *Red Star*, January 31, 2018. http://redstar.ru/operatsiya-v-sirii-pokazala-silu-rossii/.
44. "Rossya Privlekla dlya Perevozki Gruzov v Siriu Desyati Grazhdanskih Sudov [Russia Contracted Ten Civil Vessels for Cargo Transportation to Syria]," *RBC*, November 15, 2015. https://www.rbc.ru/politics/15/10/2015/561fb5539a79471d00663b1e.
45. "Russia's New Armament Program to Focus on Precision Weapons," ITAR-Tass, December 27, 2017. http://tass.com/defense/983376.
46. "Russia's State Armament Programme 2027: A More Measured Course on Procurement," *IISS Military Balance Blog*, February 13, 2018. https://www.iiss.org/en/militarybalanceblog/blogsections/2018-f256/february-1c17/russia-state-armament-programme-d453.

5 The Nonwar on Daesh

1. Official website of the President of Russia, "Direct Line with Vladimir Putin," April 16, 2015. http://en.kremlin.ru/events/president/news/49261.

2. "Russian Air Strikes on Syrian Targets Raise 'Grave Concerns' in US," *Financial Times*, September 30, 2015. https://www.ft.com/content/a72cee0a-674e-11e5-a57f-21b88f7d973f.

3. "'More Than 90%' of Russian Airstrikes in Syria Have Not Targeted Isis, US Says," *The Guardian*, October 7, 2015. https://www.theguardian.com/world/2015/oct/07/russia-airstrikes-syria-not-targetting-isis; "Lawmakers Authorize Use of Russian Military Force for Anti-IS Airstrikes in Syria," *ITAR-Tass*, September 30, 2015. http://tass.ru/en/politics/824795; *Atlantic Council*, "Distract Deceive Destroy: Putin at War in Syria," April 2016. http://publications.atlanticcouncil.org/distract-deceive-destroy/assets/download/ddd-report.pdf.

4. Levada Center, "Syria and the Plane Crash in Egypt," November 23, 2015. https://www.levada.ru/en/2015/11/23/syria-the-plane-crash-in-egypt/; Levada Center, "Syria," July 10, 2016. https://www.levada.ru/en/2016/06/10/syria-2/.

5. "Russian Anti-Terrorist op in Syria," *RT*. https://www.rt.com/trends/russia-syria-op/; "Syria War: What the Mainstream Media Isn't Telling You about Eastern Ghouta," *RT*, March 5, 2018. https://www.rt.com/op-ed/420521-syria-eastern-ghouta-aleppo-media/.

6. "How Syria's White Helmets Became Victims of an Online Propaganda Machine," *The Guardian*, December 18, 2017. https://www.theguardian.com/world/2017/dec/18/syria-white-helmets-conspiracy-theories; BBC Monitoring, "Syrian President Condemns West, Vows to Survive Protests," January 11, 2012.

7. Vladimir Putin, "A Plea for Caution From Russia," *New York Times*, September 11, 2013. https://www.nytimes.com/2013/09/12/opinion/putin-plea-for-caution-from-russia-on-syria.html.

8. Official website of the President of Russia, "Vladimir Putin Answered Russian Journalists' Questions," September 4, 2015. http://en.special.kremlin.ru/events/president/transcripts/50234.

9. The Ministry of Foreign Affairs of the Russian Federation, "Foreign Minister Sergey Lavrov's Interview with Voskresnoye Vremya TV Programme, September 13, 2015," September 13, 2015. http://www.mid.ru/en/web/guest/foreign_policy/news/-/asset_publisher/cKNonkJE02Bw/content/id/1744777.

10. "Assad Poses Bigger Threat to Syrians Than Isis, Warns Thinktank," *The Guardian*, September 15, 2015. https://www.theguardian.com/world/2015/sep/15/syrian-president-bashar-al-assad-bigger-threat-than-isis; Charles Lister, "The West Is Walking into the Abyss on Syria," September 28, 2015. https://www.brookings.edu/blog/markaz/2015/09/28/the-west-is-walking-into-the-abyss-on-syria/.

11. "Syria's Bashar Assad Is Not a Perfect Leader, But Certainly Better Than Islamic State," *RT*, March 31, 2017. https://www.rt.com/op-ed/382958-assad-turkey-us-rex-tillerson/.

12. Fox News Poll, "Syria, Benghazi and the US Economy," October 14, 2015. http://www.foxnews.com/politics/interactive/2015/10/14/fox-news-poll-syria-benghazi-and-us-economy.html; "More Than 70% Support for Vladimir Putin's Bombing Campaign Despite Middle East Tensions," *Express*, October 13, 2015. https://www.express.co.uk/news/uk/611495/Vladimir-Putin-bombing-campaign-poll-support-syria-middle-east.

13. "Pour Bachar Al-Assad, la Position de François Fillon Sur la Syrie Est 'Une Très Bonne Chose,'" *Le Monde*, January 9, 2017. https://www.lemonde.fr/election-presidentielle-2017/article/2017/01/09/pour-bachar-al-assad-la-position-de-francois-fillon-sur-la-syrie-est-une-tres-bonne-chose_5059694_4854003.html#57QmCkAtQhPxfZ92.99.

14. "For Average Syrians, All Members of Opposition Are Terrorists—State Senator Richard Black," *RT*, January 27, 2017. https://www.rt.com/op-ed/375287-syria-draft-constitution-rebels/.

15. "Vladimir Putin Accuses US of Backing Terrorism in Middle East," *The Guardian*, October 22, 2015. https://www.theguardian.com/world/2015/oct/22/vladimir-putin-accuses-us-backing-terrorism-middle-east.

16. "Le Pen Says Assad May Be Lesser of Two Evils for Syria's Future," *Bloomberg*, February 20, 2017. https://www.bloomberg.com/news/articles/2017-02-20/le-pen-says-assad-may-be-lesser-of-two-evils-for-syria-s-future.

17. "Accept the Uncomfortable Truth: It's Time to Support Assad," *National Review*, January 7, 2016. https://www.nationalreview.com/2016/01/supporting-assad-best-option/; RTL, "Syrie: 'Il Faut se Rapprocher de Bachar al-Assad Pour Mieux Détruire Daesh', Dit Thierry Mariani," May 22, 2015. http://www.rtl.fr/actu/international/syrie-il-faut-se-rapprocher-de-bachar-al-assad-pour-mieux-detruire-daesh-dit-thierry-mariani-7778439575.

18. "Faut-il Choisir Entre Bachar el-Assad Et l'État Islamique?," *Le Figaro*, May 26, 2015. http://www.lefigaro.fr/vox/monde/2015/05/26/31002-20150526ARTFIG00196-faut-il-choisir-entre-bachar-el-assad-et-l-etat-islamique.php.

19. Jeremy Shapiro, "Bashar al-Assad Is a Monster. But Getting Rid of Him Won't Fix Syria," *European Council on Foreign Relations*, March 3, 2016. https://www.ecfr.eu/article/commentary_bashar_al_assad_is_a_monster_but_getting_rid_of_him_wont_fix_sy; Michael E. O'Hanlon, "Deconstructing Syria: A New Strategy for America's Most Hopeless War," Brookings, June 30, 2015. https://www.brookings.edu/blog/order-from-chaos/2015/06/30/deconstructing-syria-a-new-strategy-for-americas-most-hopeless-war/.

20. "U.N. Envoy Says Assad Is Crucial to Defusing Conflict in Syria," *New York Times*, February 13, 2015. https://www.nytimes.com/2015/02/14/world/middleeast/un-envoy-to-syria-says-assad-is-crucial-to-hopes-to-end-war.html.

21. "Reports on US Training 'Ex-Terrorists' in Syria Concerning," *RT*, December 25, 2017. https://www.rt.com/news/414189-syria-terrorists-training-lavrov/; *ITAR-Tass*, "Washington Uses Terror Groups in Syria for Its Own Goals," TASS, November 21, 2017. http://tass.com/politics/976604.

22. Levada Center, "Syria," October 22, 2014. https://www.levada.ru/en/2014/10/22/syria/.

23. "Syria War: What the Mainstream Media Isn't Telling You about Eastern Ghouta," *RT*, March 5, 2018. https://www.rt.com/op-ed/420521-syria-eastern-ghouta-aleppo-media/.

24. IFOP, "Enquête Sur le Complotisme," December 2017, 69. https://jean-jaures.org/sites/default/files/redac/commun/productions/2018/0108/115158_-_rapport_02.01.2017.pdf.

25. "US Protecting Syria Jihadist Group—Russia's Lavrov," *BBC News*, September 30, 2016. http://www.bbc.com/news/world-europe-37520793; "Russia Accuses US of Training ex-ISIS Fighters in Syria," *New York Post*, December 27, 2017. https://nypost.com/2017/12/27/russia-accuses-us-of-training-former-islamic-state-fighters-in-syria/.

26. "'Go Back to Raqqa & Bury Bodies': Putin Calls for Investigation into Strikes on Civilians in Syria," *RT*, March 10, 2018. https://www.rt.com/news/420923-raqqa-crimes-investigation-putin/; "US Destroying Syrian Cities Liberated from ISIS to Obstruct Pro-Assad Forces–Analyst," *RT*, October 15, 2017.https://www.rt.com/news/406751-mayadeen-syria-liberation-isis/.

27. Official website of the president of Russia, "Meeting with President of Syria Bashar al-Assad," December 11, 2017. http://en.kremlin.ru/events/president/transcripts/56353; "Russia Bewildered at France's Statement on Syria," *AMN*, December 10, 2017. https://mobile.almasdarnews.com/article/russia-bewildered-frances-statement-syria/.

28. Zogby Research Services, "Middle East 2016: Current Conditions and the Road Ahead," November 2016. https://static1.squarespace.com/static/52750dd3e4b08c252c723404/t/58509580ff7c5039b9505e67/1481676164948/SBY2016+FINAL.pdf.

29. Arab Center Washington DC, "2016 Arab Opinion Index," 11; Zogby Research Services, "Sir Bani Yas Forum—Public Opinion 2017," 7.

6 Russian Arms Exports in the Middle East

1. Mikhail Barabanov, Konstantin Makienko, Ruslan Pukhov, and Aleksandr Rybas, "Voenno-Tehnicheskoe Sotrudnichestvo Rossii s Zarubezhnymi Gosudarstvami: Analiz Rynkov [Military-Technical Cooperation between Russia and Foreign Countries: A Market Analysis]," Centre for Analysis of Strategies and Technologies (Moscow: Nauka, 2008), 42–3.

2. Ibid.

3. Robert O. Freedman, *Soviet Policy towards the Middle East since 1970* (New York: Praeger, 1982).

4. "Interviu Zamestitelya Direktora FSVTS Rossii M.V. Petuhova [Interview with Mikhail Petukhov, Deputy Director of the Federal Service for Military-Technical Cooperation of Russia]," August 26, 2010. http://www.fsvts.gov.ru/materials/26795A8AD42B3137C325778B0042FB8B.html.

5. "Aljir Priobretiot v Rossii Eshio Dve Podlodki [Algeria Will Acquire Two More Submarines in Russia]," *Kommersant*, May 18, 2006. https://www.kommersant.ru/doc/674444.

6. According to NATO's classification the Kilo-class refers to Russian-made attack submarines powered by diesel-electric propulsion.

7. "Ukaz Prezidenta Rossiiskoi Federatsii no.1154 [Decree of the President of the Russian Federation no.1154]," *Kremlin.ru*, September 22, 2010. http://kremlin.ru/acts/bank/31772.

8. "Ukaz Prezidenta Rossiiskoi Federatsii no.286 "O Merah po Vypolneniu Rezoliutsii Soveta Bezopasnosti OON 1970 ot 26 fevralia 2011 g. [Decree of the President of the Russian Federation no. 286 on Measures to Implement UN Security Council Resolution No. 1970 from 26 February 2011]," *Rossiiskaya Gazeta*, March 11, 2011. https://rg.ru/2011/03/11/livia-site-dok.html.

9. Andrey Frolov, "Itogi Voenno-Tehnicheskogo Sotrudnichestva Rossii s Inostrannymi Gosudarstvami v 2015 godu [The Results of the Military-Technical Cooperation of Russia with Foreign States in 2015]," *CAST*, January 2016. http://cast.ru/products/

articles/itogi-voenno-tekhnicheskogo-sotrudnichestva-rossii-s-inostrannymi-gosudarstvami-v-2015-godu.html.

10. "Meeting of Commission for Military-Technical Cooperation with Foreign States," *Kremlin.ru*, March 5, 2018. http://en.kremlin.ru/events/president/news/56981.

11. "Rosoboroneksport Polnostiu Vypolnit Godovoi Plan po Eksportu Vooruzhenia [Rosoboronexport Will Fully Implement the Annual Plan for Arms Exports]," *ITAR-Tass*, November 15, 2017. http://tass.ru/armiya-i-opk/4731347.

12. "Direktor FSVTS Dmitri Shugaev o Sushestvuiushih Slozhnostiyah i Otkryvaiushihsya Perespektivah Oruzheinogo Eksporta [Director of FSMTC Dmitry Shugaev on the Existing Difficulties and the Emerging Prospects of Arms Exports]," *Kommersant*, February 6, 2019. https://www.kommersant.ru/doc/3874641.

13. Alexey Nikolsky, "Blizhnii Vostok Stanovitsya Krupneishim Rynkom dlya Rossiiskih Vooruzhenii [Middle East Is Becoming the Largest Market for Russian Weapons]," *Vedomosti*, February 18, 2019. https://www.vedomosti.ru/politics/articles/2019/02/18/794445-blizhnii-vostok-stanovitsya-krupneishim-rinkom-vooruzhenii.

14. Ibid.

15. "Glava FSVTS Dmitrij Shugaev o potenciale eksporta rossijskogo vooruzheniya ["Dmitry Shugaev, the Head of the FSMTC, on the Potential on the Prospects of Russian Arms Exports]," *RT*, November 21, 2019. https://russian.rt.com/russia/article/689034-dmitrii-shugaev-intervyu-vystavka-dubai-airshow-2019.

16. "Aljir Poluchil Pervye Vosemi Istrebitelei Su-30MKI(A) po Tretiemu Kontraktu [Algeria Received the First Eight Su-30MKI(A) Fighters under the Third Contract]," *BMPD*, January 1, 2017. https://bmpd.livejournal.com/2355958.html.

17. "Rossya Postavila OTRK Iskander-E v Odnu iz Stran Severnoi Afriki [Russia Has Delivered Iskander-E Ballistic Missile Systems to a Country in the MENA region]," *RIA Novosti*, November 15, 2017. https://ria.ru/defense_safety/20171115/1508832294.html.

18. Alexey Nikolsky, "Zakliuchen Kontrakt po Litsenzionnomu Proizvodstvu Tankov T-90 v Aljire [The Contract on Licensed Production of T-90 Tanks in Algeria Concluded]," *Vedomosti*, February 20, 2015. https://www.vedomosti.ru/newspaper/articles/2015/02/20/tank-alzhirskoi-sborki.

19. "Algeria Is the First Export Client for the Russian Su-57 Stealth Fighter and the Su-34 Bomber," *MENA Defense*, December 27, 2019. https://www.menadefense.net/non-classe-en/algeria-is-the-first-export-client-for-the-russian-su-57-stealth-fighter-and-the-su-34-bomber.

20. Elena Chernenko, Sergey Goryashko, and Ivan Safronov, "Bagdad Vyshel v Chislo Liderov po Zakupkam Vooruzhenii u Moskvy [Baghdad Was among the Leaders in Arms Procurement from Moscow]," *Kommersant*, March 28, 2015. https://www.kommersant.ru/doc/2697125.

21. "V Irak Dostavlena Pervaya Partya BMP-3 [The First Batch of BMP-3's Delivered to Iraq]," *BMPD*, August 29, 2018. https://bmpd.livejournal.com/3322045.html.

22. "Irak i Saudovskaya Aravya Hotyat Kupiti Pochiti 1,5 tysyachi BMP-3 [Iraq and Saudi Arabia Want to Buy Almost 1500 BMP-3's]," *ITAR-Tass*, September 30, 2015. https://tass.ru/armiya-i-opk/2302766.

23. "Iraqi Defense Ministry Receives T90S Tanks from Russia," *ITAR-Tass*, February 19, 2018. http://tass.com/defense/990795.

24. "Bondarev Rasskazal o Vozmozhnyh Pretendentah na Pokupku S-400 [Bondarev Told about Possible Candidates for the Purchase of S-400]," *Ria Novosti*, January 2018. https://ria.ru/defense_safety/20180123/1513157260.html.

25. "Iraq to Purchase Russia's S-400 Missile Systems," *ITAR-Tass*, May 15, 2019. https://tass.com/defense/1058382.

26. Alexey Nikolsky, "Soglasovan Kontrakt na Postavku 46 Istrebitelei MiG-29 v Egipet [The Contract for the Supply of 46 MiG-29 Fighters to Egypt Signed]," *Vedomosti*, May 24, 2015. https://www.vedomosti.ru/politics/articles/2015/05/25/593348-soglasovan-kontrakt-na-postavku-46-istrebitelei-mig-29-v-egipet.

27. "Rosoboroneksport Oproverg Nalichie Kontrakta na Postavku Su-35 Egiptu [Rosoboronexport Denied the Signing of a Contract for the Supply of Su-35 Fighters to Egypt]," *Interfax*, March 26, 2019. https://www.interfax.ru/russia/655788.

28. "Rossia Protestirovala v Sirii 316 Obraztsov Vooruzhenya [Russia Tested in Syria 316 Types of Military Hardware]," *RIA Novosti*, March 11, 2019. https://ria.ru/20190311/1551688108.html.

29. "Putin Zayavil o Primenenii v Sirii 215 Sovremennyh Vidov Vooruzhenii [Putin Noted That Russian Forces Used Some 215 New Types of Advanced Weapons Systems in Syria]," *Interfax*, January 30, 2018. http://www.interfax.ru/russia/597769.

30. Ivan Safronov, "Kakim Sprosom Polizuetsya Rossiiskoe Oruzhie posle Sirii [What Is the Demand for Russian Weapons after Syria?]," *Kommersant*, March 28, 2016. https://www.kommersant.ru/doc/2932551.

31. "Glava Rosoboroneksporta: v 2018 godu Prodadim Oruzhiya Bolee Chem na $13 mlrd [The Head of Rosoboronexport: in 2018 We Will Sell Weapon on More Than $13 billion]," *RIA Novosti*, April 16, 2018. https://ria.ru/20180416/1518588740.html.

32. Alexandra Dzhordzhevich and Ivan Safronov, "Rossya i Saudovskaya Aravya Kak Nikogda Sblizilisi v Voprosah Postavok S-400 [Russia and Saudi Arabia Brought Together Their Views on the Supply of S-400 Systems as Never Before]," *Kommersant*, October 6, 2017. https://www.kommersant.ru/doc/3429985.

33. "Rossia Postavila Saudovskoi Aravii Vooruzhenie i Voennuiu Tehniku [Russia Supplied Weapons and Military Equipment to Saudi Arabia]," *Interfax*, June 27, 2019. https://www.interfax.ru/russia/666791.

34. Konstantin Makienko, "Rossiiskii Eksport Vooruzhenii v 2014–2018 gg.: Stagnatsya, Rost Riskov, Uhudshenie Vneshnei Sredy [Russian Arms Exports in 2014–2018: Stagnation, Increased Risks, External Factors]," *Export Vooruzheniy* 2 (2019): 9.

35. Ivan Safronov and Svetlana Bocharova, "Ataka Dronov Pomozhet Rossii Prodat' Sistemy PVO Stranam Persidskogo Zaliva [Drone Attack Will Help Russia Sell its Air Defense Systems to Gulf Countries]," *Vedomosti*, October 2019. https://www.vedomosti.ru/politics/articles/2019/10/23/814508-ataka-dronov-pomozhet-rossii.

36. "Glava FSVTS Dmitrij Shugaev o Potenciale Eksporta Rossijskogo Vooruzheniya ["Dmitry Shugaev, the Head of the FSMTC, on the Potential on the Prospects of Russian Arms Exports]," *RT*, November 21, 2019. https://russian.rt.com/russia/article/689034-dmitrii-shugaev-intervyu-vystavka-dubai-airshow-2019.

37. "Russia's Rostec to Co-develop 5th-gen Fighter with UAE," *Defense News*, February 20, 2017. https://www.defensenews.com/digital-show-dailies/idex/2017/02/20/russia-s-rostec-to-co-develop-5th-gen-fighter-with-uae.

38. "Rossya i Katar Vedut Peregovory po Vozmozhnym Postavkam Su-35 [Russia and Qatar Are Negotiating the Possible Supplies of Su-35 Fighters]," *ITAR-Tass*, March 1, 2018. http://tass.ru/armiya-i-opk/4999532.

39. "V FSVTS Zayavili o Peregovorah s Katarom po Postavkam S-400 [FSMTC Announced Talks with Qatar on the Delivery of the S-400's]," *ITAR-Tass*, February 19, 2019. https://tass.ru/armiya-i-opk/6133932.

40. "Putin Podpisal Ukaz ob Ucherezdenii Voennogo Attashata pri Posolistve Rossii v Katare [Putin Signed a Decree on the Establishment of a Military Attaché Office at the Russian Embassy in Qatar]," *ITAR-Tass*, June 24, 2019. https://tass.ru/armiya-i-opk/6584844.

41. "Russia to Supply Turkey with Four S-400 Missile Batteries for $2.5 Billion," *Reuters*, December 27, 2017. https://www.reuters.com/article/us-russia-turkey-missiles/russia-to-supply-turkey-with-four-s-400-missile-batteries-for-2-5-billion-kommersant-idUSKBN1EL0H6.

42. "Vneseno Izmenenie v Ukaz o Merah po Vypolneniu Rezoliutsii Soveta Bezopasnosti OON No.1929 [President of Russia, Amendment to Executive Order on Measures for Implementing UN Security Council Resolution no. 1929]," *Kremlin.ru*, April 13, 2015. http://en.kremlin.ru/events/president/news/49248.

43. United Nations, "Security Council Resolution 2231 (2015)," July 20, 2015. http://www.un.org/en/ga/search/view_doc.asp?symbol=S/RES/2231(2015).

44. "Rossya Gotova Postaviti Iranu S-400, Zayavili v FSVTS [Russia Ready to Deliver S-400 to Iran, Declared Federal Service for Military-Technical Cooperation of Russia]," *RIA Novosti*, June 28, 2019. https://ria.ru/20190628/1556012154.html.

45. Makienko, "Rossiiskii Eksport Vooruzhenii v 2014–2018 gg.: Stagnatsya, Rost Riskov, Uhudshenie Vneshnei Sredy [Russian Arms Exports in 2014–2018: Stagnation, Increased Risks, External Factors]," 7.

46. "Countering America's Adversaries through Sanctions Act, H.R. 3364," February 8, 2017. https://www.congress.gov/bill/115th-congress/house-bill/3364/text.

47. "Kuwaiti Army Officer Says Russian Tanks Purchase Postponed," *Xinhua*, March 5, 2019. http://www.xinhuanet.com/english/2019-03/05/c_137871438.htm.

48. "Egypt Faces Sanctions If It Buys Su-35s from Russia, U.S. Warns," *Jane's Defence Weekly*, April 10, 2019. https://www.janes.com/article/87808/egypt-faces-sanctions-if-it-buys-su-35s-from-russia-us-warns.

49. Idrees Ali and Phil Stewart, "U.S. Removing Turkey from F-35 Program after Its Russian Missile Defense Purchase," *Reuters*, July 18, 2019. https://www.reuters.com/article/us-turkey-security-usa-idUSKCN1UC2DD.

50. "Rossia Perevela Nekotorye Oruzheinie Eksportnye Kontrakty na Rashiot v Nationalnyh Valiutah [Russia Switched Some Arms Export Contracts for the Calculation in National Currencies]," *ITAR-Tass*, September 14, 2018. https://tass.ru/politika/5564237.

51. Aleksey Nikolskii, "Gosbanki Rossii i Indii Obespechiat Raschioty za Rossiiskoe Oruzhie v Natsionalinyh valiutah [Russian and Indian State Banks Will Ensure Payments for Russian Weapons in the National Currencies]," *Vedomosti*, July 16, 2019. https://www.vedomosti.ru/politics/articles/2019/07/15/806604-gosbanki-rossii-i-indii-obespechat-rascheti-za-oruzhie.

52. "Rossya Ushla ot Ispolizovaniya SWIFT i Dollara po Oruzheinym Kontraktam [Russia Abandoned the Use of SWIFT and Dollar in Arms Contracts]," *Interfax*, June 26, 2019. https://www.interfax.ru/business/666701.

7 Russia's Energy Diplomacy in the Middle East

1. Ministry of Energy of the Russian Federation, *Energy Strategy of Russia for the Period Up to 2030*, November 2009. http://www.energystrategy.ru/projects/docs/ ES-2030_(Eng).pdf.

2. BP, *BP Statistical Review of World Energy*, 2018. https://www.bp.com/content/dam/ bp/en/corporate/pdf/energy-economics/statistical-review/bp-stats-review-2018-full-report.pdf.

3. Tight oil "is a type of oil found in impermeable shale and limestone rock deposits ...; extracted using hydraulic fracturing, or fracking." "What Is Tight Oil?," *UCSUSA.org*, March 3, 2015. https://www.ucsusa.org/resources/what-tight-oil.

4. Jennifer Gnana, "Iraq's Dependence on Oil to Continue as Reform Pace Slows, Says Moody's," *The National*, October 3, 2019. https://www.thenational.ae/business/economy/ iraq-s-dependence-on-oil-tocontinue-as-reform-pace-slows-says-moody-s-1.918725.

5. World Bank, *From Recession to Recovery: Russia Economic Report*, May 2017. http://documents.worldbank.org/curated/en/782451497437509084/ Russia-economic-report-2017-from-recession-to-recovery.

6. In January 2019, Qatar left OPEC after being a member for about sixty years. Julia Kollewe, "Qatar Pulls Out of OPEC to Focus on Gas Production," *The Guardian*, December 3, 2018. https://www.theguardian.com/business/2018/dec/03/ qatar-pulls-out-of-opec-to-focus-on-gas-production.

7. International Energy Agency, *Monthly Oil Market Report*, January 2020. https://www. iea.org/reports/oil-market-report-january-2020.

8. Commitments of other non-OPEC parties have not been meaningful or credible, with the exception of Oman. For example, Mexican production had been on a strong downward trend, so the promised cuts had already been fully reflected in market expectation. And Kazakhstan actually increased its production by 260 kb/d from 2016 to 2018.

9. Rania El Gamal, Parisa Hafezi, and Dmitry Zhdannikov, "How Putin, Khamenei and Saudi Prince Got OPEC Deal Done," *Reuters*, December 1, 2016. https://www.reuters. com/article/us-opec-meeting/exclusive-how-putin-khamenei-and-saudi-prince-got-opec-deal-done-idUSKBN13Q4WG.

10. "BP Statistical Review of World Energy 2019," 68th edition, 2019. https://www. bp.com/content/dam/bp/business-sites/en/global/corporate/pdfs/energy-economics/ statistical-review/bp-stats-review-2019-full-report.pdf.

11. World Bank, *From Recession to Recovery*, 2017.

12. Joshua Yaffa, "How the Russian-Saudi Oil War Went Awry—for Putin Most of All," *New Yorker*, April 15, 2020. https://www.newyorker.com/news/dispatch/ how-the-russian-saudi-oil-war-went-awry-for-putin-most-of-all.

13. Energy Information Administration, 2020. https://www.eia.gov/dnav/pet/pet_pri_ spt_s1_d.htm.

14. Clearly, the 11 mb/d for both key producers was a compromise meant to signal equal importance and sacrifice. In fact, it gave a slight advantage to Saudi Arabia, which had threatened to ratchet production up to 12.3 mb/d after the fallout in early March. If that would have been taken as the benchmark, Saudi Arabia's cuts would have been higher than Russia's, which produces around 11.3 mb/d. On the other hand, Saudi Arabia had produced only around 9.7 mb/d before the fallout in March, as they

shouldered more production than required, while Russia's production over the entire period was relatively stable at around 11.5 mb/d, because it did not adhere to the latest production targets agreed within OPEC+ in December.

15. The Energy Information Administration defines spare capacity as the volume of production that can be brought on within thirty days and sustained for at least ninety days. https://www.eia.gov/finance/markets/crudeoil/supply-opec.php.

16. BP, *BP Statistical Review*, 2018.

17. The fiscal breakeven oil price is the minimum oil price needed to meet the spending commitments of an oil-exporting country while balancing public budgets.

18. IMF, *Regional Economic Outlook: Middle East and Central Asia*, November 2018. https://www.imf.org/en/Publications/REO/MECA/Issues/2018/10/02/mreo1018.

19. S&P Global, *Hooked on Oil: Is Russia Breaking*, March 2019. Free?https://www. allnews.ch/sites/default/files/files/Hooked%20on%20Oil_Is%20Russia%20 Breaking%20Free_14%20March%202019.pdf.

20. Joshua Yaffa, "How the Russian-Saudi Oil War Went Awry-for Putin Most of All."

21. Sovereign Wealth Fund Institute, *Sovereign Wealth Fund Rankings*, 2018. https://www. swfinstitute.org/sovereign-wealth-fund-rankings/.

22. Russia Direct Investment Fund, *Partnerships*, 2019. https://rdif.ru/Eng_Partnership/.

23. In April 2016, Saudi Arabia published its first long-term reform plan, "Vision 2030," which presents a roadmap for the kingdom's economic and social policies and aspirations.

24. The Public Investment Fund Program (2018–20). https://vision2030.gov.sa/sites/ default/files/attachments/PIF%20Program_EN_0.pdf.

25. "UAE's Russian Community Is Most Active in MENA Region," *Gulf News*, January 12, 2018. https://gulfnews.com/going-out/society/ uaes-russian-community-is-most-active-in-mena-region-1.2155824.

26. "NOC of Libya Signs Agreement with Rosneft of Russia," *National Oil Company*, February 21, 2017. https://noc.ly/index.php/en/new-4/2095-noc-and-rosneft-sign-cooperation-framework-agreement-at-london-ip-week.

27. "Russia Obtains 30% Stake in Egyptian Zohr Gas Field," *Rosneft*, October 9, 2017. https://www.rosneft.com/press/today/item/188235/.

28. "Russia Delivers LNG to Egypt under a Contract," *ITAR-Tass*, August 4, 2017. https:// tass.com/economy/959129.

29. "Rosneft Enters into an Agreement for Operational Management of an Oil Products Terminal in Lebanon," *Rosneft*, January 24, 2019. https://www.rosneft.com/press/ releases/item/193617/.

30. Henry Foy, "Rosneft's Iraqi Kurdistan Oil and Gas Play Angers Baghdad," *Financial Times*, October 30, 2018. https://www.ft.com/content/ ace52dd2-4f0c-11e8-ac41–759eee1efb74.

31. "Rosneft Pulls Out of $30 bln Iran Oil Project over Fears of U.S. Sanctions," *Moscow Times*, December 13, 2018. https://www.themoscowtimes.com/2018/12/13/rosneft-pulls-out-of-30-bln-iran-oil-project-over-fears-us-sanctions-media-reports-a63811.

32. "Igor Sechin Makes Key Report at X Eurasian Economic Forum in Verona," *Rosneft*, October 19, 2017. https://www.rosneft.com/press/today/item/188249/.

33. Rosatom, 2019. http://www.rosatom.ru/en/about-us/.

34. "Rosatom Opens a Branch in Saudi Arabia," *Rosatom*, June 11, 2019. https://www. rosatom.ru/en/press-centre/news/rosatom-opens-a-branch-in-saudi-arabia/.

35. World Nuclear Association, *Nuclear Power in Jordan*, 2017. http://www.world-nuclear. org/information-library/country-profiles/countries-g-n/jordan.aspx.

36. Asma Alsharif, "Russia to Lend Egypt $25 billion to Build Nuclear Power Plant," *Reuters*, May 19, 2016. https://www.reuters.com/article/us-egypt-russia-nuclear/russia-to-lend-egypt-25-billion-to-build-nuclear-power-plant-idUSKCN0YA1G5.

37. Nikita Minin and Tomas Vlcek, "Determinants and Considerations of Rosatom's External Strategy," *Energy Strategy Reviews*, no. 17 (2017): 37–44.

38. "Rosatom Opens a Branch," 2019.

8 Russia and Iran: It's Complicated

1. Irina Zviagelskaya and Nikolay Surkov, "Russian Policy in the Middle East: Dividends and Cost of the Big Game," *Russian International Affairs Council Working Paper 51* (2019): 4.

2. See, for example, Andrej Krickovic, "Russia's Challenge: A Declining Power's Quest for Status," *PONARS*, no. 543, October 2018. http://www.ponarseurasia.org/memo/russia-challenge-declining-power-quest-status.

3. Nikita Smagin, "Strategicheskoe Nedoverie. Pochemy u Rossii i Irana ne Polychaetsia Stati Soiuznikami [Strategic Mistrust. Why Russia and Iran Are Not Able to Become Allies]," *Moscow Carnegie Center*, June 4, 2019. https://carnegie.ru/commentary/79251.

4. Ibid.

5. Brenton Clark, "Persian Games: Iran's strategic Foothold in Tajikistan," *Open Democracy*, April 10, 2012. https://www.opendemocracy.net/en/odr/persian-games-irans-strategic-foothold-in-tajikistan/.

6. For Russia and other allies Nagorno-Karabakh is outside the CSTO remit as it is not a part of Armenia. Azad Garibov, "Pashinyan Tries to Leverage Armenia's CSTO Membership against Azerbaijan," *Eurasia Daily Monitor* 16, no. 174, December 13, 2009. https://jamestown.org/program/pashinyan-tries-to-leverage-armenias-csto-membership-against-azerbaijan/.

7. "Iran, Azerbaijan Sign Agreement on Defense Cooperation," *Press TV*, January 17, 2019. https://www.presstv.com/Detail/2019/01/17/586006/Iran-Azerbaijan-defense-MoU-Major-General-Mohammad-Baqeri-Baqeri--Zakir-Hasanov?fbclid=IwAR2pCt QlQsR_0yvKCeblDYtmZsy5reKLCPCozAKkQxTt70FSzspMtU-iRc0.

8. The North–South Corridor envisions three directions of interest for Iran and Azerbaijan: Caucasus–Persian Gulf, Central Asia–Persian Gulf, Caspian Sea– Iran. "North-South International Transport Corridor," *Ministry of Transport, Communication and High Technologies of the Republic of Azerbaijan*. https://mincom. gov.az/en/view/pages/104/.

9. Fariz Ismailzada, "The North-South Transport Corridor Finally Kicks Off," *The Central Asia-Caucasus Analyst*, September 27, 2016. https://www.cacianalyst. org/publications/analytical-articles/item/13395-the-%E2%80%9Cnorth-south%E2%80%9D-transport-corridor-finally-kicks-off.html.

10. Paul Goble, "Can the Kremlin Finally Realize the North-South Transit Corridor?," The Jamestown Foundation, February 16, 2019. https://jamestown.org/program/can-the-kremlin-finally-realize-the-north-south-transit-corridor/.

11. "Five States Sign Convention on Caspian Legal Status," *RFE/RL*, August 12, 2018. https://www.rferl.org/a/russia-iran-azerbaijan-kazakhstan-turkmenistan-caspian-sea-summit/29428300.html.

12. Douglas Frantz, "Iran and Azerbaijan Argue over Caspian's Riches," *New York Times*, August 30, 2001. https://www.nytimes.com/2001/08/30/world/iran-and-azerbaijan-argue-over-caspian-s-riches.html.

13. "Five States Sign …"

14. Dina Khrennikova, "Caspian Sea Breakthrough Treaty Set to Boost Oil, Pipeline Plans," *Bloomberg News*, August 12, 2018. https://www.bloomberg.com/news/articles/2018-08-12/caspian-sea-breakthrough-treaty-set-to-boost-oil-pipeline-plans.

15. Ilgar Gurbanov, "Caspian Convention Signing and Implications for the Trans-Caspian Gas Pipeline," *Eurasia Daily Monitor*, September 12, 2018. https://jamestown.org/program/caspian-convention-signing-and-the-implications-for-the-trans-caspian-gas-pipeline/. See also the full document: http://kremlin.ru/supplement/5328.

16. Olzhas Auyezov, "Russia, Iran, and Three Others Agree Caspian Status, but Not Borders," *Reuters*, August 12, 2018. https://www.reuters.com/article/us-kazakhstan-caspian-borders-idUSKBN1KX0CI.

17. Hamidreza Azizi, "Caspian Sea Convention Moves Iran Closer to Northern Neighbors," *Al-Monitor*, August 22, 2018. www.al-monitor.com/pulse/originals/2018/08/Caspian-sea-convention-iran-russia-us-sanctions-pipeline.html.

18. As cited in Carol R. Saivetz, "Moscow's Iranian Policies: Opportunities and Dangers," Crown Center, Brandeis University, *Middle East Brief*, 2007. https://www.brandeis.edu/crown/author/saivetz.html.

19. Author's Interviews in Moscow, November 2011.

20. Andrey Sushentsov, "A Russian View on America's Withdrawal from the Iran Deal," *National Interest*, May 15, 2018. https://nationalinterest.org/feature/russian-view-americas-withdrawal-the-iran-deal-25836.

21. "Timeline of Nuclear Diplomacy with Iran," *Arms Control*, July 2019. https://www.armscontrol.org/factsheet/Timeline-of-Nuclear-Diplomacy-With-Iran.

22. As cited in Mark N. Katz, "Russia and the Iran Crisis," *Lobelog*, May 17, 2019. https://lobelog.com/russia-and-the-iran-crisis/.

23. "Russia Is Not a 'Fire Brigade' to Save Disintegrating Iran Deal, Says Putin," *Times of Israel*, May 16, 2019. https://www.timesofisrael.com/russia-not-fire-brigade-to-save-disintegrating-iran-deal-says-putin/.

24. "Intel: Why Russia Dispatched Top Diplomatic to Teheran," *Al-Monitor*, May 30, 2019. www.al-monitor.com/pulse/originals/2019/05/intel-russia-sergey-ryabov-tehran-iran-nuclear-deal.html.

25. Robin Wright, "A Tanker War in the Middle East—Again?" *New Yorker*, June 13, 2019. https://www.newyorker.com/news/our-columnists/a-tanker-war-in-the-middle-eastagain.

26. Noa Landau, "Contradicting Trump, Top Putin Advisor Says U.S. Drone Downed in Iranian Airspace," *Ha'aretz*, June 26, 2019. https://www.haaretz.com/middle-east-news/at-israel-russia-meeting-bolton-says-u-s-awaits-real-negotiations-with-iran-1.7408293.

27. Thomas Buonomo, "Russia's Potential Response to a U.S.-Iran Conflict," *Lobelog*, July 5, 2019. https://lobelog.com/russias-potential-response-to-a-u-s-iran-conflict/.

28. "Caspian Sea Deal Benefits Russia, Troubles Iran," *DW.com*, August 15, 2018. https://www.dw.com/en/caspian-sea-deal-benefits-russia-troubles-iran/a-45051799.

29. Ibid.

30. Alireza Noori, "Iran Seeks Relief from U.S. Sanctions in Asia," *Al-Monitor*, June 28, 2019. www.al-monitor.com/pulse/originals/2019/06/iran-seeks-relief-us-sanctions-asia.html.

31. Alireza Noori, "Can Iran Rely on Russia to Dodge U.S. Pressure," *Al-Monitor*, May 21, 2019. www.al-monitor.com/pulse/originals/2019/05/iran-russia-nuclear-deal-jcpoa-trump-us-sanctions-oil.html.

32. Reese Erlich, "Trump Is Driving Iran into Russia's Arms," *Foreign Policy*, May 29, 2019. https://foreignpolicy.com/2019/05/29/trump-is-driving-iran-into-russias-arms-nuclear-deal-putin-rouhani-sanctions/.

33. Thomas Buonomo, "Russia's Potential Response to a U.S.-Iran Conflict," *Lobelog*, July 5, 2019. https://lobelog.com/russias-potential-response-to-a-u-s-iran-conflict/.

34. Tom Miles, "Russia Sees Closer Iran Ties as U.S. Exits Nuclear Deal: Official," *Reuters*, May 4, 2018. http://www.reuters.com/article/us-iran-nuclear-russia-idUSKBN11516Z.

35. "Lukoil Puts Iran Plans on Hold Due to Threat of US Sanctions," *Reuters*, May 29, 2018. https://www.reuters.com/article/us-russia-lukoil-iran/lukoil-puts-iran-plans-on-hold-due-to-threat-of-u-s-sanctions-idUSKCN1IU1M7.

36. Alireza Noori, "Can Iran Rely on Russia to Dodge US Pressure," *Al-Monitor*, May 21, 2019. www.al-monitor.com/pulse/originals/2019/05/iran-russia-nuclear-deal-jcpoa-trump-us-sanctions-oil.html.

37. Mark N. Katz, "Russia and the Iran Crisis," *Lobelog*, May 17, 2019. https://lobelog.com/russia-and-the-iran-crisis/.

38. Maxim A. Suchkov, "How Russia Is Reading the Killing of Qassem Suleimani," *Al-Monitor*, January 3, 2020, www.al-monitor.com/pulse/originals/2020/01/russia-soleimani-iran-us-strikes-ira1.html.

39. Konstantin von Eggert, "Opinion: Putin Power Games May Get Out of Hand," DW, January 6, 2020. https://www.dw.com/en/opinion-putins-power-games-may-get-out-of-hand/a-51907064.

40. "Russia Reacts to Claims of Iranian Missile Downing Ukrainian Plane," *Moscow Times*, January 10, 2020. https://www.themoscowtimes.com/2020/01/10/russia-reacts-to-claims-of-iranian-missile-downing-ukrainian-plane-a68859.

41. "Lavrov Blames Washington's 'Aggressive' Policies for Rise in Global Tensions," *RFE/RL*, January 17, 2020. https://www.rferl.org/a/lavrov-blames-washington-s-aggressive-policies-for-rise-in-global-tensions/30383167.html.

42. Alexey Khlebnikov, "Iran, Russia, and the Impact of U.S. Sanctions," Middle East Institute, July 17, 2019. https://www.mei.edu/publications/iran-russia-and-impact-us-sanctions.

43. Alireza Noori, "Can Iran Rely on Russia to Dodge U.S. Pressure," *Al-Monitor*, May 21, 2019. www.al-monitor.com/pulse/originals/2019/05/iran-russia-nuclear-deal-jcpoa-trump-us-sanctions-oil.html.

44. Nikolay Pakhomov, "Russia's Grand Plan to Gain Power in the Shadow of U.S. Sanctions," *National Interest*, May 7, 2019. https://nationalinterest.org/feature/russias-grand-plan-gain-power-shadow-us-sanctions-56427.

45. "Russia's Security Concept for the Gulf Area," *MID.ru*, July 23, 2019. http://www.mid.ru/ru/foreign_policy/international_safety/conflicts/-/asset_publisher/xIEMTQ3OvzcA/content/id/3733575?p_p_id=101_INSTANCE_xIEMTQ3OvzcA&_101_INSTANCE_xIEMTQ3OvzcA_languageId=en_GB.

46. Maxim A. Suchkov, "Intel: Why Russia Is Calling for Rethinking Gulf Security," *Al-Monitor*, July 24, 2019. www.al-monitor.com/pulse/originals/2019/07/intel-russia-proposal-gulf-security-iran-tensions.html.

47. Andrei Baklanov, "Security in the Gulf Area: Russia's New Initiative," *Valdai Club*, August 6, 2019. valdaiclub.com/a/highlights/security-in-the-gulf-area-russia's-new-initiative/.

48. Cited in Robin Wright, "Russia and Iran Deepen Ties to Challenge Trump and the United States," *New Yorker*, March 2, 2018. https://www.newyorker.com/news/news-desk/russia-and-iran-deepen-ties-to-challenge-trump-and-the-united-states.

9 Russia and the "Resistance Axis"

1. "Trump Expected to Seek Putin's Help to Curb Iran's Military in Syria," *Wall Street Journal*, June 28, 2018. https://www.wsj.com/articles/trump-to-meet-russias-putin-in-finland-on-july-16-1530187901?emailToken=17a77cd4d4aa6965efbdc228b00f6a39Na bkwZUR0oRaoZreVrS0uL/IflEuI9Z5nzSZZ0rb1vjZhrq11RjTZaOdRg+QMkuSBfhJ7 3at7urD+G2PjjBfZFYklDNqEn3iF4OKiQuLBNk%3D&reflink=article_email_share.
2. "How Iranian General Plotted Out Syrian Assault in Moscow," *Reuters*, October 6, 2015. https://www.reuters.com/article/us-mideast-crisis-syria-soleimani-insigh/how-iranian-general-plotted-out-syrian-assault-in-moscow-idUSKCN0S02BV20151006.
3. After Russia made public the use of Hamadan base, Teheran revoked the permission granted to Russian military aircrafts to operate from the base. For more, see Anne Barnard and Andrew E. Kramer, "Iran Revokes Russia's Use of Air Base, Saying Moscow 'Betrayed Trust'," *New York Times*, August 22, 2016. https://www.nytimes.com/2016/08/23/world/middleeast/iran-russia-syria.html.
4. "Iraq, Russia, Iran and Syria Coordinate against ISIS," *Al Jazeera*, September 27, 2015. https://www.aljazeera.com/news/2015/09/iraq-russia-iran-syria-coordinate-isil-150927125919507.html.
5. Julian Barnes-Dacey, "To End a War: Europe's Role in Bringing Peace to Syria," *ECFR Policy Brief*, September 12, 2017. http://www.ecfr.eu/publications/summary/to_end_a_war_europes_role_in_bringing_peace_to_syria7223.
6. Ellie Geranmayeh and Kadri Liik, "The New Power Couple: Russia and Iran in the Middle East," *ECFR Policy Brief*, September 13, 2016. http://www.ecfr.eu/publications/summary/iran_and_russia_middle_east_power_couple_7113.
7. Author's Interview with Arab Government Official, Moscow, June 2019.
8. Author's Interviews with Iranian Officials and Analysts, 2014.
9. See Julien Barnes-Dacey, "Russia's Policy in Syria: Efforts to Pivot to a Political Track," *Valdai Discussion Club*, December 15, 2017. http://valdaiclub.com/a/highlights/russian-policy-in-syria/.
10. "Russian-drafted New Constitution for Syria Promises Kurds Greater Autonomy," *New Arab*, January 26, 2017. https://www.alaraby.co.uk/english/news/2017/1/26/russia-drafted-new-constitution-for-syria-promises-kurds-greater-autonomy.
11. Author's Interview with Iranian Officials and Analysts, 2016 and 2017.
12. "Russian-Sponsored Syrian Agency to 'Protect Government Facilities'," *Asharq Al-Awsat*, July 11, 2019. https://aawsat.com/english/home/article/1808021/russian-sponsored-syrian-agency-%E2%80%98protect-government-facilities%E2%80%99.
13. Author's Interview with Western Diplomat, 2016.
14. "Russian-Sponsored Syrian Agency to 'Protect Government Facilities'."
15. Author's Interview with Iranian Officials and Analysts, 2016 and 2017.
16. "Iran-Backed Militias Block Aleppo Evacuation as Shelling Resumes," *The Guardian*, December 14, 2016. https://www.theguardian.com/world/2016/dec/14/aleppo-residents-evacuation-uncertainty-ceasefire-deal-assad.
17. "Tensions Flare between Syrian Leader's Foreign Backers," *SFGATE*, June 9, 2018. https://www.sfgate.com/world/article/Tensions-flare-between-Syrian-leader-s-foreign-12981371.php.

18. "Iran-Backed Militias Block ..."
19. "Assad Offers Russia Reconstruction Benefits at Iran's Expense," *Syrian Observer*, February 28, 2018. http://syrianobserver.com/EN/Features/33899/ Assad_Offers_Russia_Reconstruction_Benefits_Iran_Expense.
20. Ibrahim Hamidi, "Damascus' Allies, Opponents Race over Strategic Gains," *Asharq Al-Awsat*, April 25, 2019. https://aawsat.com/english/home/article/1694476/ damascus%E2%80%99-allies-opponents-race-over-strategic-gains.
21. Rohollah Faghihi, "Iranian Mistrust of Russia Surges as Syrian War Winds Down," *Al-Monitor*, March 12, 2018. https://www.al-monitor.com/pulse/en/originals/2018/03/ iran-syria-russia-sentiment-reconstruction-spoils-safavi.html.
22. Author's Interview with Senior Gulf Official, March 2018.
23. Author's Interview with Senior Israeli Official, March 2018.
24. Author's Interview with Senior Saudi and Israeli Officials, January and March 2018.
25. Author Interview with Russian Official, Moscow, June 2019.
26. "We Can't Force Iran Out of Syria, Russia Tells Israelis," *Reuters*, July 30, 2018. https://uk.reuters.com/article/uk-mideast-crisis-syria-israel-russia/ we-cant-force-iran-out-of-syria-russia-tells-israelis-idUKKBN1KK29A?il=0.
27. "Putin's Envoy Briefs Tehran about Russia-Israel-U.S. Meeting," PressTV, July 8 2019. https://www.presstv.com/Detail/2019/07/09/600561/ Iran-Russia-Putin-envoy-brief-Jerusalem-alQuds-meeting-Israel.
28. "Russia's Military Offer Stalls in Lebanon, for Now," *Asia Times*, April 8, 2018. http://www.atimes.com/article/russias-military-offer-stalls-lebanon-now/.

10 Russia and Turkey: The Promise and the Limits of Partnership

1. For an overview of Turkey's relations with Russia, see Pavel Baev, "Turkey and Russia," in *The Routledge Handbook of Turkish Politics*, ed. Alparslan Özerdem and Matthew Whiting (London: Routledge, 2019), 413–24. Also Gençer Özcan, Evren Balta, and Burç Beşgül (eds.), *Kuşku ile Komşuluk: Türkiye ve Rusya İlişkilerinde Değişen Dinamikler* (İstanbul: İletişim, 2017).
2. Chris Drake, "Cyprus Bows to Pressure and Drops Missile Plan," *The Guardian*. December 29, 1998. F. Stephen Larrabee and Ian Lesser, *Turkish Foreign Policy in an Age of Uncertainty* (Santa Monica, CA: RAND, 2003), ch. 4.
3. Boris Yeltsin never came to Turkey on an official visit, though he did attend the launch of BSEC hosted by President Turgut Özal in 1992 as well as the 1998 OSCE summit in Istanbul. Dimitar Bechev, *Rival Power: Russia in Southeast Europe* (New Haven: Yale University Press), ch. 5.
4. Turkey imported about 23.96 bcm in 2018 of which 7.86 bcm from Iran and 7.52 bcm from Azerbaijan. Data by Gazprom Export and the Turkish Statistical Institute (TÜİK) http://www.tuik.gov.tr/.
5. By comparison, 3.5 million arrived in 2014. Numbers went down in 2015 because of terrorist attacks and in 2016 as a result of Russian sanctions. Turkish 2015 tourism revenues fall 8.3 pct to $31.46 billion. *Hürriyet Daily News*, January 29, 2016.
6. Trade volume is still well under $37.7 billion recorded in 2008, the last year before the global financial crisis.
7. Suat Kınıklıoğlu and Valeriy Morkva, "An Anatomy of Russian-Turkish Relations," *Journal of Southeast European and Black Sea Studies* 7, no. 1 (2007): 533–53.

8. Russia began the physical delivery of S-400 missiles in mid-July 2019, the third-year anniversary of the coup attempt.
9. See Kemal Kirişci, *Turkey and the West: Faultlines in a Troubled Alliance* (Washington, DC: Brookings Institution, 2017). Also Soner Çağaptay, *Erdoğan's Empire: Turkey and the Politics of the Middle East* (London: Bloomsbury, 2019).
10. Erdoğan has pointed out at Russia's Su-57 as an alternative.
11. At the same time, it is true that Russian state media such as the Turkish-language version of the Sputnik agency often take an antigovernment line in their coverage of domestic affairs and Turkey's foreign policy. "Russian Propaganda Outlets Prosper in Turkey," *Economist*, February 28, 2019.
12. Dimitar Bechev, "Turkey's View of the U.S.–Iran Crisis," *Ahval*, May 24, 2019. https://ahvalnews.com/us-turkey/turkeys-view-us-iran-crisis.
13. About 500 US troops remain deployed in the Deir ez Zor governorate, with a mission to fight ISIS and protect oil wells. See Luke Morgelson, "America's Abandonment of Syria," *New Yorker*, April 20, 2020.
14. See the chapters by Julien Barnes-Dacey and Dmitriy Frolovskiy in this volume.
15. Aslı Aydıntaşbaş, "A New Gaza: Turkey's Border Policy in Northern Syria." Policy Brief, European Council on Foreign Relations, May 2020. https://www.ecfr.eu/publications/summary/a_new_gaza_turkeys_border_policy_in_northern_syria.
16. "Where Does the Syrian Regime Get Foreign Currency From?" *Enab Baladi*, July 8, 2020. https://english.enabbaladi.net/archives/2020/07/where-does-the-syrian-regime-get-foreign-currency-from/.
17. Alan Makovsky, "Turkey's Refugee Dilemma," *Center for American Progress*, March 13, 2019. https://www.americanprogress.org/issues/security/reports/2019/03/13/467183/turkeys-refugee-dilemma/.
18. Charles Lister, "Assad Hasn't Won Anything," *Foreign Policy*, July 11, 2019. https://foreignpolicy.com/2019/07/11/assad-hasnt-won-anything-syria/.
19. Galip Dalay, "How Long Will the Russian-Turkish Deal on Idlib Last?" *Al Jazeera*, March 20, 2020. https://www.aljazeera.com/indepth/opinion/long-turkish-russian-deal-idlib-200316135110613.html.
20. The Libyan campaign has tested and showcased to potential customers weapons systems developed by the Turkish defense industry, such as the Bayraktar T2 drone (also used in Idlib and, in the autumn of 2020, in Nagorno-Karabakh), the same way Syria did for Russian arms exporters.
21. "Russian Snipers, Missiles and Warplanes Try to Tilt Libyan Conflict," *New York Times*, November 5, 2019. https://www.nytimes.com/2019/11/05/world/middleeast/russia-libya-mercenaries.html; Jalel Harchaoui, The Pendulum: How Russia Sways Its Way into More Influence in Libya, War on the Rocks, 7 January 2021. https://warontherocks.com/2021/01/the-pendulum-how-russia-sways-its-way-to-more-influence-in-libya/.
22. "*Turkey Wades into Libya's Troubled Waters, International Crisis Group*," Report 257. Europe and Central Asia. April 30, 2020. https://www.crisisgroup.org/europe-central-asia/western-europemediterranean/turkey/257-turkey-wades-libyas-troubled-waters.
23. Brian Katz and Joseph Bermudez Jr., "Moscow's Next Front: Russia's Expanding Footprint in Libya," *Center for Strategic and International Studies*, June 17, 2020. https://www.csis.org/analysis/moscows-next-front-russias-expanding-military-footprint-libya.

24. Erdogan expressed skepticism whether the ceasefire would last. "Libyan Factions Sign 'Permanent' Ceasefire, Erdogan Casts Doubt," *The Arab Weekly*, October 23, 2020. https://thearabweekly.com/ libyan-factions-sign-permanent-ceasefire-erdogan-casts-doubt.
25. Elena Milashina, "Khalifat? Primanka dlia Durakov [Khalifate? Trap for Fools]," *Novaya Gazeta*, July 29, 2015. https://www.novayagazeta.ru/ articles/2015/07/29/65056-171-halifat-primanka-dlya-durakov-187.
26. Shaun Walker, "Murder in Istanbul: Kremlin's Hand Suspected in Shooting of a Chechen," *The Guardian*, January 10, 2016. https://www.theguardian.com/world/2016/ jan/10/murder-istanbul-chechen-kremlin-russia-abdulvakhid-edelgireyev.
27. Together with HTS, Ahrar al-Sham played a key role in the capture of Idlib in 2015. Jaish al-Islam, once dominant in the eastern suburbs of Damascus, has relocated to the Euphrates Shield area in northern Aleppo controlled by Turkey.
28. The target date for the first unit is 2023, the centennial from the establishment of the Republic of Turkey.
29. The main fields are located in the exclusive economic zones of Cyprus, Israel, and Egypt. Turkey has been opposing exploration commissioned by Cyprus, arguing that it violates the sovereign rights of Turkish Cypriots.
30. Turkey has invested heavily in capacity. A new floating storage and regasification unit (FSRU) entered into service in July 2019. It is located close to Izmir, on the Turkish Aegean coast. That is added to an FSRU off the coast of the Hatay province, which began operating in February 2018. Turkey now has five LNG import facilities. "Turkey's New LNG Storage, Regasification Unit to Dock in İzmir Today," *Daily Sabah*, July 5, 2019. https://www.dailysabah.com/energy/2019/07/05/ turkeys-new-lng-storage-regasification-unit-to-dock-in-izmir-today.
31. Purchases from Azerbaijan rose by a third and reached 9.2 bcm while LNG, from a variety of suppliers including the United States, went up to 11 bcm or about a quarter of all natural gas imports. Brenda Shaffer, "Turkey's Westward Energy Shift," Middle East Institute, January 15, 2020. See TÜİK's website for up-to-date data.
32. Eser Özdil, "How Turkey Benefits from the Global LNG Glut," *Atlantic Council*, May 7, 2020. https://www.atlanticcouncil.org/blogs/turkeysource/ how-turkey-benefits-from-global-lng-glut/.
33. In June 2019, Turkish authorities froze plans for a second nuclear power plant near the Black Sea city of Sinop.
34. Moscow followed with unease the brief thaw in relations between Turkey and Armenia between 2009 and 2010 culminating in a deal on opening the border that however remained unimplemented. Personal communication with a former Turkish policymaker active at the time.
35. "Russia and Turkey in the Black Sea and the South Caucasus," *International Crisis Group*, Europe and Central Asia Report no. 250, June 28, 2018. https:// www.crisisgroup.org/europe-central-asia/western-europemediterranean/ turkey/250-russia-and-turkey-black-sea-and-south-caucasus.
36. Turkey has been upgrading and expanding its naval forces and developing plans for a new base near the Black Sea coastal town of Zonguldak, about 100 nautical miles east of the Bosphorus entry point.

11 Understanding Russia–GCC Relations

1. Charter of the Gulf Cooperation Council (GCC)," May 25, 1981. https://www.files. ethz.ch/isn/125347/1426_GCC.pdf.
2. "Federalnaya Sluzhba Bezopasnosti Rossii Raspolagaet Dostovernoi Informatsiei o Putyah i Sposobah Finansovoi Podderzhki Voorujennyh Formirovanii Mezhdunarodnyh Terroristov, Voiuyuschih na Territorii Chechenskoi Respubliki [Federal Security Service of Russia Disclaims Reliable Information on the Ways and Methods of Financial Support for Armed Formations of International Terrorists in the Chechen Republic]," *FSB.ru*, May 19, 2000. http://www.fsb.ru/fsb/press/message/ single.htm%21id%3D10340914%40fsbMessage.html.
3. "President Vladimir Putin Held Negotiations with Abdullah Ibn Abdul Aziz Al Saud, the Crown Prince of Saudi Arabia," *Kremlin.ru*, September 2, 2003. http://en.kremlin. ru/ events/president/news/29294.
4. Alexey Malashenko, "Russia and the Arab Spring," *Carnegie Moscow Center*, October 2013. https://carnegieendowment.org/files/russia_arab_spring2013.pdf.
5. "How Qatar Seized Control of the Syrian Revolution," *Financial Times*, May 17, 2013. https://www.ft.com/content/f2d9bbc8-bdbc-11e2–890a-00144feab7de.
6. "Russia to Extend Tartus and Hmeimim Military Bases in Syria," *Deutsche Welle*, December 26, 2017. http://www.dw.com/en/ russia-to-extend-tartus-and-hmeimim-military-bases-in-syria/a-41938949.
7. Dmitriy Frolovskiy, "Chego Hotyat Drug ot Druga Rossia i Monarhii Zaliva" [What Russia and the Gulf Monarchies Want from Each Other]," *Carnegie Moscow Center*, August 27, 2017. http://carnegie.ru/commentary/72897.
8. Giorgio Cafiero and Theodore Karasik, "Yemen War and Qatar Crisis Challenge Oman's Neutrality," *Middle East Institute*, July 6, 2017. http://www.mei.edu/content/ article/oman-s-high-stakes-yemen.
9. Holly Ellyatt, "Russia Rolls Out the Red Carpet for Saudi King with Billion-Dollar Deals on the Table," *CNBC*, October 5, 2017. https://www.cnbc.com/2017/10/05/ saudi-king-visits-russia-as-billion-dollar-deals-on-the-table.html.
10. "Qatari Emir in Russia to Discuss Syrian Crisis," *Al Jazeera*, March 25, 2018. https://www.aljazeera.com/news/2018/03/qatari-emir-russia-discuss-syrian-crisis-180325195253621.html.
11. Dmitri Trenin, "Russia's Policy in the Middle East: Prospects for Consensus and Conflict with the United States," *The Century Foundation*, March 2, 2010. https:// carnegieendowment.org/files/trenin_middle_east.pdf.
12. Leonid Issaev, "Russia and the GCC Crisis," *Al Jazeera*, June 13, 2017. https://www. aljazeera.com/indepth/opinion/2017/06/russia-gcc-crisis-170613073826800.html.
13. "Lavrov Prokommentiroval Diplomaticheski Skandal Vokrug Katara [Lavrov Commented on the Qatari Diplomatic Scandal]," *RIA Novosti*, June 5, 2017. https:// ria.ru/world/20170605/1495842179.html.
14. Alexey Malashenko, "Islamic Challenges to Russia, From the Caucasus to the Volga and the Urals," *American Enterprise Institute*, May 13, 2015. http://carnegie.ru/2015/05/13/ islamic-challenges-to-russia-from-caucasus-to-volga-and-urals-pub-60334.
15. Zogby Research Services, "Middle East Public Opinion 2018," December 11, 2018. https://www.zogbyresearchservices.com/new-gallery-71.

16. Zogby Research Services, "Looking to the Next Decade," November 2019. http://www.
    zogbyresearchservices.com/s/2019-SBY-standalone.pdf.
17. ASDA'A Burston-Marsteller, "Arab Youth Survey," 2018. http://www.arabyouthsurvey.
    com/findings.html.
18. Zogby Research Services, 2019.
19. Theodore Karasik, "Why Is Qatar Investing so Much in Russia?," *Middle East Institute*,
    March 8, 2017. http://www.mei.edu/content/article/why-qatar-investing-so-much-
    russia; Frank Kane, " 'Reset' for Russian-GCC Trade Relations, but Still a Long Way to
    Go," *Arab News*, June 4, 2017. http://www.arabnews.com/node/1110241.
20. Vitaliy Naumkin, *Nesostoyavsheesya Partniorstvo. Sovetskaya Diplomatya v Saudovskoi
    Araviy mezhdu Mirovymi Voynami* [Failed Partnership. Soviet Diplomacy in Saudi
    Arabia between World Wars] (Moscow: Aspekt Press, 2018), 130, 142, 207.
21. Evelina Zakamskaya, "Glava MID Saudovskoi Aravii ob Otnosheniyah c Rossiei
    [Head of the Ministry of Foreign Affairs of Saudi Arabia Talks about Relations
    with Russia]," *Russia 24-Mnenie*, October 7, 2017. https://www.youtube.com/
    watch?v=VsItopYU-M0.
22. "Unemployment, Youth Total (percent of total labor force ages 15–24) (modeled
    ILO estimate)," data from World Bank. https://data.worldbank.org/indicator/
    SL.UEM.1524.ZS; "Corruption Perceptions Index 2017," *Transparency International*.
    https://www.transparency.org/news/feature/corruption_perceptions_index_2017;
    Frederic Wehrey, "The Forgotten Uprising in Eastern Saudi Arabia," *Carnegie
    Endowment for International Peace*, June 14, 2013. http://carnegieendowment.
    org/2013/06/14/forgotten-uprising-in-eastern-saudi-arabia-pub-52093;
    John Kemp, "Saudi Arabia's Oil Reserves: How Big Are They Really?,"
    Reuters, July 11, 2016. https://www.reuters.com/ article/us-saudi-oil-kemp/
    saudi-arabias-oil-reserves-how-big-are-they-really-kemp-idUSKCN0ZL1X6.
23. Saudi Vision 2030, "Our Vision: Saudi Arabia, the Heart of the Arab and Islamic
    Worlds, the Investment Powerhouse, and the Hub Connecting Three Continents."
    http://vision2030.gov.sa/en.
24. David Ignatius, "A Young Prince Is Reimagining Saudi Arabia: Can He Make His
    Vision Come True?," *Washington Post*, April 20, 2017. https://www.washingtonpost.
    com/opinions/global-opinions/a-young-prince-reimagines-saudi-arabia-can-he-
    make-his-vision-come-true/2017/04/20/.
25. Sune Engel Rasmussen, "In Syria, Foreign Powers' Scramble for Influence
    Intensifies," *Wall Street Journal*, February 28, 2018. https://www.wsj.com/articles/
    in-syria-foreign-powers-scramble-for-influence-intensifies-1519817348.
26. "V 2019 Hadj Sovershat 20,5 tysyachi Rossiskih Musulman [In 2019, 20.5 thousand
    Russian Muslims Will Make the Hajj]," *ITAR-Tass*, January 16, 2019. https://tass.ru/
    obschestvo/6007479.
27. "SPIEF 2018 to be Attended by Biggest Saudi Delegation in Forum's History," *Russian
    Exports National Information Portal*, March 27, 2018. http://www.rusexporter.com/
    news/detail/5286/.
28. "Saudovskaya Araviya Investiruet v Bolee Chem 25 Rossiiskih Proektov [Saudi Arabia
    Will Invest in More Than 25 Projects in Russia]," *RIA Novosti*, October 4, 2017.
    https://ria.ru/economy/20171004/1506213502.html.
29. "RDIF, PIF and Saudi Aramco Announce the Establishment of a New Platform for
    Russian-Saudi Energy Investment," *Russian Direct Investment Fund*, October 5, 2017.
    https://rdif.ru/Eng_fullNews/2660/.

30. Kathrin Hille, "Saudi Sovereign Fund to Invest $10bn in Russia," *Financial Times*, July 6, 2015. https://www.ft.com/content/0205a0d6-2412-11e5-bd83–71cb60e8f08c.

31. Darya Korsunskaya and Polina Nikolskaya, "Russian Fund Builds Investors Pool for Saudi Aramco IPO," *Reuters*, February 15, 2018. https://www.reuters.com/article/us-russia-sarabia-novatek/russian-fund-builds-investors-pool-for-saudi-aramco-ipo-idUSKCN1FZ0PV.

32. "RDIF and Saudi Aramco Agree Terms of Investment in Novomet," *Russian Direct Investment Fund*, February 20, 2019. https://rdif.ru/Eng_fullNews/3943/.

33. Henry Meyer and Ilya Arkhipov, "Saudis, Russia Fund to Sign $2 Billion in Deals During Putin's Visit," *Bloomberg*, October 10, 2019. https://www.bloomberg.com/news/articles/2019-10-10/saudis-russia-fund-to-sign-2-billion-deals-during-putin-visit.

34. "Falih: Saudi Aramco Extends Offer to Buy Stake in Arctic LNG 2," *Reuters*, June 10, 2019. https://www.reuters.com/article/lng-novatek-saudi-aramco/falih-saudi-aramco-extends-offer-to-buy-stake-in-arctic-lng-2-tass-idUSR4N23D08Z.

35. Dmitriy Frolovskiy, "Russia and Qatar: The Middle East's Newest Pragmatic Friendship?" *Jerusalem Post*, April 1, 2019. https://www.jpost.com/Opinion/Russia-and-Qatar-The-Middle-Easts-newest-pragmatic-friendship-585461.

36. Steven Lee Myers, "Qatar Court Convicts 2 Russians in Top Chechen's Death," *New York Times*, July 1, 2004. http://www.nytimes.com/2004/07/01/world/qatar-court-convicts-2-russians-in-top-chechen-s-death.html.

37. "Russia Withdraws Envoy to Katar after Attack," *Reuters*, December 5, 2011. https://af.reuters.com/article/commoditiesNews/idAFL3E7N535820111205; "Rossia i Qatar Ssoriatsya iz-za Rukoprikladstva [Russia and Qatar Are Quarrelling over a Physical Fight]," *Interfax*, December 5, 2011. http://www.interfax.ru/russia/220228.

38. Dmitriy Frolovskiy, "Seryi Kardinal Blizhnego Vostoka. Kak Malenkii Qatar Pokoril Bolshoi Region [Eminence Grise of the Middle East. How Small Qatar Conquered the Giant Region]," *Carnegie Moscow Center*, May 11, 2017. http://carnegie.ru/commentary/69917.

39. "Rossia Gotova Narastit Postavki Prodovolstviya v Qatar [Russia Is Ready to Increase Food Supplies to Qatar]," *ITAR-Tass*, June 8, 2017. http://tass.ru/ekonomika/4323794; Kinninmont, Jane. "The Gulf Divided: The Impact of the Qatar Crisis." Middle East and North Africa Programme, Chatham House, May 2019. https://www.chathamhouse.org/sites/default/files/publications/research/2019-05-30-Gulf%20Crisis_0.pdf.

40. "Russian Foreign Minister Sergey Lavrov to Hold Talks in Qatar," *Al Jazeera*, March 3, 2019. https://www.aljazeera.com/news/2019/03/russian-foreign-minister-sergey-lavrov-hold-talks-qatar-190304070458781.html.

41. Mohammed Sergie, "The Tiny Gulf Country with a $335 Billion Global Empire," *Bloomberg*, January 11, 2017. https://www.bloomberg.com/news/articles/2017-01-11/qatar-sovereign-wealth-fund-s-335-global-empire.

42. Henry Meyer, "Qatar Seeks More Russian Deals after 'Great' Rosneft Investment," *Bloomberg*, March 11, 2019. https://www.bloomberg.com/news/articles/2019-03-11/qatar-seeks-more-russia-deals-after-great-rosneft-investment.

43. Theodore Karasik, "Why Is Qatar Investing so Much in Russia?," *Middle East Institute*, March 8, 2017. http://www.mei.edu/content/article/why-qatar-investing-so-much-russia.

44. Jack Farchy and Neil Hume, "Glencore and Qatar Take 19.5 percent Stake in Rosneft," *Financial Times*, December 10, 2016. https://www.ft.com/content/d3923b08-bf09-11e6-9bca-2b93a6856354.

45. Voronova, Tatiana. "Exclusive: Russian State Bank Secretly Financed Rosneft Sale after Foreign Buyers Balked." *Thomson Reuters*, November 9, 2018. https://www.reuters.com/article/us-rosneft-privatisation-exclusive/exclusive-russian-state-bank-secretly-financed-rosneft-sale-after-foreign-buyers-balked-idUSKCN1NE132.

46. "QF and Rosneft Unveil New R&D Hub at QSTP," *Qatar Foundation*, March 28, 2018. https://www.qf.org.qa/news/qf-and-rosneft-unveil-new-rd-hub-at-qstp.

47. "Russia and Qatar Hold Discussions on Collaborating at International Multilateral Events in 2019–2020," *SPIEF*, June 11, 2019. https://www.forumspb.com/en/news/news/russia-and-qatar-hold-discussions-on-collaborating-at-international-multilateral-events-in-20192020/.

48. "Qatar Waives Entry Visa Requirements for Citizens of 80 Countries," *Qatar Airways*, August 9, 2017. https://www.qatarairways.com/en/press-releases/2017/Aug/qatar-waives-entry-visa-requirements-for--citizens-of-80-countri.html#.

49. "Upravlenie po Turismu Qatara Prezentovalo Rossiiskoe Predstavitelstvo i Oboznachilo Prioritety [Qatar Tourism Authority Opened Representation in Russia and Outlined Its Priorities]," *Vesti.ru*, March 30, 2018. http://travel.vesti.ru/article_37356.

50. James Dorsey, "Fighting for the Soul of Islam: A Battle of the Paymasters," *Huffington Post*, September 30, 2017. https://www.huffingtonpost.com/james-dorsey/fighting-for-the-soul-of_b_12259312.html; "Islamic Conference in Chechnya: Why Sunnis Are Disassociating Themselves from Salafists," *Firstpost*. September 9, 2016. https://www.firstpost.com/world/islamic-conference-in-chechnya-why-sunnis-are-disassociating-themselves-from-salafists-2998018.html.

51. Jumana Khamis, "UAE's Long-Term Food Security Strategy under Study," *Gulf News*, February 8, 2018. http://gulfnews.com/news/uae/society/uae-s-long-term-food-security-strategy-under-study-1.2170588; "Russian Visitors to GCC to Increase 38 Percent by 2020," *Gulf News*, January 13, 2018. http://gulfnews.com/business/sectors/tourism/russian-visitors-to-gcc-to-increase-38-by-2020-1.2156253.

52. Gnana Jennifer. "Adnoc Awards 5 Percent Stake in Ghasha Concession to Russia's Lukoil," *The National*, October 15, 2019. https://www.thenational.ae/business/energy/adnoc-awards-5-stake-in-ghasha-concession-to-russia-s-lukoil-1.924175.

53. "Flydubai Launches New Route to Russia," *Russian Aviation Insider*, April 24 2019. http://www.rusaviainsider.com/flydubai-launches-new-route-russia/; "Loukoster Pobeda Nachiniot Letati v Eilat i Dubai [Low-Cost Company Podeda Will Start Flying to Eilat and Dubai]," *Meduza*, July 10, 2019. https://meduza.io/news/2019/07/10/loukoster-pobeda-nachnet-letat-v-eylat-i-dubay.

54. Anne-Sylvaine Chassany, "Abu Dhabi Plans to Invest Up to $5bn in Russian Infrastructure," *Financial Times*, September 11, 2013. https://www.ft.com/content/372b18e6-1af4-11e3-87da-00144feab7de.

55. Fareed Rahman, "RDIF in Talks with UAE Partners for Investments," *Gulf News*, December 3, 2017. https://gulfnews.com/business/sectors/investment/rdif-in-talks-with-uae-partners-for-investments-1.2134596.

12 Russia and Egypt: A Precarious Honeymoon

1. According to Russia's Foreign Ministry data, April 23, 2019. http://www.mid.ru/ru/
maps/eg/?currentpage=main-country.
2. Mohamed Heikal, *The Sphinx and the Commissar* (New York: Harper & Row,
1978), 35–55.
3. Schoenberger Erica and Stephanie Reich, "Soviet Policy in the Middle East," *MERIP
Reports*, no. 39 (1975): 3–28.
4. Ibid.
5. Evgeny Primakov, *Confidentially: The Middle East on Stage and Behind the Curtains*
(Moscow: Rossijskaya Gazeta, 2012).
6. Yuriy Zinin, "Is the Red October Legacy Still Traceable across the Middle East?,"
New Eastern Outlook, January 31, 2018. https://journal-neo.org/2018/01/31/
is-the-red-october-legacy-still-traceble-across-the-middle-east/.
7. Bogdanov Mikhail, "Russian-Egyptian Relations at the Turn of the Centuries," *Asia i
Afrika segodnya*, no. 12 (2013): 2–3.
8. BRICS stands for Brazil, Russia, India, China, and South Africa.
9. Alekxey Podtserob, *Rossia i Arabskii Mir* [Russia and Arab World] (Moscow: MGIMO
Universitet, 2015), 102–4.
10. "The First Joint Russian-Egyptian Commission on Military and Technical
Cooperation Was Held in Moscow," *Russian Ministry of Defense*, March
3, 2015. http://eng.mil.ru/en/mpc/news/more.htm?id=12009420@
egNews; "Egypt Licensed to Assemble Russian T-90S Tanks. Capacity–50
a Year," *Debka Weekly*, March 11, 2018. https://www.debka.com/
egypt-licensed-to-assemble-russian-t-90s-tanks-capacity-50-a-year/.
11. Sergey Lavrov, "Friendship and Cooperation Tested by Time," *Al Ahram*, October
13, 2018. http://www.mid.ru/en/diverse/-/asset_publisher/zwI2FuDbhJx9/content/
stat-a-ministra-inostrannyh-del-rossii-s-v-lavrova-rossia-i-egipet-druzba-i-
sotrudnicestvo-ispytannye-vremenem-opublikovannaa-v-egipetskoj-gazete-al-
a?_101_INSTANCE_zwI2FuDbhJx9_redirect=http%3A%2F%2Fwww.mid.
ru%2Fen%2Fdiverse%3Fp_p_id%3D101_INSTANCE_zwI2FuDbhJx9%26p_p_
lifecycle%3D0%26p_p_state%3Dnormal%26p_p_mode%3Dview%26p_p_col_
id%3Dcolumn-1%26p_p_col_pos%3D2%26p_p_col_count%3D6; "Russian
Federation Naval Doctrine," *Kremlin.ru*, July 26, 2015. http://en.kremlin.ru/events/
president/news/50060.
12. Rafael Daminov, "Vozobnovlenie Charterov iz Rossii Vyzvalo Likovanie v
Egipetskom Tursektore [Relaunch of Charter Flights from Russia Triggered
Cheers in Egypt's Tourist Sector]," *RIA Novosti*, October 18, 2018. https://ria.
ru/20181018/1530960714.html; Yasmin El Beih, "Russian Tourism in Egypt: What's
Next?," *Egypt Today*, July, 23, 2018. https://www.egypttoday.com/Article/3/54330/
Russian-Tourism-in-Egypt-What%E2%80%99s-Next.
13. "Egipet Otkryvaiut dlya Rossiiskih Turistov: Progress na Litso [Egypt Is Opened
for Russian Tourists: Progress Is Evident]," *Turprom*, April 9, 2019. https://www.
tourprom.ru/news/41965/.
14. Mohamed Emad, "Russian Experts Continue Inspection of Hurghada Airport
Security," *El-Balad*, April 16, 2019. https://en.el-balad.com/2416757.

15. Vladimir Isachenkov, "Russia Negotiates Deal for Its Warplanes to Use Egypt Bases," *AP*, November 30, 2017. https://apnews.com/bdfae4502ca74c1eacdbf6d32252e8f4?utm_campaign=SocialFlow&utm_source=Twitter&utm_medium=AP.

16. Phil Stewart, Idrees Ali, and Lin Noueihed, "Russia Appears to Deploy Forces in Egypt, Eyes on Libya Role–Sources," *Reuters*, March 13, 2017. https://www.reuters.com/article/us-usa-russia-libya-exclusive/exclusive-russia-appears-to-deploy-forces-in-egypt-eyes-on-libya-role-sources-idUSKBN16K2RY; "Reuters: Russia Apparently Deploys Forces near Libyan Border in Egypt," *RFE/RL*, March 14, 2017. https://www.rferl.org/a/russia-special-forces-libya-egypt/28368266.html.

17. Vickiie Oliphant, "Russia Hits Out after Being Accused of Sending Forces to Egypt to Influence Libya Conflict," *Express*, March 14, 2017. https://www.express.co.uk/news/world/778864/Russia-DENIES-deploying-special-forces-Egypt-influence-Libya-conflict.

18. "Gaddafi Fall Cost Russia Tens of Billions in Arms Deals," *Reuters*, November 2, 2011. https://www.reuters.com/article/russia-libya-arms/gaddafi-fall-cost-russia-tens-of-blns-in-arms-deals-idUSL5E7M221H20111102.

19. "Egypt, Russia to Hold Joint Military Exercises in mid-October," *Reuters*, October 12, 2016. https://www.reuters.com/article/us-egypt-russia-military-idUSKCN12C2E0.

20. "Russia and Egypt Hold First-Ever Joint Naval Drills," *Defense News*, June 10, 2015. https://www.defensenews.com/home/2015/06/10/russia-and-egypt-hold-first-ever-joint-naval-drills/.

21. Shaul Shay, "Exercise 'Protectors of Friendship 2' and the Egyptian-Russian Strategic Relations," *Israel Defense*, September 26, 2017. https://www.israeldefense.co.il/en/node/31239; Shaul Shay, "Defenders of Friendship 2018: Egypt, Russia Conclude Joint Drills," *Israel Defense*, October 31, 2018. https://www.israeldefense.co.il/en/node/36153.

22. "Interview with Lev Dengov, Head of the Russian Contact Group on Libya," *News.ru*, July, 2, 2019. https://news.ru/afrika/lev-dengov-rossiya-v-livii-ne-delaet-stavku-na-kakuyu-libo-storonu/.

23. Ibid.

24. "Foreign Minister Sergey Lavrov's Remarks and Answers to Media Questions at a Joint News Conference Following Talks with Egyptian Foreign Minister Sameh Shoukry," *MID.ru*, August 21, 2017. http://www.mid.ru/en/foreign_policy/news/-/asset_publisher/cKNonkJE02Bw/content/id/2840676.

25. Malak Chabkoun, "What Is Left of the Syrian Opposition?," *Al Jazeera*, January 28, 2018. https://www.aljazeera.com/indepth/opinion/left-syrian-opposition-180127154708397.html.

26. Data from Russian Federal Custom Service, 2019. http://eng.customs.ru/.

27. "Torgovlia Mezhdu Rossiei i Egiptom v 2018 [Russia's Trade with Egypt in 2018]," *Vneshniya Torgovlya Rossii*, February 9, 2019. http://russian-trade.com/reports-and-reviews/2019-02/torgovlya-mezhdu-rossiey-i-egiptom-v-2018-g/.

28. "Rossiisko-Egipetskie Ekonomicheskie Otnosheniya [Russian-Egyptian Economic Relations]," *ITAR-Tass*, December 11, 2017. https://tass.ru/info/4802472.

29. "Egipet Narashivaet Eksport Selskokhozyaistvennoi Produktsii v Rossiu [Egypt Increases Export of Agro Products to Russia]," *RIA Novosti*, August 8, 2018. https://ria.ru/20180805/1525957209.html.

30. "Rosneft Closes the Deal to Acquire a 30% Stake in Zohr Gas Field," *Rosneft*, October 9, 2017. https://www.rosneft.com/press/releases/item/188045/.

31. "Egypt and Russia Sign 50-Year Industrial Zone Agreement," *Reuters*, May 23, 2018. https://af.reuters.com/article/egyptNews/idAFL5N1SU5SI.

32. Hagar Omran, "Russian-Egyptian Political Rapprochement to Propel Economic Cooperation Forward," *Daily News Egypt*, October 17, 2018. https://dailynewssegypt.com/2018/10/17/russian-egyptian-political-rapprochement-to-propel-economic-cooperation-forward/.

33. "Egypt, EAEU Can Sign Free Trade Zone Agreement in 2020: Russian Minister," *Egypt Today*, June 22, 2019. https://www.egypttoday.com/Article/3/71919/Egypt-EAEU-can-sign-free-trade-zone-agreement-in-2020.

34. Nikolay Kozhanov, "Arms Exports Add to Russia's Tools of Influence in Middle East," *Chatham House*, July 20, 2016. https://www.chathamhouse.org/expert/comment/arms-exports-add-russia-s-tools-influence-middle-east.

35. "Source: Egypt Buys 50 Russian Alligator Helicopters, Deck-Based Version May Be Supplied," *ITAR-Tass*, September 23, 2015. http://tass.com/defense/823140.

36. Thomas Gibbons-Neff, "Egypt to Buy French Mistral Landing Ships Originally Intended for Russia," *Washington Post*, September, 23, 2015. https://www.washingtonpost.com/news/checkpoint/wp/2015/09/23/egypt-to-buy-french-mistral-landing-ships-originally-intended-for-russia/.

37. Alexey Khlebnikov, "Russia Looks to the Middle East to Boost Arms Exports," *Middle East Institute*, April 8, 2019. https://www.mei.edu/publications/russia-looks-middle-east-boost-arms-exports.

38. "Russia Lends Egypt $25 Billion for Dabaa Nuclear Power Plant," *Al-Monitor*, February 26, 2020. https://www.al-monitor.com/pulse/originals/2020/02/power-plant-nuclear-egypt-russia-loan.html.

39. Podtserob, *Rossia i Arabskii Mir*, 103.

40. Iman K. Harb, "An Economic Explanation for Egypt's Alignment in the GCC Crisis," *Arab Center*, August 9, 2017. http://arabcenterdc.org/policy_analyses/an-economic-explanation-for-egypts-alignment-in-the-gcc-crisis.

41. "Gulf Countries Supported Egypt with $92bn since 2011," *Middle East Monitor*, March 19, 2019. https://www.middleeastmonitor.com/20190319-gulf-countries-supported-egypt-with-92bn-since-2011/.

42. Lesley Wroughton and Patricia Zengerle, "U.S. Sanctions China for Buying Russian Fighter Jets, Missiles," *Reuters*, September 20, 2018. https://www.reuters.com/article/us-usa-russia-sanctions/u-s-sanctions-china-for-buying-russian-fighter-jets-missiles-idUSKCN1M02TP.

43. Jeremy Binnie, "Egypt Faces Sanctions If It Buys Su-35s from Russia, US Warns," *Jane's 360*, April 10, 2019. https://www.janes.com/article/87808/egypt-faces-sanctions-if-it-buys-su-35s-from-russia-us-warns.

13 The "Comrades" in the Maghreb

1. "Otvet Ministra Inostrannyh Del Rossii S.V. Lavrova na Vopros Korrespondenta RIA Novosti o Situatsii v Egipte [The Foreign Minister of Russia Sergei Lavrov's Answer to the RIA Novosti Reporter's Question about the Situation in Egypt]," *MID. ru*, February 3, 2011. http://www.mid.ru/ru/press_service/minister_speeches/-/asset_publisher/7OvQR5KJWVmR/content/id/220434.

2. "Vyderzhki iz Stenograficheskogo Otchiota o Zasedanii Natsionalinogo Anti-terroristicheskogo Komiteta [Extracts from the Report on the Meeting of National Counter-terrorist Committee of Russia]," *Kremlin.ru*, February 22, 2011. http://kremlin.ru/events/president/news/10408.

3. This chapter is an expanded and updated version of the contribution coauthored by Dalia Ghanem and Vasily Kuznetsov for the EUISS Chaillot paper No. 146, "Russia's Return to the Middle East Building Sandcastles?," July 2018, Paris.

4. Robert O. Freedman, *Soviet Policy towards the Middle East since 1970* (New York: Praeger, 1982), 17, 19, 37.

5. Mark N. Katz, "Russia and Algeria: Partners or Competitors?," *Middle East Policy Council* 14, no. 4 (Winter 2017). http://www.mepc.org/journal/russia-and-algeria-partners-or-competitors.

6. "Trends in International Arms Transfers, 2016," *SIPRI Fact Sheet*, February 2017. https://www.sipri.org/sites/default/files/Trends-in-international-arms-transfers-2016.pdf.

7. "Coopération: la Russie Annule une Dette Algérienne de 4,7 milliards de dollars," *Algérie Monde Infos*, January 13, 2018. http://www.algeriemondeinfos.com/2018/01/13/cooperation-russie-annule-dette-algerienne-de-47-milliards-de-dollars/.

8. Andrew McGregor, "Defense or Domination? Building Algerian Power with Russian Arms," *Eurasia Daily Monitor*, September 5, 2018. https://jamestown.org/program/defense-or-domination-building-algerian-power-with-russian-arms/.

9. "Trends in International Arms Transfers, 2018," *SIPRI Fact Sheet*, February 2018. https://www.sipri.org/sites/default/files/2019-03/fs_1903_at_2018.pdf.

10. "Russian Trade with Algeria in 2018," *Russian Foreign Trade*, February 10, 2019. http://en.russian-trade.com/reports-and-reviews/2019-02/russian-trade-with-algeria-in-2018/.

11. "Trends in International Arms Transfers, 2018."

12. "Alexey Shatilov, Représentant Commercial de la Russie: 'Nous Pouvons Aider l'Algérie dans le Domaine des Hautes Technologies,'" *Algerie Eco*, June 22, 2017. https://www.algerie-eco.com/2017/06/22/alexeyshatilov-representant-commercial-de-russie-pouvons-aider-lalgerie-domaine-hautes-technologies/.

13. "Russian Trade with Algeria in 2018."

14. "Russian Trade with Tunisia, 2018," *Russian Foreign Trade*, February 10, 2019. http://en.russian-trade.com/reports-and-reviews/2019-02/russian-trade-with-tunisia-in-2018/; "Russian Trade with Egypt, 2018," *Russian Foreign Trade*, February 10, 2019. http://en.russian-trade.com/reports-and-reviews/2019-02/russian-trade-with-egypt-in-2018/.

15. "L'Algérie a Importé 4,6 millions de tonnes de Blé Français," *El Watan.com*, May 30, 2019. https://www.elwatan.com/edition/economie/lalgerie-a-importe-46-millions-de-tonnes-de-ble-francais-30-05-2019.

16. Polina Ivanova, "Russia Sends Test Shipment of Wheat to Algeria," *ZAWYA*, March 21, 2019. https://www.zawya.com/mena/en/story/Russia_sends_test_shipment_of_wheat_to_Algeria-TR20190321nL8N2184PPX1.

17. Anatoly Medetsky, "Soviet-Era Grain Record Seen Tumbling on Bumper Russian Crop," *Bloomberg*, August 21, 2017. https://www.bloomberg.com/news/articles/2017-08-21/soviet-era-grain-record-seen-tumbling-on-bumper-russian-harvest.

18. "Algeria," *Gazprom*. http://www.gazprom.com/about/production/projects/deposits/algeria/; "Gazprom's Next Acquisition—Algeria?," *Oilprice.com*, February 22, 2014. https://oilprice.com/Energy/Natural-Gas/Gazproms-Next-Acquisition-Algeria.html.

19. "Accord Algéro-Russe pour la Construction d'une 1re Centrale Nucléaire," *Le Matin d'Algerie*, September 3, 2014. http://www.lematindz.net/news/15106-accord-algero-russe-pour-la-construction-dune-1re-centrale-nucleaire.html; "Algeria, Russia Ink Five Cooperation Agreements," *Algeria Press Service*, June 27, 2018. http://www.aps.dz/en/economy/20532-algeria-russia-ink-five-cooperation-agreements.

20. Dalia Ghanem, "Another Battle of Algiers," *New York Times*, March 13, 2019. https://www.nytimes.com/2019/03/13/opinion/algeria-protests-president-military.html.

21. "Russia Hopes Algeria Will Resolve Its Issues in Constructive Manner," *Russia News Agency*, March 12, 2019. https://tass.com/world/1048369.

22. The peaceful and civil nature of these protests is important to note. For more information, read Dalia Ghanem, "A Protest Made in Algeria," *Carnegie*, April 2, 2019. https://carnegie-mec.org/2019/04/02/protest-made-in-algeria-pub-78748. In addition, it should be said that at the time when these lines are being written, the demonstrators agreed upon a truce with the government because of the COVID-19 pandemic.

23. Freedman, *Soviet Policy towards the Middle East*, 19.

24. "Morocco, Russia Promote Cooperation with Signing of 11 Agreements," *Asharq Al-Awsat*, October 12, 2017. https://aawsat.com/english/home/article/1050066/morocco-russia-promote-cooperation-signing-11-agreements.

25. Freedman, *Soviet Policy towards the Middle East*, 221–2; "La Position de la Russie sur le Conflit du Sahara Occidental, Selon une Note Confidentielle Marocaine," *Diaspora Saharaui*, January 2016. http://diasporasaharaui.blogspot.com/2016/01/la-position-de-la-russie-sur-le-conflit.html.

26. "King Mohammed Makes a Strategic Visit to Russia," *Submit 123 Press Release*, March 16, 2016. https://newsreleases.submitpressrelease123.com/2016/03/18/king-mohammed-vi-makes-a-strategic-visit-to-russia/.

27. Habibulah Mohamed Lamin, "How Polisario Front Hopes to Partner with Russia in Western Sahara," *Al-Monitor*, April 11, 2017. https://www.al-monitor.com/pulse/ru/contents/articles/originals/2017/04/western-sahara-polisario-sell-russia-moscow-visit.html.

28. "Russian Trade with Morocco in 2018," *Russian Foreign Trade*, February 10, 2019. http://en.russian-trade.com/reports-and-reviews/2019-02/russian-trade-with-morocco-in-2018/.

29. "Medvedev au Maroc: Onze Accords Signés pour Renforcer le Partenariat Stratégique Maroco-Russe," *HuffPost Maghreb*, October 11, 2017. https://www.huffpostmaghreb.com/2017/10/11/medvedev-au-maroconze-accords-signes-pour-renforcer-le-partenariat-strategique-maroco-russe_n_18237080.html.

30. "Russian Trade with Morocco"; "What Does Morocco Export to Russia?," *OEC*, 2017. https://oec.world/en/visualize/tree_map/hs92/export/mar/rus/show/2017/.

31. "Russian Trade with Morocco."

32. Ibid.

33. "Morocco to Train Russian Imams," *Morocco World News*, March 19, 2016. http://www.moroccoworldnews.com/2016/03/182434/182434/.

34. The Troika was an alliance between three parties, the Islamist-inspired Ennahda [the Renaissance party], the social-democratic Democratic Forum for Labour and Liberties (FDTL) or Ettakatol, and the center-left secular, the Congress for

the Republic (CPR) or El Mottamar that ruled Tunisia after the 2011 constituent Assembly election.

35. "Tunisia, Russia Contemplate Setting Up of Free Trade Area," *North Africa Post*, April 26, 2019. http://northafricapost.com/30351-tunisia-russia-contemplate-setting-up-of-free-trade-area.html.

36. "Russian Trade with Tunisia."

37. "La Tunisie et la Russie Cherchent à Lancer une Zone de Libre-échange," *Xinhuanet*, April 27, 2019. http://french.xinhuanet.com/2019-04/27/c_138013696.htm.

38. Imène Zine, "Coopération entre Deux Univeristés Tunisiennes et Leurs Homologues Russes," *L'économiste Maghrébin*, April 4, 2018. https://www.leconomistemaghrebin.com/2018/04/04/cooperation-universite-tunis-manar-sfax-russes/.

39. Karolina Prokopovič, "Russian Tourists May Swap Turkey for Asia," *Aviation Voice*, March 12, 2015. https://aviationvoice.com/russian-tourists-may-swap-turkey-for-asia-201512030959/; "Posol RF: Turpotok v Tunis Sokratilsya Pochti v Piati Raz v 2015 godu [Ambassador of Russia: The Tourist Flow to Tunisia Has Decreased Five Times in 2015]," *RIA Novosti*, February 3, 2016. https://ria.ru/tourism/20160203/1369189221.html.

40. "Posol RF: Turpotok v Tunis Sokratilsya."

41. "Afflux Russe sur les Plages de Tunisie," *Le Point Afrique*, October 3, 2016. http://afrique.lepoint.fr/economie/afflux-russe-sur-les-plages-de-tunisie-03-10-2016-2073228_2258.php.

42. "Turpotok iz Rossii v Tunis Sokratilsya, no Pokazal Organicheskii Rost [The Number of Russian Tourists in Tunisia Has Decreased, But the Flow Proves Its Organic Growth]," *Association of Tour Operators*, December 28, 2017. http://www.atorus.ru/ru/main/news/press-centre/new/41799.html; "Tunisie: Les Touristes Russes Arrivent en Masse," *Espace Manager*, May 27, 2019. https://www.espacemanager.com/tunisie-les-touristes-russes-arrivent-en-masse.html.

43. Hatem Bourial, "Tunisie-Russie: 800.000 Touristes Russes en 2019 et D'autres Motifs de Satisfaction," *Webdo*, June 12, 2019. http://www.webdo.tn/2019/06/12/tunisie-russie-800-000-touristes-russes-en-2019-et-dautres-motifs-de-satisfaction/.

14 Russia and Israel: An Improbable Friendship

1. For examples of such statements, see Committee for Accuracy in Middle East Reporting in America (CAMERA), "Precursors to War: Arab Threats against Israel," The Six-Day War. http://www.sixdaywar.org/content/threats.asp.

2. Robert O. Freedman, "Russia and the Middle East: The Primakov era," *Middle East Review of International Affairs* 2, no. 2 (May 1998): 1–8. http://www.rubincenter.org/meria/1998/05/freedman.pdf.

3. Mark N. Katz, "Putin's Pro-Israel Policy," *Middle East Quarterly* 12, no. 1 (Winter 2005), 51–9. https://www.meforum.org/articles/2005/putin-s-pro-israel-policy.

4. Mark N. Katz, "Implications of the Georgian Crisis for Israel, Iran, and the West," *Middle East Review of International Affairs* 12, no. 4 (December 2008): 4–5. http://mars.gmu.edu/bitstream/handle/1920/5585/Meria_katz_Dec_2008.pdf?sequence=1&isAllowed=y.

5. Patrick Hilsman, "Drone Deals Heighten Military Ties between Israel and Russia," *Middle East Eye*, October 4, 2015. http://www.middleeasteye.net/news/analysis-drone-deals-highlight-military-ties-between-israel-and-russia-24061368.

6. Anna Borshchevskaya, "The Maturing of Israeli-Russian Relations," *Washington Institute for Near East Policy*, Spring 2016. http://www.washingtoninstitute.org/policy-analysis/view/the-maturing-of-israeli-russian-relations; Aleksey Golubovych, "K Vizitu Netanyahu: Chto Rossia Mozhet Poluchyt ot Ekonomiki Izrailia [Towards the Netanyahu Visit: What Russia Can Obtain from the Israeli Economy]," *Forbes.ru*, March 9, 2017. http://www.forbes.ru/finansy-i-investicii/340519-rossiysko-izrailskie-ekonomicheskie-svyazi-ne-tolko-neft-na; Jessica Steinberg, "Mother Russia Returns to Grand Duke's Jerusalem Compound," *Times of Israel*, July 13, 2017. https://www.timesofisrael.com/mother-russia-returns-to-grand-dukes-jerusalem-compound/.

7. Jeffrey Martini, Erin York, and William Young, "Syria as an Arena of Strategic Competition," *RAND Corporation*, 2013. https://www.rand.org/content/dam/rand/pubs/research_reports/RR200/RR213/RAND_RR213.pdf.

8. Ian Black, "Israelis Watch Intently as Syrian Rebel Forces Approach Golan Heights Border," *The Guardian*, June 19, 2015. https://www.theguardian.com/world/on-the-middle-east/2015/jun/19/israelis-watch-intently-as-syrian-rebel-forces-approach-golan-heights-border.

9. Cnaan Liphshiz, "Can Israel Benefit from Sheriff Putin Policing the Middle East?," *Times of Israel*, October 13, 2015. https://www.timesofisrael.com/can-israel-benefit-from-sheriff-putin-policing-the-middle-east/.

10. Judah Ari Gross, "Netanyahu: Israel Acts to Keep Game-changing Arms Away from Hezbollah," *Times of Israel*, January 9, 2018. https://www.timesofisrael.com/netanyahu-israel-acts-to-keep-game-changing-arms-away-from-hezbollah/.

11. Samuel Ramani, "Why Russia and Israel Are Cooperating in Syria," *Huffpost*, June 23, 2016. https://www.huffingtonpost.com/ entry/why-russia-and-israel-are-cooperating-in-syria_us_576bdb68e4b083e0c0235e15?guccounter=1.Putin, of course, did not withdraw Russian forces from Syria either on this or subsequent occasions when he announced that he would.

12. In February 2018, though, a Putin phone call to Netanyahu reportedly halted the escalation of direct conflict between Israeli and Iranian forces. Amos Harel, "Putin's Phone Call with Netanyahu Put End to Israeli Strikes in Syria," *Haaretz*, February 15, 2018. https://www.haaretz.com/middle-east-news/iran/putin-s-call-with-netanyahu-called-time-on-israel-s-syrian-strikes-1.5809118.

13. Joost Hiltermann, "Russia Can Keep the Peace between Israel and Iran—But Following the Hostilities over the Weekend, Does Putin Want to?," *The Atlantic*, February 13, 2018. https://www.theatlantic.com/international/archive/2018/02/israel-syria-iran-hezbollah-putin-assad/553217/; Jonathan Marcus, "Is Israel Driving a Wedge between Russia and Iran?," *BBC News*, May 31, 2018. https://www.bbc.co.uk/news/world-middle-east-44313744.

14. On the overall convergence of Russian-Israeli interests, see Nikolay Pakhomov, "The Russia-Israel Relationship Is Perfect Realpolitik," *National Interest*, March 23, 2017. http:// nationalinterest.org/feature/the-russia-israel-relationship-perfect-realpolitik-19881.

15. On Saudi-UAE-Israeli cooperation, see Adam Hanieh, "Israel, Saudi Arabia and the United Arab Emirates: New Regional Alliances and the Palestinian Struggle," *Middle East in London blog* (SOAS University of London), January 27, 2018. https://blogs.soas.ac.uk/the-middle-east-in-london/2018/01/27/

israel-saudi-arabia-and-the-united-arab-emirates-new-regional-alliances-and-the-palestinian-struggle/.

16. Raziye Akkoc and Ezzedine Said, "Iran, Russia, Turkey Team Up to Hold Sway in Syria," *Times of Israel*, April 2, 2018. https://www.timesofisrael.com/iran-russia-turkey-team-up-to-hold-sway-in-syria/; Shira Efron, "The Future of Israeli-Turkish Relations," *RAND Corporation*, 2018. https://www.rand.org/content/dam/rand/pubs/research_reports/RR2400/RR2445/RAND_RR2445.pdf; Mark N. Katz, "Putin's Courtship of Both Assad and Erdogan Is Spinning Out of Control in Syria," *Responsible Statecraft*, March 2, 2020. https://responsiblestatecraft.org/2020/03/02/putins-assad-erdogan-spinning-out-of-control-in-syria/.

17. According to one of Moscow's leading analysts of Russian foreign policy, Dmitri Trenin, Russia is "no longer a sponsor of the PLO, which is now mainly supported by the European Union." Dmitri Trenin, *What Is Russia Up to in the Middle East?* (Cambridge: Polity, 2018), 90.

18. David Choi, "Syria Accidentally Shot Down a Russian Plane While Fending Off an Israeli Missile Strike, Report Says," *Business Insider*, September 18, 2018. http://www.businessinsider.fr/us/syria-accidentally-shoots-down-russian-aircraft-report-2018-9.

19. Liz Sly, Anton Troianovski, and Ruth Eglash, "Russia Revives Allegations of Israeli Culpability in Downed Plane in Syria," *Washington Post*, September 23, 2018. https://www.washingtonpost.com/world/middle_east/russia-revives-allegations-of-israeli-culpability-in-downed-plane-in-syria/2018/09/23/ac6741de-bf36-11e8-9f4f-a1b7af255aa5_story.html?utm_term=.a3adbe20f361.

20. Krishnadev Calamur, "An Unlikely Alliance in Syria Comes under Strain," *The Atlantic*, September 24, 2018. https://www.theatlantic.com/international/archive/2018/09/russia-israel-syria/571138/; "Syria Says Russian Missile Defence System 'Ineffective,'" *MEMO—Middle East Monitor*, May 1, 2020.https://www.middleeastmonitor.com/20200501-syria-says-russian-missile-defence-system-ineffective/.

21. "Israel v Iran in Syria: Heating Up," *The Economist*, April 14, 2018. 40 (US edition). https://www.economist.com/ news/middle-east-and-africa/21740471-conflict-between-two-powers-escalating-israel-determined-stop.

22. Trenin, *What Is Russia Up*, 89–90.

23. Sebastien Roblin, "Israeli F-16s Wiped Out a Syrian Missile Complex (Russian Didn't Fire Back)," *National Interest*, June 3, 2019. https://nationalinterest.org/blog/buzz/israeli-f-16s-wiped-out-syrian-missile-complex-russian-didn%E2%80%99t-fire-back-60732.

24. Anaïs LLobet, "Russia Seeks Mediator Role between Israel and Iran," *Times of Israel*, May 10, 2018. https://www.timesofisrael.com/russia-seeks-mediator-role-between-israel-and-iran/; and "Russia's Intentions Behind Mediating Iran, Israel Explained," *Persia Digest*, October 7, 2018. https://persiadigest.com/Russia's-intentions-behind-mediating-Iran,-Israel-explained.

25. Michel Duclos, "Russia and Iran in Syria—A Random Partnership or an Enduring Alliance?," *Atlantic Council*, June 2019. https://www.atlanticcouncil.org/images/publications/Russia_and_Iran_in_Syria_a_Random_Partnership_or_an_Enduring_Alliance.pdf.

26. Julian Borger and Patrick Wintour, "Donald Trump Tells Iran 'Call Me' over Lifting Sanctions," *The Guardian*, May 9, 2019. https://www.theguardian.com/world/2019/may/09/eu-rejects-iran-two-month-ultimatum-on-nuclear-deal.

15 Russia in the Middle East and
North Africa: A Balance Sheet

1. "Russian Military, UN Mission Conduct First Joint Patrol of Israeli-Syrian Border," *ITAR-Tass*, October 26, 2018. https://tass.com/world/1027954.
2. "Libya's Eastern Parliament Speaker Praises Russia's Training of Haftar-Led Forces," *Libyan Express*, January 7, 2018. http://www.libyanexpress.com/libyas-eastern-parliament-speaker-praises-russias-training-of-haftar-led-forces/; "Russian Mercenaries Are Fighting in Libya, UN diplomats Confirm," *Moscow Times*, May 7, 2020. https://www.themoscowtimes.com/2020/05/07/russian-mercenaries-are-fighting-in-libya-un-diplomats-confirm-a70204.
3. Anna Boitsova, Inna Sidorkova, and Anton Baev, "Glava ChVK Rasskazal o Rabote Rossiiskih Spetsialistov v Livii [The Head of ChVK Informed about the Work of Russian Specialists in Libya]," *RBC*, March 13, 2017. https://www.rbc.ru/politics/13/03/2017/58c69ef59a7947e8a7c2ea63.
4. "Rossia Vstupila v Peregovory s Egiptom ob Ispolizovanii Voennyh Aviabaz [Russia Entered the Talks with Egypt on Use of Military Air Bases]," *Meduza*, November 30, 2017. https://meduza.io/news/2017/11/30/rossiya-vstupila-v-peregovory-s-egiptom-ob-ispolzovanii-voennyh-aviabaz.
5. Omid Shamizi, "Iran Allows Russia to Use Airbase for Refuelling," *Anadolu Agency*, April 14, 2018. https://www.aa.com.tr/en/europe/iran-allows-russia-to-use-airbase-for-refueling/1117681.
6. Oleg Grinevskii, *Tainy Sovetskoi Diplomatii [The Secrets of Soviet Diplomacy]* (Moscow: Vagrius, 2000), 11.
7. "Egypt Imported 10 Million Tonnes of Wheat in 2018: Ministry Report," *Ahram Online*, November 8, 2018. http://english.ahram.org.eg/NewsContent/3/12/315983/Business/Economy/Egypt-imported--million-tonnes-of-wheat--in--Minis.aspx.
8. "Russia's VTB Bank Buys 19% Stake in Qatar's CQUR Bank–Ifax," *Nasdaq.com*, August 15, 2019. http://www.nasdaq.com/article/russias-vtb-bank-buys-19-stake-in-qatars-cqur-bank--ifax-20190815-00122.
9. "Russian Ambitions for Syrian Phosphates," *Syrian Observer*, August 3, 2018. https://syrianobserver.com/EN/features/19755/russian_ambitions_syrian_phosphates.html; "Russian Firm to Take over Syria Port for 49 Years: Damascus," *Arab News*, April 25, 2019. http://www.arabnews.com/node/1488161/middle-east.
10. "Russian Investors Want to Reconstruct Damascus Airport," *Russia Business Today*, January 21, 2019. https://russiabusinesstoday.com/infrastructure/russian-investors-want-to-reconstruct-damascus-airport/.
11. "Direct Line with Vladimir Putin," *Kremlin.ru*, June 7, 2018. http://en.kremlin.ru/events/president/news/57692.
12. Between 2015 and 2017 Russia officially confirmed forty-three casualties. In the first five months of 2018 Russia officially confirmed forty-eight casualties. "Chto Izvestno o pogibshih v Sirii Rossiiskih Voennyh [What Is Known about Russian Military Who Perished in Syria]," *Kommersant*, May 27, 2018. https://www.kommersant.ru/doc/3460282.
13. Kimberly Marten, "Russia's Use of Semi-state Security Forces: The Case of the Wagner Group," *Post-Soviet Affairs* 35, no. 3 (2019): 181–204.
14. "Assad Otsenil Zatraty na Vosstanovlenie Siriiskoi Ekonomiki v 400 Milliardov Dollarov" [Assad Estimated Syria Will Need $400 billion to Rebuild Its

Economy]," *Novaya Gazeta*, April 15, 2018. https://www.novayagazeta.ru/news/2018/04/15/141010-asad-otsenil-zatraty-na-vosstanovlenie-siriyskoy-ekonomiki-v-400-milliardov-dollarov.

15. Olga Bozhieva, "Ekspert Rasskazal Kakoi Budet Rossiiskaya Armiya Cherez Desyati Let [Expert Told How Russian Army Will Look Like in 10 years-time]," *Moskovskii Komsomolets*, July 1, 2018. https://www.mk.ru/politics/2018/07/01/ekspert-rasskazal-kakoy-budet-rossiyskaya-armiya-cherez-desyat-let.html.

16. Pew Research Center, "Publics Worldwide Unfavourable toward Putin, Russia," Global Attitudes & Trends, August 16, 2017. http://www.pewglobal.org/2017/08/16/publics-worldwide-unfavorable-toward-putin-russia/.

17. Pavel Aptekari, "Kak Rossiane Ustali ot Vnesheni Politiki [How Russians Got Tired of the Foreign Policy]," *Vedomosti*, June 21, 2019. http://www.vedomosti.ru/opinion/articles/2019/06/21/804715-rossiyane-ustali.

18. "Sobytia v Sirii [Events in Syria]," Levada-Center, May 6, 2019. http://www.levada.ru/2019/05/06/sobytiya-v-sirii/.

Bibliography

Personal Correspondence

Barnes-Dacey, Julien, Author's Interview with Arab Government Official, June 2019.
Barnes-Dacey, Julien, Author's Interview with Iranian Officials and Analysts, 2016 and 2017.
Barnes-Dacey, Julien, Author's Interview with Iranian Officials and Analysts, 2016 and 2017.
Barnes-Dacey, Julien, Author's Interviews with Iranian Officials and Analysts, 2014.
Barnes-Dacey, Julien, Author's Interview with Russian Official, June 2019.
Barnes-Dacey, Julien, Author's Interview with Senior Gulf Official, March 2018.
Barnes-Dacey, Julien, Author's Interview with Senior Israeli Official, March 2018.
Barnes-Dacey, Julien, Author's Interview with Senior Saudi and Israeli Officials, January and March 2018.
Barnes-Dacey, Julien, Author's Interview with Western Diplomat, 2016.
Saivetz, Carol R., Author's Interviews, November 2011.

Official Documents

Cabinet of Kingdom of Saudi Arabia, "Saudi Vision 2030. Our Vision: Saudi Arabia, the Heart of the Arab and Islamic Worlds, the Investment Powerhouse, and the Hub Connecting Three Continents." http://vision2030.gov.sa/en.
Department of Defense, "Soviet Military Power," Washington, DC, 1984. http://www.dtic.mil/dtic/tr/fulltext/u2/a152445.pdf.
Gulf Cooperation Council, "Charter of the Gulf Cooperation Council (GCC)," May 25, 1981. https://www.files.ethz.ch/isn/125347/1426_GCC.pdf.
Ministry of Energy of the Russian Federation, "Energy Strategy of Russia for the Period up to 2030," November 2009. http://www.energystrategy.ru/projects/docs/ES-2030_(Eng).pdf.
Ministry of Foreign Affairs, "Russia's Security Concept for the Gulf Area," MID.ru, July 23, 2019. http://www.mid.ru/ru/foreign_policy/international_safety/conflicts/-/asset_publisher/xIEMTQ3OvzcA/content/id/3733575?p_p_id=101_INSTANCE_xIEMTQ3OvzcA&_101_INSTANCE_xIEMTQ3OvzcA_languageId=en_GB.
Organization for the Prohibition of Chemical Weapons, "Fact-Finding Mission Report," April 2018. https://www.opcw.org/sites/default/files/documents/2019/03/s-1731-2019%28e%29.pdf.
Russian President, "Convention on Legal Status of the Caspian Sea," *Kremlin.ru*, August 12, 2018. http://kremlin.ru/supplement/5328.
Russian President, "Russian Federation Naval Doctrine," Kremlin.ru, July 26, 2015. http://en.kremlin.ru/events/president/news/50060.

Russian President, "Ukaz Prezidenta Rossiiskoi Federatsii no.286 "O Merah po Vypolneniu Rezoliutsii Soveta Bezopasnosti OON 1970 ot 26 fevralia 2011 g. [Decree of the President of the Russian Federation no. 286 on Measures to Implement UN Security Council Resolution No. 1970 from 26 February 2011]," Rossiiskaya Gazeta, March 11, 2011. https://rg.ru/2011/03/11/livia-site-dok.html.

Russian President, "Ukaz Prezidenta Rossiiskoi Federatsii no.1154 [Decree of the President of the Russian Federation no.1154]," Kremlin.ru, September 22, 2010. http://kremlin.ru/acts/bank/31772.

Russian President, "Vneseno Izmenenie v Ukaz o Merah po Vypolneniu Rezoliutsii Soveta Bezopasnosti OON No.1929 [President of Russia, Amendment to Executive Order on Measures for Implementing UN Security Council Resolution no. 1929]," Kremlin.ru, April 13, 2015. http://en.kremlin.ru/events/president/news/49248.

United Nations, "Security Council Resolution 2231 (2015)," July 20, 2015. http://www.un.org/en/ga/search/view_doc.asp?symbol=S/RES/2231 (2015).

US Congress, "Countering America's Adversaries through Sanctions Act, H.R. 3364," February 8, 2017. https://www.congress.gov/bill/115th-congress/house-bill/3364/text.

Documentaries and Videos

Zakamskaya, Evelina, "Glava MID Saudovskoi Aravii ob Otnosheniyah c Rossiei [Head of the Ministry of Foreign Affairs of Saudi Arabia Talks about Relations with Russia]," *Russia 24-Mnenie*, October 7, 2017. https://www.youtube.com/watch?v=VsItopYU-M0.

Web Pages

"Algeria," Gazprom. http://www.gazprom.com/about/production/projects/deposits/algeria/.

"What Does Morocco Export to Russia?," OEC, 2017. https://oec.world/en/visualize/tree_map/hs92/export/mar/rus/show/2017/.

"BP Statistical Review of World Energy 2019," 68th edition, 2019. https://www.bp.com/content/dam/bp/business-sites/en/global/corporate/pdfs/energy-economics/statistical-review/bp-stats-review-2019-full-report.pdf.

British Petroleum, BP Statistical Review of World Energy, 2018. https://www.bp.com/content/dam/bp/en/corporate/pdf/energy-economics/statistical-review/bp-stats-review-2018-full-report.pdf.

Committee for Accuracy in Middle East Reporting in America (CAMERA), "Precursors to War: Arab Threats against Israel," The Six-Day War. http://www.sixdaywar.org/content/threats.asp.

Data on Turkish Gas Imports, Turkish Statistical Institute (TÜİK). http://www.tuik.gov.tr/.

Data from Russian Federal Custom Service, 2019. http://eng.customs.ru/.

"Direct Line with Vladimir Putin," Kremlin.ru, June 7, 2018. http://en.kremlin.ru/events/president/news/57692.

"Direct Line with Vladimir Putin," Kremlin.ru, April 16, 2015. http://en.kremlin.ru/events/president/news/49261.

"DOD Puts Military-to-Military Activities with Russia on Hold," U.S. Department of Defense, March 3, 2014. http://archive.defense.gov/news/newsarticle.aspx?id=121759.

Energy Information Administration, 2020. https://www.eia.gov/dnav/pet/pet_pri_spt_s1_d.htm.

"Federalnaya Sluzhba Bezopasnosti Rossii Raspolagaet Dostovernoi Informatsiei o Putyah i Sposobah Finansovoi Podderzhki Voorujennyh Formirovanii Mezhdunarodnyh Terroristov, Voiuyuschih na Territorii Chechenskoi Respubliki [Federal Security Service of Russia Disclaims Reliable Information on the Ways and Methods of Financial Support for Armed Formations of International Terrorists in the Chechen Republic]," FSB.ru, May 19, 2000. http://www.fsb.ru/fsb/press/message/single.htm%21id%3D10340914%40fsbMessage.html.

"Foreign Minister Sergey Lavrov's Interview with Voskresnoye Vremya TV Programme, MID.ru, September 13, 2015," September 13, 2015. http://www.mid.ru/en/web/guest/foreign_policy/news/-/asset_publisher/cKNonkJE02Bw/content/id/1744777.

"Foreign Minister Sergey Lavrov's Remarks and Answers to Media Questions at a Joint News Conference Following Talks with Egyptian Foreign Minister Sameh Shoukry," MID.ru, August 21, 2017. http://www.mid.ru/en/foreign_policy/news/-/asset_publisher/cKNonkJE02Bw/content/id/2840676.

Fox News Poll, "Syria, Benghazi and the US Economy," October 14, 2015. http://www.foxnews.com/politics/interactive/2015/10/14/fox-news-poll-syria-benghazi-and-us-economy.html.

"Igor Sechin Makes Key Report at X Eurasian Economic Forum in Verona," Rosneft, October 19, 2017. https://www.rosneft.com/press/today/item/188249/.

IMF, Regional Economic Outlook: Middle East and Central Asia, November 2018. https://www.imf.org/en/Publications/REO/MECA/Issues/2018/10/02/mreo1018.

International Energy Agency, Monthly Oil Market Report, January 2020. https://www.iea.org/reports/oil-market-report-january-2020.

"Interview to American TV Channel CBS and PBS," Kremlin.ru, September 29, 2015. http://en.kremlin.ru/events/president/news/50380.

"Interview with Alexey Pushkov," *Europe1*, October 2, 2015. http://www.europe1.fr/emissions/l-interview-politique/la-coalition-americaine-a-fait-semblant-de-bombarder-daech-pendant-une-annee-2523383.

"Interviu Zamestitelya Direktora FSVTS Rossii M.V. Petuhova [Interview with Mikhail Petukhov, Deputy Director of the Federal Service for Military-Technical Cooperation of Russia]," August 26, 2010. http://www.fsvts.gov.ru/materials/26795A8AD42B3137C325778B0042FB8B.html.

Levada-Center, "Sobytia v Sirii [Events in Syria]," May 6, 2019. http://www.levada.ru/2019/05/06/sobytiya-v-sirii/.

Levada Center, "Syria," July 10, 2016. https://www.levada.ru/en/2016/06/10/syria-2/.

Levada Center, "Syria and the Plane Crash in Egypt," November 23, 2015. https://www.levada.ru/en/2015/11/23/syria-the-plane-crash-in-egypt/.

Levada Center, "Syria," October 22, 2014. https://www.levada.ru/en/2014/10/22/syria/.

"News Conference Following Talks with Austrian Federal President Alexander Der Bellen," Kremlin.ru, May 15, 2019. http://en.kremlin.ru/events/president/news/60527.

"Meeting of Commission for Military-Technical Cooperation with Foreign States," Kremlin.ru, March 5, 2018. http://en.kremlin.ru/events/president/news/56981.

"Meeting with President of Syria Bashar al-Assad," Kremlin.ru, December 11, 2017. http://en.kremlin.ru/events/president/transcripts/56353.

"NOC of Libya Signs Agreement with Rosneft of Russia," National Oil Compnay, February 21, 2017. https://noc.ly/index.php/en/new-4/2095-noc-and-rosneft-sign-cooperation-framework-agreement-at-london-ip-week.

"North-South International Transport Corridor," Ministry of Transport, Communication and High Technologies of the Republic of Azerbaijan. https://mincom.gov.az/en/view/pages/104/.

Official Data by the Central Election Commission of the Russian Federation, March 2018. http://www.foreign-countries.vybory.izbirkom.ru/region/foreign-countries?action=show&global=true&root=994001256&tvd=499400168175&vrn=100100084849062&prver=0&pronetvd=null&region=99&sub_region=99&type=226&vibid=499400168175.

"Otvet Ministra Inostrannyh Del Rossii S.V. Lavrova na Vopros Korrespondenta RIA Novosti o situatsii v Egipte [The Foreign Minister of Russia Sergei Lavrov's Answer to the RIA Novosti Reporter's Question about the Situation in Egypt]," MID.ru, February 3, 2011. http://www.mid.ru/ru/press_service/minister_speeches/-/asset_publisher/7OvQR5KJWVmR/content/id/220434.

"President Putin's Remarks during the Direct Line Phone-in Session," Kremlin.ru, June 20, 2019. http://en.kremlin.ru/events/president/news/60795.

"President Vladimir Putin Held Negotiations with Abdullah Ibn Abdul Aziz Al Saud, The Crown Prince Of Saudi Arabia," Kremlin.ru, September 2, 2003. http://en.kremlin.ru/events/president/news/29294.

The Public Investment Fund Program (2018–20). https://vision2030.gov.sa/sites/default/files/attachments/PIF%20Program_EN_0.pdf.

"Qatar Waives Entry Visa Requirements for Citizens of 80 Countries," Qatar Airways, August 9, 2017. https://www.qatarairways.com/en/press-releases/2017/Aug/qatar-waives-entry-visa-requirements-for--citizens-of-80-countri.html#.

"QF and Rosneft Unveil New R&D Hub at QSTP," Qatar Foundation, March 28, 2018. https://www.qf.org.qa/news/qf-and-rosneft-unveil-new-rd-hub-at-qstp.

"RDIF and Saudi Aramco Agree Terms of Investment in Novomet," Russian Direct Investment Fund, February 20, 2019. https://rdif.ru/Eng_fullNews/3943/.

"RDIF, PIF and Saudi Aramco Announce the Establishment of a New Platform for Russian-Saudi Energy Investment," Russian Direct Investment Fund, October 5, 2017. https://rdif.ru/Eng_fullNews/2660/.

Rosatom, 2019. http://www.rosatom.ru/en/about-us/.

"Rosatom Opens a Branch in Saudi Arabia," Rosatom, June 11, 2019. https://www.rosatom.ru/en/press-centre/news/rosatom-opens-a-branch-in-saudi-arabia/.

"Rosneft Closes the Deal to Acquire a 30% Stake in Zohr Gas Field," Rosneft, October, 9, 2017. https://www.rosneft.com/press/releases/item/188045/.

"Rosneft Enters into an Agreement for Operational Management of an Oil Products Terminal in Lebanon," Rosneft, January 24, 2019. https://www.rosneft.com/press/releases/item/193617/.

Russia Direct Investment Fund, "Partnerships," 2019. https://rdif.ru/Eng_Partnership/.

Russia's Foreign Ministry data, April, 23, 2019. http://www.mid.ru/ru/maps/eg/?currentpage=main-country.

"Russia Obtains 30% Stake in Egyptian Zohr Gas Field," Rosneft, October 9, 2017. https://www.rosneft.com/press/today/item/188235/.

"Russia and Qatar Hold Discussions on Collaborating at International Multilateral Events in 2019–2020," SPIEF, June 11, 2019. https://www.forumspb.com/en/news/news/russia-and-qatar-hold-discussions-on-collaborating-at-international-multilateral-events-in-20192020/.

"Russian Trade with Algeria in 2018," Russian Foreign Trade, February
    10, 2019. http://en.russian-trade.com/reports-and-reviews/2019-02/
    russian-trade-with-algeria-in-2018/.
"Russian Trade with Egypt, 2018," Russian Foreign Trade, February 10
    2019. http://en.russian-trade.com/reports-and-reviews/2019-02/
    russian-trade-with-egypt-in-2018/.
"Russian Trade with Morocco in 2018," Russian Foreign Trade, February
    10, 2019. http://en.russian-trade.com/reports-and-reviews/2019-02/
    russian-trade-with-morocco-in-2018/.
"Russian Trade with Tunisia, 2018," Russian Foreign Trade, February
    10, 2019. http://en.russian-trade.com/reports-and-reviews/2019-02/
    russian-trade-with-tunisia-in-2018/.
"Sergey Lavrov's Press Conference Following Russia's Presidency of the UN Security
    Council, New York," MID.ru, October 1, 2015. http://www.mid.ru/en/foreign_policy/
    news/-/asset_publisher/cKNonkJE02Bw/content/id/1825252.
"Speech and the Following Discussion at the Munich Conference on Security
    Policy," Kremlin.ru, February 10, 2007. http://en.kremlin.ru/events/president/
    transcripts/24034.
"SPIEF 2018 to Be Attended by Biggest Saudi Delegation in Forum's History," Russian
    Exports National Information Portal, March 27, 2018. http://www.rusexporter.com/
    news/detail/5286/.
"The First Joint Russian-Egyptian Commission on Military and Technical Cooperation
    Was Held in Moscow," Russian Ministry of Defense, March 3 2015. http://eng.mil.ru/
    en/mpc/news/more.htm?id=12009420@egNews.
"Torgovlia Mezhdu Rossiei i Egiptom v 2018 [Russia's Trade with Egypt in 2018],"
    Vneshniya Torgovlya Rossii, February 9, 2019. http://russian-trade.com/
    reports-and-reviews/2019-02/torgovlya-mezhdu-rossiey-i-egiptom-v-2018-g/.
"Unemployment, Youth Total (percent of total labor force ages 15–24) (modeled ILO
    estimate)," data from World Bank. https://data.worldbank.org/indicator/SL.UEM.1524.
    ZS.
"Vladimir Putin Answered Russian Journalists' Questions," Kremlin.ru, September 4,
    2015. http://en.special.kremlin.ru/events/president/transcripts/50234.
"Vyderzhki iz Stenograficheskogo Otchiota o Zasedanii Natsionalinogo Anti-
    terroristicheskogo Komiteta [Extracts from the Report on the Meeting of National
    Counter-terrorist Committee of Russia]," Kremlin.ru, February 22, 2011. http://
    kremlin.ru/events/president/news/10408.
"What Is Tight Oil?," UCSUSA.org, March 3, 2015. https://www.ucsusa.org/resources/
    what-tight-oil.
Wikileaks, "The Global Intelligence Files." https://wikileaks.org/gifiles/docs/24/2436109_-
    os-syria-lebanon-security-wikileaks-france-said-syrian.html.
World Nuclear Association, Nuclear Power in Jordan, 2017. http://www.world-nuclear.
    org/information-library/country-profiles/countries-g-n/jordan.aspx.

Policy Analysis and Reports

"2016 Arab Opinion Index," Arab Center, April 12, 2017. http://arabcenterdc.org/survey/arab-opinion-index-2016/.

"Arab Youth Survey," ASDA'A Burston-Marsteller 2018. http://www.arabyouthsurvey.com/findings.html.

Aydıntaşbaş, Aslı, "A New Gaza: Turkey's Border Policy in Northern Syria." Policy Brief, European Council on Foreign Relations, May 2020. https://www.ecfr.eu/publications/summary/a_new_gaza_turkeys_border_policy_in_northern_syria.

Baklanov, Andrei, "Security in the Gulf Area: Russia's New Initiative," Valdai Club, August 6, 2019. valdaiclub.com/a/highlights/security-in-the-gulf-area-russia's-new-initiative/.

Barnes-Dacey, Julian, 'To End a War: Europe's Role in Bringing Peace to Syria," ECFR Policy Brief, September 12, 2017. https://ecfr.eu/publication/to_end_a_war_europes_role_in_bringing_peace_to_syria7223/.

Barnes-Dacey, Julien, "Russia's Policy in Syria: Efforts to Pivot to a Political Track," Valdai Discussion Club, December 15, 2017. http://valdaiclub.com/a/highlights/russian-policy-in-syria/.

Borshchevskaya, Anna, "The Maturing of Israeli-Russian Relations," Washington Institute for Near East Policy, Spring 2016. http://www.washingtoninstitute.org/policy-analysis/view/the-maturing-of-israeli-russian-relations.

Cafiero, Giorgio and Theodore Karasik, "Yemen War and Qatar Crisis Challenge Oman's Neutrality," Middle East Institute, July 6, 2017. http://www.mei.edu/content/article/oman-s-high-stakes-yemen.

"Corruption Perceptions Index 2017," Transparency International. https://www.transparency.org/news/feature/corruption_perceptions_index_2017.

"Distract Deceive Destroy: Putin at War in Syria," Atlantic Council, April 2016. http://publications.atlanticcouncil.org/distract-deceive-destroy/assets/download/ddd-report.pdf.

Duclos, Michel, "Russia and Iran in Syria—A Random Partnership or an Enduring Alliance?," Atlantic Council, June 2019. https://www.atlanticcouncil.org/images/publications/Russia_and_Iran_in_Syria_a_Random_Partnership_or_an_Enduring_Alliance.pdf.

Efron, Shira, "The Future of Israeli-Turkish Relations," RAND Corporation, 2018. https://www.rand.org/content/dam/rand/pubs/research_reports/RR2400/RR2445/RAND_RR2445.pdf.

"Enquête Sur le Complotisme," IFOP, December 2017, 69. https://jean-jaures.org/sites/default/files/redac/commun/productions/2018/0108/115158_-_rapport_02.01.2017.pdf.

"Foreign Fighters in Syria and Iraq," The Soufan Group, December 2015. http://soufangroup. com/wp-content/uploads/2015/12/TSG_ForeignFightersUpdate3.pdf.

Frolovskiy, Dmitriy, "Chego Hotyat Drug ot Druga Rossia i Monarhii Zaliva" [What Russia and the Gulf Monarchies Want from Each Other], Carnegie Moscow Center, August 27, 2017. http://carnegie.ru/commentary/72897.

Frolovskiy, Dmitriy, "Seryi Kardinal Blizhnego Vostoka. Kak Malenkii Qatar Pokoril Bolshoi Region [Eminence Grise of the Middle East. How Small Qatar Conquered the Giant Region]," Carnegie Moscow Center. May 11, 2017. http://carnegie.ru/commentary/69917.

Frolov, Andrey, "Itogi Voenno-Tehnicheskogo Sotrudnichestva Rossii s Inostrannymi Gosudarstvami v 2015 godu [The Results of the Military-Technical Cooperation of

Russia with Foreign States in 2015]," *CAST*, January 2016. http://cast.ru/products/articles/itogi-voenno-tekhnicheskogo-sotrudnichestva-rossii-s-inostrannymi-gosudarstvami-v-2015-godu.html.

"From Recession to Recovery: Russia Economic Report," World Bank, May 2017. http://documents.worldbank.org/curated/en/782451497437509084/Russia-economic-report-2017-from-recession-to-recovery.

Garibov, Azad, "Pashinyan Tries to Leverage Armenia's CSTO Membership against Azerbaijan," Eurasia Daily Monitor 16, no. 174, December 13, 2019. https://jamestown.org/program/pashinyan-tries-to-leverage-armenias-csto-membership-against-azerbaijan/.

Geranmayeh, Ellie, and Kadri Liik, "The New Power Couple: Russia and Iran in the Middle East," ECFR Policy Brief, September 13, 2016. http://www.ecfr.eu/publications/summary/iran_and_russia_middle_east_power_couple_7113.

Ghanem, Dalia, "A Protest Made in Algeria," Carnegie, April 2, 2019. https://carnegie-mec.org/2019/04/02/protest-made-in-algeria-pub-78748.

"Global Arms Trade: USA Increases Dominance; Arms Flows to the Middle East Surge," Stockholm International Peace Research Institute (SIPRI), March 11, 2019. https://www.sipri.org/media/press-release/2019/global-arms-trade-usa-increases-dominance-arms-flows-middle-east-surge-says-sipri.

Goble, Paul, "Can the Kremlin Finally Realize the North-South Transit Corridor?," The Jamestown Foundation, February 16, 2019. https://jamestown.org/program/can-the-kremlin-finally-realize-the-north-south-transit-corridor/.

Gurbanov, Ilgar, "Caspian Convention Signing and Implications for the Trans-Caspian Gas Pipeline," Eurasia Daily Monitor, September 12, 2018. https://jamestown.org/program/caspian-convention-signing-and-the-implications-for-the-trans-caspian-gas-pipeline/.

Hanieh, Adam, "Israel, Saudi Arabia and the United Arab Emirates: New Regional Alliances and the Palestinian Struggle," Middle East in London blog (SOAS University of London), January 27, 2018. https://blogs.soas.ac.uk/the-middle-east-in-london/2018/01/27/israel-saudi-arabia-and-the-united-arab-emirates-new-regional-alliances-and-the-palestinian-struggle/.

Harb, Iman K., "An Economic Explanation for Egypt's Alignment in the GCC Crisis," Arab Center, August 9, 2017. http://arabcenterdc.org/policy_analyses/an-economic-explanation-for-egypts-alignment-in-the-gcc-crisis.

"Hooked on Oil: Is Russia Breaking," S&P Global March 2019. Free?https://www.allnews.ch/sites/default/files/files/Hooked%20on%20Oil_Is%20Russia%20Breaking%20Free_14%20March%202019.pdf.

Ismailzada, Fariz, "The North-South Transport Corridor Finally Kicks Off," The Central Asia-Caucasus Analyst, September 27, 2016. https://www.cacianalyst.org/publications/analytical-articles/item/13395-the-%E2%80%9Cnorth-south%E2%80%9D-transport-corridor-finally-kicks-off.html.

Karasik, Theodore, "Why Is Qatar Investing so Much in Russia?," Middle East Institute, March 8, 2017. http://www.mei.edu/content/article/why-qatar-investing-so-much-russia.

Kinninmont, Jane. "The Gulf Divided. The Impact of the Qatar Crisis." Middle East and North Africa Programme, Chatham House, May 2019. https://www.chathamhouse.org/sites/default/files/publications/research/2019-05-30-Gulf%20Crisis_0.pdf.

Khlebnikov, Alexey, "Iran, Russia, and the Impact of U.S. Sanctions," Middle East Institute, July 17, 2019. https://www.mei.edu/publications/iran-russia-and-impact-us-sanctions.

Khlebnikov, Alexey, "Russia Looks to the Middle East to Boost Arms Exports," Middle East Institute, April 8, 2019. https://www.mei.edu/publications/ russia-looks-middle-east-boost-arms-exports.

Kozhanov, Nikolay, "Arms Exports Add to Russia's Tools of Influence in Middle East," Chatham House, July 20, 2016. https://www.chathamhouse.org/expert/comment/arms-exports-add-russia-s-tools-influence-middle-east.Katz, Brian and Joseph Bermudez Jr.

Krickovic, Andrej, "Russia's Challenge: A Declining Power's Quest for Status," PONARS, No. 543, October 2018. http://www.ponarseurasia.org/memo/ russia-challenge-declining-power-quest-status.

Kuimova, Alexandra, "Russia's Arms Exports to the MENA Region: Trends and Drivers," EuroMeSco Policy Brief, No. 95, 2019. https://www.euromesco.net/wp-content/ uploads/2019/03/Brief95-Russia-Arms-transfer-to-the-MENA-region.pdf.

Lister, Charles, "The West Is Walking into the Abyss on Syria," September 28, 2015. https://www.brookings.edu/blog/markaz/2015/09/28/ the-west-is-walking-into-the-abyss-on-syria/.

"Looking to the Next Decade," Zogby Research Services, November 2019. http://www. zogbyresearchservices.com/s/2019-SBY-standalone.pdf.

Makovsky, Alan, "Turkey's Refugee Dilemma," Center for American Progress, March 13, 2019. https://www.americanprogress.org/issues/security/reports/2019/03/13/467183/ turkeys-refugee-dilemma/.

Malashenko, Alexey, "Islamic Challenges to Russia, from the Caucasus to the Volga and the Urals," American Enterprise Institute, May 13, 2015. http://carnegie.ru/2015/05/13/ islamic-challenges-to-russia-from-caucasus-to-volga-and-urals-pub-60334.

Malashenko, Alexey, "Russia and the Arab Spring," Carnegie Moscow Center, October 2013. https://carnegieendowment.org/files/russia_arab_spring2013.pdf.

"Map of Control and Influence in Syria: February 16, 2018," Omran Center for Strategic Studies. http://en.omrandirasat.org/publications/reports/map-of-control-and-influence-syria-16-february-2018.html.

Martini, Jeffrey, Erin York, and William Young, "Syria as an Arena of Strategic Competition," RAND Corporation, 2013. https://www.rand.org/content/dam/rand/ pubs/research_reports/RR200/RR213/RAND_RR213.pdf.

McGregor, Andrew, "Defense or Domination? Building Algerian Power with Russian Arms," Eurasia Daily Monitor, September 5, 2018. https://jamestown.org/program/ defense-or-domination-building-algerian-power-with-russian-arms/.

"Middle East 2016: Current Conditions and the Road Ahead," Zogby Research Services, November 2016. https://static1.squarespace.com/static/52750dd3e4b08c252c723404/ t/58509580ff7c5039b9505e67/1481676164948/SBY2016+FINAL.pdf.

"Middle East Public Opinion 2018," Zogby Research Services, December 11, 2018. https:// www.zogbyresearchservices.com/new-gallery-71.

"Moscow's Next Front: Russia's Expanding Footprint in Libya," Center for Strategic and International Studies, June 17, 2020. https://www.csis.org/analysis/ moscows-next-front-russias-expanding-military-footprint-libya.

O'Hanlon, Michael E., "Deconstructing Syria: A New Strategy for America's Most Hopeless War," Brookings, June 30, 2015. https://www.brookings.edu/blog/order-from-chaos/2015/06/30/ deconstructing-syria-a-new-strategy-for-americas-most-hopeless-war/.

"Opposition Party's Report on Russia's Syria Campaign Costs Dismissed by Government," The Jamestown Foundation, July 31, 2017. https://jamestown.org/program/opposition-partys-report-on-russias-syria-campaign-costs-dismissed-by-government/.

Özdil, Eser, "How Turkey Benefits from the Global LNG Glut," Atlantic Council, May 7, 2020. https://www.atlanticcouncil.org/blogs/turkeysource/how-turkey-benefits-from-global-lng-glut/.

Popescu, Nicu and Stanislav Secrieru (eds.), "Russia's Return to the Middle East: Building Sandcastles?," EUISS Chaillot Paper no.146, July, 2018.

"Publics Worldwide Unfavourable toward Putin, Russia—Global Attitudes & Trends," Pew Research Center, August 16, 2017. http://www.pewglobal.org/2017/08/16/publics-worldwide-unfavorable-toward-putin-russia/.

"Russia's State Armament Programme 2027: A More Measured Course on Procurement," IISS Military Balance Blog, February 13, 2018. https://www.iiss.org/en/militarybalanceblog/blogsections/2018-f256/february-1c17/russia-state-armament-programme-d453.

"Russia and Turkey in the Black Sea and the South Caucasus," International Crisis Group, Europe and Central Asia Report no. 250, June 28, 2018. https://www.crisisgroup.org/europe-central-asia/western-europemediterranean/turkey/250-russia-and-turkey-black-sea-and-south-caucasus.

Saivetz, Carol R., "Moscow's Iranian Policies: Opportunities and Dangers," Crown Center, Brandeis University, Middle East Brief, 2007. https://www.brandeis.edu/crown/author/saivetz.html.

Schoenberger, Erica, and Stephanie Reich. "Soviet Policy in the Middle East." *MERIP Reports*, no. 39 (1975): 3–28.

Shapiro, Jeremy, "Bashar al-Assad Is a Monster. But Getting Rid of Him Won't Fix Syria," European Council on Foreign Relations, March 3, 2016. https://www.ecfr.eu/article/commentary_bashar_al_assad_is_a_monster_but_getting_rid_of_him_wont_fix_sy.

"Sir Bani Yas Forum-Public Opinion 2017," Zogby Research Services. http://www.zogbyresearchservices.com/new-gallery-56/2017/11/26/k3awx7fy6r1s5k5ekxmvn70rh9tyfx.

Smagin, Nikita, "Strategicheskoe Nedoverie. Pochemy u Rossii i Irana ne Poluchaetsia Stati Soiuznikami [Strategic Mistrust. Why Russia and Iran Are Not Able to Become Allies]," Moscow Carnegie Center, June 4, 2019. https://carnegie.ru/commentary/79251.

"Sovereign Wealth Fund Rankings," Sovereign Wealth Fund Institute 2018. https://www.swfinstitute.org/sovereign-wealth-fund-rankings/.

Sushentsov, Andrey, "A Russian View on America's Withdrawal from the Iran Deal," National Interest, May 15, 2018. https://nationalinterest.org/feature/russian-view-americas-withdrawal-the-iran-deal-25836.

"Timeline of Nuclear Diplomacy with Iran," Arms Control, July 2019. https://www.armscontrol.org/factsheet/Timeline-of-Nuclear-Diplomacy-With-Iran.

"Trends in International Arms Transfers, 2016," SIPRI Fact Sheet, February 2017. https://www. sipri.org/sites/default/files/Trends-in-international-arms-transfers-2016.pdf.

"Trends in International Arms Transfers, 2018," SIPRI Fact Sheet, February 2018. https://www.sipri.org/sites/default/files/2019-03/fs_1903_at_2018.pdf.

Trenin, Dmitri, "Russia's Policy in the Middle East: Prospects for Consensus and Conflict with the United States," The Century Foundation, March 2, 2010. https://carnegieendowment.org/files/trenin_middle_east.pdf.

"Turkey Wades into Libya's Troubled Waters," International Crisis Group, Report 257. Europe and Central Asia. April 30, 2020. https://www.crisisgroup.org/europe-central-asia/western-europemediterranean/turkey/257-turkey-wades-libyas-troubled-waters.

Wehrey, Frederic, "The Forgotten Uprising in Eastern Saudi Arabia," Carnegie Endowment for International Peace, June 14, 2013. http://carnegieendowment.org/2013/06/14/forgotten-uprising-in-eastern-saudi-arabia-pub-52093.

Zviagelskaya, Irina, and Nikolay Surkov, "Russian Policy in the Middle East: Dividends and Cost of the Big Game," Russian International Affairs Council Working Paper 51 (2019): 4.

Newspaper, Magazine and Website Articles

"Accept the Uncomfortable Truth: It's Time to Support Assad," *National Review*, January 7, 2016. https://www. nationalreview.com/2016/01/supporting-assad-best-option/.

"Accord Algéro-Russe pour la Construction d'une 1re Centrale Nucléaire," *Le Matin d'Algerie*, September 3, 2014. http://www.lematindz.net/news/15106-accord-algero-russe-pour-la-construction-dune-1re-centrale-nucleaire.html.

"Afflux Russe sur les Plages de Tunisie," *Le Point Afrique*, October 3, 2016. http://afrique.lepoint. fr/economie/afflux-russe-sur-les-plages-de-tunisie-03-10-2016-2073228_2258.php.

Akkoc, Raziye, and Ezzedine Said, "Iran, Russia, Turkey Team Up to Hold Sway in Syria," *Times of Israel*, April 2, 2018. https://www.timesofisrael.com/iran-russia-turkey-team-up-to-hold-sway-in-syria/.

"Algeria Is the First Export Client for the Russian Su-57 Stealth Fighter and the Su-34 Bomber," *MENA Defense*, December 27, 2019. https://www.menadefense.net/non-classe-en/algeria-is-the-first-export-client-for-the-russian-su-57-stealth-fighter-and-the-su-34-bomber.

"Algeria, Russia Ink Five Cooperation Agreements," *Algeria Press Service*, June 27, 2018. http://www.aps.dz/en/economy/20532-algeria-russia-ink-five-cooperation-agreements.

Ali, Idrees, Phil Stewart, "U.S. Removing Turkey from F-35 Program after Its Russian Missile Defense Purchase," *Reuters*, July 18, 2019. https://www.reuters.com/article/us-turkey-security-usa-idUSKCN1UC2DD.

"Aljir Priobretiot v Rossii Eshio Dve Podlodki [Algeria Will Acquire Two More Submarines in Russia]," *Kommersant*, May 18, 2006. https://www.kommersant.ru/doc/674444.

"Aljir Poluchil Pervye Vosemi Istrebitelei Su-30MKI(A) po Tretiemu Kontraktu [Algeria Received the First Eight Su-30MKI(A) Fighters under the Third Contract]," *BMPD*, January 1, 2017. https://bmpd.livejournal.com/2355958.html.

Alsharif, Asma, "Russia to Lend Egypt $25 billion to Build Nuclear Power Plant," *Reuters*, May 19, 2016. https://www.reuters.com/article/us-egypt-russia-nuclear/russia-to-lend-egypt-25-billion-to-build-nuclear-power-plant-idUSKCN0YA1G5.

Aptekari, Pavel, "Kak Rossiane Ustali ot Vnesheni Politiki [How Russians Got Tired of the Foreign Policy]," *Vedomosti*, June 21, 2019. http://www.vedomosti.ru/opinion/articles/2019/06/21/804715-rossiyane-ustali.

"Assad Offers Russia Reconstruction Benefits at Iran's Expense," *Syrian Observer*, February 28, 2018. http://syrianobserver.com/EN/Features/33899/Assad_Offers_Russia_Reconstruction_Benefits_Iran_Expense.

"Assad Otsenil Zatraty na Vosstanovlenie Siriiskoi Ekonomiki v 400 Milliardov Dollarov" [Assad Estimated Syria Will Need $400 billion to Rebuild Its Economy]," *Novaya Gazeta*, April 15, 2018. https://www.novayagazeta.ru/news/2018/04/15/141010-asad-otsenil-zatraty-na-vosstanovlenie-siriyskoy-ekonomiki-v-400-milliardov-dollarov.

"Assad Poses Bigger Threat to Syrians Than Isis, Warns Thinktank," *The Guardian*, 15 September, 2015. https://www.theguardian.com/world/2015/sep/15/syrian-president-bashar-al-assad-bigger-threat-than-isis.

Auyezov, Olzhas, "Russia, Iran, and Three Others Agree Caspain Status, but Not borders," *Reuters*, August 12, 2018. https://www.reuters.com/article/us-kazakhstan-caspian-borders-idUSKBN1KX0CI.

Azizi, Hamidreza, "Caspian Sea Convention Moves Iran Closer to Northern Neighbors," *Al-Monitor*, August 22, 2018. www.al-monitor.com/pulse/originals/2018/08/Caspian-sea-convention-iran-russia-us-sanctions-pipeline.html.

Bechev, Dimitar, "Turkey's View of the U.S.—Iran Crisis," *Ahval*, May 24, 2019. https://ahvalnews.com/us-turkey/turkeys-view-us-iran-crisis.

Binnie, Jeremy, "Egypt Faces Sanctions If It Buys Su-35s from Russia, US Warns," *Jane's 360*, April, 10, 2019. https://www.janes.com/article/87808/egypt-faces-sanctions-if-it-buys-su-35s-from-russia-us-warns.

Black, Ian, "Israelis Watch Intently as Syrian Rebel Forces Approach Golan Heights Border," *The Guardian*, June 19, 2015. https://www.theguardian.com/world/on-the-middle-east/2015/jun/19/israelis-watch-intently-as-syrian-rebel-forces-approach-golan-heights-border.

"Bogdanov: Operatsiya VKS v Sirii Dolzhna Byla Prodlitsya Neskoliko Mesyatsev [Bogdanov: the Operation of the VKS in Syria Was Expected to Last Several Months]," *RIA Novosti*, September 26, 2016. https://ria.ru/syria/20160926/1477859123.html.

Boitsova, Anna, Inna Sidorkova, and Anton Baev, "Glava ChVK Rasskazal o Rabote Rossiiskih Spetsialistov v Livii [The Head of ChVK Informed about the Work of Russian Specialists in Libya]," *RBC*, March 13, 2017. https://www.rbc.ru/politics/13/03/2017/58c69ef59a7947e8a7c2ea63.

"Bolishoe Interviu Chlenov ChVK Vagnera [A Big Interview with Wagner's PMC Members]," *Onpress.info*, November 2017. https://onpress.info/bolshoe-yntervyu-chlenov-chvk-vagnera-112488.

"Bondarev Rasskazal o Vozmozhnyh Pretendentah na Pokupku S-400 [Bondarev Told about Possible Candidates for the Purchase of S-400]," *Ria Novosti*, January 2018. https://ria.ru/defense_safety/20180123/1513157260.html.

Borger, Julian, and Patrick Wintour, "Donald Trump Tells Iran 'Call Me' over Lifting Sanctions," *The Guardian*, May 9, 2019. https://www.theguardian.com/world/2019/may/09/eu-rejects-iran-two-month-ultimatum-on-nuclear-deal.

Bourial, Hatem, "Tunisie-Russie: 800.000 Touristes Russes en 2019 et D'Autres Motifs de Satisfaction," *Webdo*, June 12, 2019. http://www.webdo.tn/2019/06/12/tunisie-russie-800-000-touristes-russes-en-2019-et-dautres-motifs-de-satisfaction/

Bozhieva, Olga, "Ekspert Rasskazal Kakoi Budet Rossiiskaya Armiya Cherez Desyati Let [Expert Told How Russian Army Will Look Like in 10 years-time]," *Moskovskii Komsomolets*, July 1, 2018. https://www.mk.ru/politics/2018/07/01/ekspert-rasskazal-kakoy-budet-rossiyskaya-armiya-cherez-desyat-let.html.

"Breaking of Idlib Siege Leaves Three Russian Servicemen Wounded," *ITAR-Tass*, September 20, 2017. https://tass.com/defense/966624.

Bryanski, Gleb, "Putin Likens U.N. Libya Resolution to Crusades," *Reuters*, March 21, 2011. https://www.reuters.com/article/us-libya-russia-idUSTRE72K3JR20110321.

Buonomo, Thomas, "Russia's Potential Response to a U.S.-Iran Conflict," *Lobelog*, July 5, 2019. https://lobelog.com/russias-potential-response-to-a-u-s-iran-conflict/.

Calamur, Krishnadev, "An Unlikely Alliance in Syria Comes under Strain," *The Atlantic*, September 24, 2018. https://www.theatlantic.com/international/archive/2018/09/russia-israel-syria/571138/.

"Caspian Sea Deal Benefits Russia, Troubles Iran," *DW.com*, August 15, 2018. https://www.dw.com/en/caspian-sea-deal-benefits-russia-troubles-iran/a-45051799.

Chabkoun, Malak, "What Is Left of the Syrian Opposition?," *Al Jazeera*, January 28, 2018. https://www.aljazeera.com/indepth/opinion/left-syrian-opposition-180127154708397.html.

Chassany, Anne-Sylvaine, "Abu Dhabi Plans to Invest Up to $5bn in Russian Infrastructure," *Financial Times*, September 11, 2013. https://www.ft.com/content/372b18e6-1af4-11e3-87da-00144feab7de.

Chernenko, Elena, Sergey Goryashko, and Ivan Safronov, "Bagdad Vyshel v Chislo Liderov po Zakupkam Vooruzhenii u Moskvy [Baghdad Was among the Leaders in Arms Procurement from Moscow]," *Kommersant*, March 28, 2015. https://www.kommersant.ru/doc/2697125.

Choi, David, "Syria Accidentally Shot Down a Russian Plane While Fending off an Israeli Missile Strike, Report Says," *Business Insider*, September 18, 2018. http://www.businessinsider.fr/us/syria-accidentally-shoots-down-russian-aircraft-report-2018-9.

"Chto Izvestno o Pogibshih v Sirii Rossiiskih Voennyh [What Is Known about Russian Military Personnel Killed in Syria]," *Kommersant*, May 27, 2018. https://www.kommersant.ru/doc/3460282.

Clark, Brenton, "Persian Games: Iran's Strategic Foothold in Tajikistan," *Open Democracy*, April 10, 2012. https://www.opendemocracy.net/en/odr/persian-games-irans-strategic-foothold-in-tajikistan/.

"Coopération: la Russie Annule une Dette Algérienne de 4,7 milliards de dollars," *Algérie Monde Infos*, January 13, 2018. http://www.algeriemondeinfos.com/2018/01/13/cooperation-russie-annule-dette-algerienne-de-47-milliards-de-dollars/.

Dalay, Galip, "How Long Will the Russian-Turkish Deal on Idlib Last?," *Al Jazeera*, March 20, 2020. https://www.aljazeera.com/indepth/opinion/long-turkish-russian-deal-idlib-200316135110613.html.

Daminov, Rafael, "Vozobnovlenie Charterov iz Rossii Vyzvalo Likovanie v Egipetskom Tursektore [Relaunch of Charter Flights from Russia Triggered Cheers in Egypt's Tourist Sector]," *RIA Novosti*, October 18, 2018. https://ria.ru/20181018/1530960714.html.

"Direktor FSVTS Dmitri Shugaev o Sushestvuiushih Slozhnostiyah i Otkryvaiushihsya Perespektivah Oruzheinogo Eksporta [Director of FSMTC Dmitry Shugaev on the

Existing Difficulties and the Emerging Prospects of Arms Exports]," *Kommersant*, February 6, 2019. https://www.kommersant.ru/doc/3874641.

Dorsey, James, "Fighting for the Soul of Islam: A Battle of the Paymasters," *Huffington Post*, September 30, 2017. https://www.huffingtonpost.com/james-dorsey/fighting-for-the-soul-of_b_12259312.html.

Drake, Chris "Cyprus Bows to Pressure and Drops Missile Plan," *The Guardian*, December 29, 1998.

Dzhordzhevich, Alexandra, and Ivan Safronov, "Rossya i Saudovskaya Aravya Kak Nikogda Sblizilisi v Voprosah Postavok S-400 [Russia and Saudi Arabia Brought Together Their Views on the Supply of S-400 Systems as Never Before]," *Kommersant*, October 6, 2017. https://www.kommersant.ru/doc/3429985.

"Egipet Otkryvaiut dlya Rossiiskih Turistov: Progress na Litso [Egypt Is Opened for Russian Tourists: Progress Is Evident]," *Turprom*, April 9 2019. https://www.tourprom.ru/news/41965/.

"Egipet Narashivaet Eksport Selskokhozyaistvennoi Produktsii v Rossiu [Egypt Increases Export of Agro Products to Russia]," *RIA Novosti*, August, 8, 2018. https://ria.ru/20180805/1525957209.html.

"Egypt and Russia Sign 50-Year Industrial Zone Agreement," *Reuters*, May 23, 2018. https://af.reuters.com/article/egyptNews/idAFL5N1SU5SI.

"Egypt, EAEU Can Sign Free Trade Zone Agreement in 2020: Russian Minister," *Egypt Today*, June 22, 2019. https://www.egypttoday.com/Article/3/71919/Egypt-EAEU-can-sign-free-trade-zone-agreement-in-2020.

"Egypt Faces Sanctions If It Buys Su-35s from Russia, U.S. Warns," *Jane's Defence Weekly*, April 10, 2019. https://www.janes.com/article/87808/egypt-faces-sanctions-if-it-buys-su-35s-from-russia-us-warns.

"Egypt Imported 10 Million Tonnes of Wheat in 2018: Ministry Report," *Ahram Online*, November 8, 2018. http://english.ahram.org.eg/NewsContent/3/12/315983/Business/Economy/Egypt-imported--million-tonnes-of-wheat--in--Minis.aspx.

"Egypt Licensed to Assemble Russian T-90S Tanks. Capacity—50 a Year," *Debka Weekly*, March 11 2018. https://www.debka.com/egypt-licensed-to-assemble-russian-t-90s-tanks-capacity-50-a-year/.

"Egypt, Russia to Hold Joint Military Exercises in mid-October," *Reuters*, October 12, 2016. https://www.reuters.com/article/us-egypt-russia-military-idUSKCN12C2E0.

El Beih, Yasmin, "Russian Tourism in Egypt: What's Next?," *Egypt Today*, July 23, 2018. https://www.egypttoday.com/Article/3/54330/Russian-Tourism-in-Egypt-What%E2%80%99s-Next.

Ellyatt, Holly, "Russia Rolls out the Red Carpet for Saudi King with Billion-dollar Deals on the Table," *CNBC*, October 5, 2017. https://www.cnbc.com/2017/10/05/saudi-king-visits-russia-as-billion-dollar-deals-on-the-table.html.

Emad, Mohamed, "Russian Experts Continue Inspection of Hurghada Airport Security," *El-Balad*, April 16, 2019. https://en.el-balad.com/2416757.

Erlich, Reese, "Trump is Driving Iran into Russia's Arms," *Foreign Policy*, May 29, 2019. https://foreignpolicy.com/2019/05/29/trump-is-driving-iran-into-russias-arms-nuclear-deal-putin-rouhani-sanctions/.

Faghihi, Rohollah, "Iranian Mistrust of Russia Surges as Syrian War Winds Down," *Al-Monitor*, March 12, 2018. https://www.al-monitor.com/pulse/en/originals/2018/03/iran-syria-russia-sentiment-reconstruction-spoils-safavi.html.

"Falih: Saudi Aramco Extends Offer to Buy Stake in Arctic LNG 2," *Reuters*, June 10, 2019. https://www.reuters.com/article/lng-novatek-saudi-aramco/falih-saudi-aramco-extends-offer-to-buy-stake-in-arctic-lng-2-tass-idUSR4N23D08Z.

Farchy, Jack, and Neil Hume, "Glencore and Qatar Take 19.5 percent Stake in Rosneft," *Financial Times*, December 10, 2016. https://www.ft.com/content/d3923b08-bf09-11e6-9bca-2b93a6856354.

"Faut-il Choisir Entre Bachar el-Assad Et l'État Islamique?," *Le Figaro*, May 26, 2015. http://www.lefigaro.fr/vox/monde/2015/05/26/31002-20150526ARTFIG00196-faut-il-choisir-entre-bachar-el-assad-et-l-etat-islamique.php.

"Five States Sign Convention on Caspian Legal Status," *RFE/RL*, August 12, 2018. https://www.rferl.org/a/russia-iran-azerbaijan-kazakhstan-turkmenistan-caspian-sea-summit/29428300.html.

"Flydubai Launches New Route to Russia," *Russian Aviation Insider*, April 24, 2019. http://www.rusaviainsider.com/flydubai-launches-new-route-russia/.

"For Average Syrians, All Members of Opposition Are Terrorists—State Senator Richard Black," *Russia Today*, January 27, 2017. https://www.rt.com/op-ed/375287-syria-draft-constitution-rebels/.

"Four-fifths of Russia's Syria Strikes Don't Target Islamic State: Reuters Analysis," *Reuters*, October 21, 2015. https://www.reuters.com/article/us-mideast-crisis-syria-russia-strikes/four-fifths-of-russias-syria-strikes-dont-target-islamic-state-reuters-analysis-idUSKCN0SF24L20151021.

Foy, Henry, "Rosneft's Iraqi Kurdistan Oil and Gas Play Angers Baghdad," *Financial Times*, October 30, 2018. https://www.ft.com/content/ace52dd2-4f0c-11e8-ac41-759eee1efb74.

Frantz, Douglas, "Iran and Azerbaijan Argue over Caspian's Riches," *New York Times*, August 30, 2001. https://www.nytimes.com/2001/08/30/world/iran-and-azerbaijan-argue-over-caspian-s-riches.html.

Frolovskiy, Dmitriy, "Russia and Qatar: The Middle East's Newest Pragmatic Friendship?," *Jerusalem Post*, April 1, 2019. https://www.jpost.com/Opinion/Russia-and-Qatar-The-Middle-Easts-newest-pragmatic-friendship-585461.

"From the Archive, 8 September 1973: Gaddafi and Castro Clash over Soviet Union," *The Guardian*, September 8, 2015. https://www.theguardian.com/world/2015/sep/08/gaddafi-castro-soviet-union-communism-1973.

"Gaddafi Fall Cost Russia Tens of Billions in Arms Deals," *Reuters*, November 2, 2011. https://www.reuters.com/article/russia-libya-arms/gaddafi-fall-cost-russia-tens-of-blns-in-arms-deals-idUSL5E7M221H20111102.

Galeotti, Mark, "Not-So-Soft Power: Russia's Military Police in Syria," *War on the Rocks*, October 2, 2017. https://warontherocks.com/2017/10/not-so-soft-power-russias-military-police-in-syria/.

Gamal, Rania El, Parisa Hafezi, and Dmitry Zhdannikov, "How Putin, Khamenei and Saudi Prince Got OPEC Deal Done," *Reuters*, December 1, 2016. https://www.reuters.com/article/us-opec-meeting/exclusive-how-putin-khamenei-and-saudi-prince-got-opec-deal-done-idUSKBN13Q4WG.

"Gazprom's Next Acquisition—Algeria?," *Oilprice.com*, February 22, 2014. https://oilprice.com/Energy/Natural-Gas/Gazproms-Next-Acquisition-Algeria.html.

Ghanem, Dalia, "Another Battle of Algiers," *New York Times*, March 13, 2019. https://www.nytimes.com/2019/03/13/opinion/algeria-protests-president-military.html.

Gibbons-Neff, Thomas, "Egypt to Buy French Mistral Landing Ships Originally Intended for Russia," *Washington Post*, September, 23, 2015. https://www.washingtonpost.com/news/checkpoint/wp/2015/09/23/egypt-to-buy-french-mistral-landing-ships-originally-intended-for-russia/.

"Glava FSVTS Dmitrij Shugaev o Potenciale Eksporta Rossijskogo Vooruzheniya ["Dmitry Shugaev, the Head of the FSMTC, on the Potential on the Prospects of Russian Arms Exports]," *RT*, November 21, 2019. https://russian.rt.com/russia/article/689034-dmitrii-shugaev-intervyu-vystavka-dubai-airshow-2019.

"Glava Rosoboroneksporta: v 2018 godu Prodadim Oruzhiya Bolee Chem na \$13 mlrd [The Head of Rosoboronexport: in 2018 We Will Sell Weapon on More Than \$13 billion]," *RIA Novosti*, April 16, 2018. https://ria.ru/20180416/1518588740.html.

Gnana, Jennifer, "Iraq's Dependence on Oil to Continue as Reform Pace Slows, Says Moody's," *The National*, October 3, 2019. https://www.thenational.ae/business/economy/iraq-s-dependence-on-oil-tocontinue-as-reform-pace-slows-says-moody-s-1.918725.

Gnana, Jennifer. "Adnoc Awards 5 Percent Stake in Ghasha Concession to Russia's Lukoil," *The National*, October 15, 2019. https://www.thenational.ae/business/energy/adnoc-awards-5-stake-in-ghasha-concession-to-russia-s-lukoil-1.924175.

Golubovych, Aleksey, "K Vizitu Netanyahu: Chto Rossia Mozhet Poluchyt ot Ekonomiki Izrailia [Towards the Netanyahu Visit: What Russia Can Obtain from the Israeli Economy]," *Forbes.ru*, March 9, 2017. http://www.forbes.ru/finansy-i-investicii/340519-rossiysko-izrailskie-ekonomicheskie-svyazi-ne-tolko-neft-na.

" 'Go Back to Raqqa & Bury Bodies': Putin Calls for Investigation into Strikes on Civilians in Syria," *RT*, March 10, 2018. https://www.rt.com/news/420923-raqqa-crimes-investigation-putin/.

Gross, Judah Ari, "Netanyahu: Israel Acts to Keep Game-changing Arms Away from Hezbollah," *Times of Israel*, January 9, 2018. https://www.timesofisrael.com/netanyahu-israel-acts-to-keep-game-changing-arms-away-from-hezbollah/.

" 'Guarantor of Peace': Russia Inserts Itself between Israel, Syria in the Golan Heights," *National Post*, August 14, 2018. https://nationalpost.com/news/world/russia-to-help-un-with-patrols-along-syria-israel-frontier.

"Gulf Countries Supported Egypt with \$92bn since 2011," *Middle East Monitor*, March, 19, 2019. https://www.middleeastmonitor.com/20190319-gulf-countries-supported-egypt-with-92bn-since-2011/.

Hamidi, Ibrahim, "Damascus' Allies, Opponents Race over Strategic Gains," *Asharq Al-Awsat*, April 25, 2019. https://aawsat.com/english/home/article/1694476/damascus%E2%80%99-allies-opponents-race-over-strategic-gains.

Harel, Amos, "Putin's Phone Call with Netanyahu Put End to Israeli Strikes in Syria," *Haaretz*, February 15, 2018. https://www.haaretz.com/middle-east-news/iran/putin-s-call-with-netanyahu-called-time-on-israel-s-syrian-strikes-1.5809118.

Hauer, Neil, "Russia's Failure at Sochi Means More War for Syria in 2018," *Middle East Eye*, February 7, 2018. https://www.middleeasteye.net/opinion/russias-failure-sochi-means-more-war-syria-2018.

Hille, Kathrin, "Saudi Sovereign Fund to Invest \$10bn in Russia," *Financial Times*, July 6, 2015. https://www.ft.com/content/0205a0d6-2412-11e5-bd83-71cb60e8f08c.

Hilsman, Patrick, "Drone Deals Heighten Military Ties between Israel and Russia," *Middle East Eye*, October 4, 2015. http://www.middleeasteye.net/news/analysis-drone-deals-highlight-military-ties-between-israel-and-russia-24061368.

Hiltermann, Joost, "Russia Can Keep the Peace between Israel and Iran—But Following the Hostilities over the Weekend, Does Putin Want to?," *The Atlantic*, February 13, 2018. https://www.theatlantic.com/international/archive/2018/02/israel-syria-iran-hezbollah-putin-assad/553217/.

"How Iranian General Plotted out Syrian Assault in Moscow," *Reuters*, October 6, 2015. https://www.reuters.com/article/us-mideast-crisis-syria-soleimani-insigh/how-iranian-general-plotted-out-syrian-assault-in-moscow-idUSKCN0S02BV20151006.

"How Qatar Seized Control of the Syrian Revolution," *Financial Times*, May 17, 2013. https://www.ft.com/content/f2d9bbc8-bdbc-11e2-890a-00144feab7de.

Holland, Steve, and Jeff Mason, "Obama, In Dig at Putin, Calls Russia 'Regional Power'," *Reuters*, March 25, 2014. https://www.reuters.com/article/us-ukraine-crisis-russia-weakness-idUSBREA2O19J20140325.

"How Syria's White Helmets Became Victims of an Online Propaganda Machine," *The Guardian*, December 18, 2017. https://www.theguardian.com/world/2017/dec/18/syria-white-helmets-conspiracy-theories.

Ignatius, David, "A Young Prince Is Reimagining Saudi Arabia. Can He Make His Vision Come True?," *Washington Post*, April 20, 2017. https://www.washingtonpost.com/opinions/global-opinions/a-young-prince-reimagines-saudi-arabia-can-he-make-his-vision-come-true/2017/04/20/.

"Intel: Why Russia Dispatched Top Diplomatic to Teheran," *Al-Monitor*, May 30, 2019. www.al-monitor.com/pulse/originals/2019/05/intel-russia-sergey-ryabov-tehran-iran-nuclear-deal.html.

"Interview with Chief of Russian General Staff" *Komsomolskaya Pravda*, December 27, 2017. https://www.kp.ru/daily/26775/3808693/.

"Interview with Lev Dengov, Head of the Russian Contact Group on Libya," *News.ru*, July, 2, 2019. https://news.ru/afrika/lev-dengov-rossiya-v-livii-ne-delaet-stavku-na-kakuyu-libo-storonu/.

"Irak i Saudovskaya Aravya Hotyat Kupiti Pochiti 1,5 tysyachi BMP-3 [Iraq and Saudi Arabia Want to Buy Almost 1500 BMP-3's]," *ITAR-Tass*, September 30, 2015. https://tass.ru/armiya-i-opk/2302766.

"Iraqi Defense Ministry Receives T90S Tanks from Russia," *ITAR-Tass*, February 19, 2018. http://tass.com/defense/990795.

'Iraq, Russia, Iran and Syria Coordinate against ISIS', *Al Jazeera*, September 27, 2015. https://www. aljazeera.com/news/2015/09/iraq-russia-iran-syria-coordinate-isil-150927125919507.html.

"Iraq to Purchase Russia's S-400 Missile Systems," *ITAR-Tass*, May 15, 2019. https://tass.com/defense/1058382.

"Iran, Azerbaijan Sign Agreement on Defense Cooperation," *Press TV*, January 17, 2019. https://www.presstv.com/Detail/2019/01/17/586006/Iran-Azerbaijan-defense-MoU-Major-General-Mohammad-Baqeri-Baqeri--Zakir-Hasanov?fbclid=IwAR2pCtQlQsR_0yvKCeblDYtmZsy5reKLCPCozAKkQxTt70FSzspMtU-iRc0.

"Iran-Backed Militias Block Aleppo Evacuation as Shelling Resumes," *The Guardian*, December 14, 2016. https://www.theguardian.com/world/2016/dec/14/aleppo-residents-evacuation-uncertainty-ceasefire-deal-assad.

Isachenkov, Vladimir, "Russia Negotiates Deal for Its Warplanes to Use Egypt Bases,"
  AP, November 30, 2017. ihttps://apnews.com/bdfae4502ca74c1eacdbf6d32252e8f4?
  utm_campaign=SocialFlow&utm_source=Twitter&utm_medium=AP.
"Islamic Conference in Chechnya: Why Sunnis Are Disassociating Themselves
  from Salafists," *Firstpost*, September 9, 2016. https://www.firstpost.com/world/
  islamic-conference-in-chechnya-why-sunnis-are-disassociating-themselves-from-
  salafists-2998018.html.
"Israel v Iran in Syria: Heating Up," *The Economist*, April 14, 2018. 40 (US edition). https://
  www.economist.com/news/middle-east-and-africa/21740471-conflict-between-two-
  powers-escalating-israel-determined-stop.
Issaev, Leonid, "Russia and the GCC Crisis," *Al Jazeera*, June 13, 2017. https://www.
  aljazeera.com/indepth/opinion/2017/06/russia-gcc-crisis-170613073826800.html.
"Isis 'Destroys' Syrian Airbase and Four Russian Helicopters," *The Independent*, May 24,
  2016. https://www.independent. co.uk/news/world/middle-east/isis-destroys-syrian-
  airbase-and-four-russian-helicopters-a7046646.html.
Ivanova, Polina, "Russia Sends Test Shipment of Wheat to Algeria," *ZAWYA*, March
  21, 2019. https://www.zawya.com/mena/en/story/Russia_sends_test_shipment_of
  _wheat_to_Algeria-TR20190321nL8N2184PPX1.
Kane, Frank, "'Reset' for Russian-GCC Trade Relations, but Still a Long Way to Go," *Arab
  News*, June 4, 2017. http://www.arabnews.com/node/1110241.
Katz, Mark N., "Putin's Courtship of Both Assad and Erdogan Is Spinning Out of
  Control in Syria," *Responsible Statecraft*, March 2, 2020. https://responsiblestatecraft.
  org/2020/03/02/putins-assad-erdogan-spinning-out-of-control-in-syria/.
Katz, Mark N., "Russia and the Iran Crisis," *Lobelog*, May 17, 2019. https://lobelog.com/
  russia-and-the-iran-crisis/.
Kemp, John, "Saudi Arabia's Oil Reserves: How Big Are They Really?,"
  Reuters, July 11, 2016. https://www.reuters.com/article/us-saudi-oil-kemp/
  saudi-arabias-oil-reserves-how-big-are-they-really-kemp-idUSKCN0ZL1X6.
Khamis, Jumana, "UAE's Long-Term Food Security Strategy under Study,"
  Gulf News, February 8, 2018. http://gulfnews.com/news/uae/society/
  uae-s-long-term-food-security-strategy-under-study-1.2170588.
Khrennikova, Dina, "Caspian Sea Breakthrough Treaty Set to Boost Oil, Pipeline
  Plans," *Bloomberg News*, August 12, 2018. https://www.bloomberg.com/news/
  articles/2018-08-12/caspian-sea-breakthrough-treaty-set-to-boost-oil-pipeline-plans.
"King Mohammed Makes a Strategic Visit to Russia," *Submit 123 Press Release*,
  March 16, 2016. https://newsreleases.submitpressrelease123.com/2016/03/18/
  king-mohammed-vi-makes-a-strategic-visit-to-russia/.
Kollewe, Julia, "Qatar Pulls Out of Opec to Focus on Gas Production," *The Guardian*,
  December 3, 2018. https://www.theguardian.com/business/2018/dec/03/
  qatar-pulls-out-of-opec-to-focus-on-gas-production.
Korsunskaya, Darya, and Polina Nikolskaya, "Russian Fund Builds
  Investors Pool for Saudi Aramco IPO," *Reuters*, February 15,
  2018. https://www.reuters.com/article/us-russia-sarabia-novatek/
  russian-fund-builds-investors-pool-for-saudi-aramco-ipo-idUSKCN1FZ0PV.
Kramer, Andrew E., "Iran Revokes Russia's Use of Air Base, Saying Moscow 'Betrayed
  Trust," *New York Times*, August 22, 2016. https://www.nytimes.com/2016/08/23/world/
  middleeast/iran-russia-syria.html.
"Kuwaiti Army Officer Says Russian Tanks Purchase Postponed," *Xinhua*, March 5, 2019.
  http://www.xinhuanet.com/english/2019-03/05/c_137871438.htm.

Lamin, Habibulah Mohamed, "How Polisario Front Hopes to Partner with Russia in Western Sahara," *Al-Monitor*, April 11, 2017. https://www.al-monitor.com/pulse/ru/contents/articles/originals/2017/04/western-sahara-polisario-sell-russia-moscow-visit.html.

Landau, Noa, "Contradicting Trump, Top Putin Advisor Says U.S. Drone Downed in Iranian Airspace," *Ha'aretz*, June 26, 2019. https://www.haaretz.com/middle-east-news/at-israel-russia-meeting-bolton-says-u-s-awaits-real-negotiations-with-iran-1.7408293.

"L'Algérie a Importé 4,6 millions de tonnes de Blé Français," *El Watan. com*, May 30, 2019. https://www.elwatan.com/edition/economie/lalgerie-a-importe-46-millions-de-tonnes-de-ble-francais-30-05-2019.

"La Position de la Russie sur le Conflit du Sahara Occidental, Selon une Note Confidentielle Marocaine," *Diaspora Saharaui*, January 2016. http://diasporasaharaui.blogspot.com/2016/01/la-position-de-la-russie-sur-le-conflit.html.

"La Tunisie et la Russie Cherchent à Lancer une Zone de Libre-échange," *Xinhuanet*, April 27, 2019. http://french.xinhuanet.com/2019-04/27/c_138013696.htm.

"Latvian President: Russia Using Syria to Divert Attention from Ukraine," *Baltic Times*, December 3, 2015. https://www.baltictimes.com/latvian_president__russia_using_syria_to_divert_attention_from_ukraine/.

"Lavrov Blames Washington's 'Aggressive' Policies for Rise in Global Tensions," *RFE/RL*, January 17, 2020. https://www.rferl.org/a/lavrov-blames-washington-s-aggressive-policies-for-rise-in-global-tensions/30383167.html.

Lavrov, Sergey, "Friendship and Cooperation Tested by Time," *Al Ahram*, October 13, 2018. http://www.mid.ru/en/diverse/-/asset_publisher/zwI2FuDbhJx9/content/stat-a-ministra-inostrannyh-del-rossii-s-v-lavrova-rossia-i-egipet-druzba-i-sotrudnicestvo-ispytannye-vremenem-opublikovannaa-v-egipetskoj-gazete-al-a?_101_INSTANCE_zwI2FuDbhJx9_redirect=http%3A%2F%2Fwww.mid.ru%2Fen%2Fdiverse%3Fp_p_id%3D101_INSTANCE_zwI2FuDbhJx9%26p_p_lifecycle%3D0%26p_p_state%3Dnormal%26p_p_mode%3Dview%26p_p_col_id%3Dcolumn-1%26p_p_col_pos%3D2%26p_p_col_count%3D6.

"Lavrov Prokommentiroval Diplomaticheski Skandal Vokrug Katara [Lavrov Commented on the Qatari Diplomatic Scandal]," *RIA Novosti*, June 5, 2017. https://ria.ru/world/20170605/1495842179.html.

"Lawmakers Authorize Use of Russian Military Force for Anti-IS Airstrikes in Syria," *ITAR-Tass*, September 30, 2015. http://tass.ru/en/politics/824795http://tass.ru/en/politics/824795.

"Le Pen Says Assad May Be Lesser of Two Evils for Syria's Future," *Bloomberg*, February 20, 2017. https://www.bloomberg.com/news/articles/2017-02-20/le-pen-says-assad-may-be-lesser-of-two-evils-for-syria-s-future.

"Libyan Factions Sign 'Permanent' Ceasefire, Erdogan Casts Doubt," *Arab Weekly*, October 23, 2020. https://thearabweekly.com/libyan-factions-sign-permanent-ceasefire-erdogan-casts-doubt.

"Libya's Eastern Parliament Speaker Praises Russia's Training of Haftar-led Forces," *Libyan Express*, January 7, 2018. http://www.libyanexpress.com/libyas-eastern-parliament-speaker-praises-russias-training-of-haftar-led-forces/.

"Libya-Soviet Ties Reported Strained," *New York Times*, May 6, 1986.

Liphshiz, Cnaan, "Can Israel Benefit from Sheriff Putin Policing the Middle East?," *Times of Israel*, October 13, 2015. https://www.timesofisrael.com/can-israel-benefit-from-sheriff-putin-policing-the-middle-east/.

Lister, Charles, "Assad Hasn't Won Anything," *Foreign Policy*, July 11, 2019. https://foreignpolicy.com/2019/07/11/assad-hasnt-won-anything-syria/.

LLobet, Anaïs, "Russia Seeks Mediator Role between Israel and Iran," *Times of Israel*, May 10, 2018. https://www.timesofisrael.com/russia-seeks-mediator-role-between-israel-and-iran/.

"Loukoster Pobeda Nachiniot Letati v Eilat i Dubai [Low-cost Company Podeda Will Start Flying to Eilat and Dubai]," *Meduza*, July 10, 2019. https://meduza.io/news/2019/07/10/loukoster-pobeda-nachnet-letat-v-eylat-i-dubay.

"Lukoil Puts Iran Plans on Hold Due to Threat of US Sanctions," *Reuters*, May 29, 2018. https://www.reuters.com/article/us-russia-lukoil-iran/lukoil-puts-iran-plans-on-hold-due-to-threat-of-u-s-sanctions-idUSKCN1IU1M7.

Luzhin, Pavel, "Ramzan Kadyrov: Russia's Top Diplomat," *Riddle*, April 19, 2018. https://www.ridl.io/en/ramzan-kadyrov-russias-top-diplomat/.

Marcus, Jonathan, "Is Israel Driving a Wedge between Russia and Iran?," *BBC News*, May 31, 2018. https://www.bbc.co.uk/news/world-middle-east-44313744.

Medetsky, Anatoly, "Soviet-Era Grain Record Seen Tumbling on Bumper Russian Crop," *Bloomberg*, August 21, 2017. https://www.bloomberg.com/news/articles/2017-08-21/soviet-era-grain-record-seen-tumbling-on-bumper-russian-harvest.

"Medvedev au Maroc: Onze Accords Signés pour Renforcer le Partenariat Stratégique Maroco-Russe," *HuffPost Maghreb*, October 11, 2017. https://www.huffpostmaghreb.com/2017/10/11/medvedev-au-marocconze-accords-signes-pour-renforcer-le-partenariat-strategique-maroco-russe_n_18237080.html.

Meyer, Henry, "Qatar Seeks More Russian Deals after 'Great' Rosneft Investment," *Bloomberg*, March 11, 2019. https://www.bloomberg.com/news/articles/2019-03-11/qatar-seeks-more-russia-deals-after-great-rosneft-investment.

Meyer, Henry, and Ilya Arkhipov, "Saudis, Russia Fund to Sign $2 Billion in Deals During Putin's Visit," *Bloomberg*, October 10, 2019. https://www.bloomberg.com/news/articles/2019-10-10/saudis-russia-fund-to-sign-2-billion-deals-during-putin-visit.

"Middle East: Top Assad Aide Assassinated at Syrian resort," *The Guardian*, August 5, 2008. https://www.theguardian.com/world/2008/aug/05/syria.lebanon.

Miles, Tom, "Russia Sees Closer Iran Ties as U.S. Exits Nuclear Deal: Official," *Reuters*, May 4, 2018. http://www.reuters.com/article/us-iran-nuclear-russia-idUSKBN11516Z.

Milashina, Elena, "Halifat? Primanka dlya durakov! [Caliphate? Trap for Fools!]," *Novaya Gazeta*, July 25, 2015. https://www.novayagazeta.ru/articles/2015/07/29/65056-171-halifat-primanka-dlya-durakov-187.

"More Russian Military Police Arrive in Syria after Moscow-Ankara Deal," *RFL*, October 25, 2019. https://www.rferl.org/a/more-russian-military-police-arrive-in-syria-after-moscow-ankara-deal/30236285.html.

"More Than 90%' of Russian Airstrikes in Syria Have Not Targeted Isis, US Says," *The Guardian*, October 7, 2015. https://www.theguardian.com/world/2015/oct/07/russia-airstrikes-syria-not-targetting-isis.

"More Than 70% Support for Vladimir Putin's Bombing Campaign Despite Middle East Tensions," *Express*, October 13, 2015. https://www.express.co.uk/news/uk/611495/Vladimir-Putin-bombing-campaign-poll-support-syria-middle-east.

Morgelson, Luke, "America's Abandonment of Syria," *New Yorker*, April 20, 2020.

"Morocco to Train Russian Imams," *Morocco World News*, March 19, 2016. http://www.moroccoworldnews.com/2016/03/182434/182434/.

"Morocco, Russia Promote Cooperation with Signing of 11 Agreements," *Asharq Al-Awsat*, October 12, 2017. https://aawsat.com/english/home/article/1050066/morocco-russia-promote-cooperation-signing-11-agreements.

Myers, Steven Lee, "Qatar Court Convicts 2 Russians in Top Chechen's Death," *New York Times*, July 1, 2004. http://www.nytimes.com/2004/07/01/world/qatar-court-convicts-2-russians-in-top-chechen-s-death.html.

Nikolsky, Alexey, "Blizhnii Vostok Stanovitsya Krupneishim Rynkom dlya Rossiiskih Vooruzhenii [Middle East Is Becoming the Largest Market for Russian Weapons]," *Vedomosti*, February 18, 2019. https://www.vedomosti.ru/politics/articles/2019/02/18/794445-blizhnii-vostok-stanovitsya-krupneishim-rinkom-vooruzhenii.

Nikolskii, Aleksey, "Gosbanki Rossii i Indii Obespechiat Raschioty za Rossiiskoe Oruzhie v Natsionalinyh Valiutah [Russian and Indian State Banks Will Ensure Payments for Russian Weapons in the National Currencies]," *Vedomosti*, July 16, 2019. https://www.vedomosti.ru/politics/articles/2019/07/15/806604-gosbanki-rossii-i-indii-obespechat-rascheti-za-oruzhie.

Nikolsky, Alexey, "Soglasovan Kontrakt na Postavku 46 Istrebitelei MiG-29 v Egipet [The Contract for the Supply of 46 MiG-29 Fighters to Egypt Signed]," *Vedomosti*, May 24, 2015. https://www.vedomosti.ru/politics/articles/2015/05/25/593348-soglasovan-kontrakt-na-postavku-46-istrebitelei-mig-29-v-egipet.

Nikolsky, Alexey, "Zakliuchen Kontrakt po Litsenzionnomu Proizvodstvu Tankov T-90 v Aljire [The Contract on Licensed Production of T-90 Tanks in Algeria Concluded]," *Vedomosti*, February 20, 2015. https://www.vedomosti.ru/newspaper/articles/2015/02/20/tank-alzhirskoi-sborki.

Noori, Alireza, "Can Iran Rely on Russia to Dodge U.S. Pressure," *Al-Monitor*, May 21, 2019. www.al-monitor.com/pulse/originals/2019/05/iran-russia-nuclear-deal-jcpoa-trump-us-sanctions-oil.html.

Noori, Alireza, "Iran Seeks Relief from U.S. Sanctions in Asia," *Al-Monitor*, June 28, 2019. www.al-monitor.com/pulse/originals/2019/06/iran-seeks-relief-us-sanctions-asia.html.

"No Sign of Obama's Predicted 'Guagmire' as Russia's Engagement in Syria Escalates," *Washington Post*, September 30, 2016. https://www.washingtonpost.com/world/no-sign-of-obamas-predicted-quagmire-as-russias-engagement-in-syria-escalates/2016/09/30/5b3e4d18-8723-11e6-ac72-a29979381495_story.html.

"Obama: Russia Heading for 'Quagmire' in Syria," *CNN*, October 2, 2015. https://edition.cnn.com/2015/10/02/politics/president-obama-syria-russia-assad/index.html.

"Obama Says Russian Strategy in Syria is 'Recipe for Disaster,'" *The Guardian*, October 2015. https://www.theguardian.com/world/2015/oct/02/us-coalition-warns-russia-putin-extremism-syria-isis.

"Obama and Putin's First Formal Meeting in Two Years Described as 'Businesslike' Despite Tensions," *ABC News*, September 28, 2015. http://abcnews.go.com/US/obama-putin-set-rare-sit-meeting-amid-tensions/story?id=34094684.

"Obama: U.S. Working to 'Isolate Russia,'" *Time*, March 3, 2014. http://time.com/11900/obama-u-s-working-to-isolate-russia/.

"Official: Russia 'Deliberately Targeting' US-Backed Forces in Syria," *Fox News*, October 14, 2018. http://www.foxnews.com/politics/2015/10/14/official-russia-deliberately-targeting-us-backed-forces-in-syria-dozens-killed.html.

Oliphant, Vickiie, "Russia Hits Out after Being Accused of Sending Forces to Egypt to Influence Libya Conflict," *Express*, March 14, 2017. https://www.express.co.uk/news/world/778864/Russia-DENIES-deploying-special-forces-Egypt-influence-Libya-conflict.

Omran, Hagar, "Russian-Egyptian Political Rapprochement to Propel Economic Cooperation Forward," *Daily News Egypt*, October 17, 2018. https://dailynewssegypt.com/2018/10/17/russian-egyptian-political-rapprochement-to-propel-economic-cooperation-forward/.

"Operatsiya v Sirii Pokazala Silu Rossii [Operation in Syria Showed the Strength of Russia]," *Red Star*, January 31, 2018. http://redstar.ru/operatsiya-v-sirii-pokazala-silu-rossii/.

"Over Half of Russian Military Police Have Syrian War Experience—Official," *Moscow Times*, February 18, 2019. https://www.themoscowtimes.com/2019/02/18/over-half-of-russian-military-police-have-syrian-war-experience-official-a64532.

Pakhomov, Nikolay, "Russia's Grand Plan to Gain Power in the Shadow of U.S. Sanctions," *National Interest*, May 7, 2019. https://nationalinterest.org/feature/russias-grand-plan-gain-power-shadow-us-sanctions-56427.

Pakhomov, Nikolay, "The Russia-Israel Relationship Is Perfect Realpolitik," *National Interest*, March 23, 2017. http://nationalinterest.org/feature/the-russia-israel-relationship-perfect-realpolitik-19881.

"Posol RF: Turpotok v Tunis Sokratilsya Pochti v Piati Raz v 2015 godu [Ambassador of Russia: the Tourist Flow to Tunisia Has Decreased Five Times in 2015]," *RIA Novosti*, February 3, 2016. https://ria.ru/tourism/20160203/1369189221.html.

"Pour Bachar Al-Assad, la Position de François Fillon Sur la Syrie Est 'Une Très Bonne Chose'," *Le Monde*, January 9, 2017. https://www.lemonde.fr/election-presidentielle-2017/article/2017/01/09/pour-bachar-al-assad-la-position-de-francois-fillon-sur-la-syrie-est-une-tres-bonne-chose_5059694_4854003.html#57QmCkAtQhPxfZ92.99.

"Proekt 'Myasorubka'. Rasskazyvaiut Tri Komandira 'ChVK Vagnera' [Project 'Meat Mincer'. Three Commanders of 'PMC Wagner' Speak Out]," *Radio Svoboda*, March 7, 2018. https://www.svoboda.org/a/29084090.html.

Prokopovič, Karolina, "Russian Tourists May Swap Turkey for Asia," *Aviation Voice*, March 12, 2015. https://aviationvoice.com/russian-tourists-may-swap-turkey-for-asia-201512030959/.

"Putin's Envoy Briefs Tehran about Russia-Israel-U.S. Meeting," *PressTV*, July 8, 2019. https://www.presstv.com/Detail/2019/07/09/600561/Iran-Russia-Putin-envoy-brief-Jerusalem-alQuds-meeting-Israel.

"Putin Is Filling the Middle East Power Vacuum," *Bloomberg*, October 3, 2017. https://www.bloomberg.com/news/articles/2017-10-03/putin-is-now-mr-middle-east-a-job-no-one-ever-succeeds-at.

Putin, Vladimir, "A Plea for Caution from Russia," *New York Times*, September 11, 2013. https://www.nytimes.com/2013/09/12/opinion/putin-plea-for-caution-from-russia-on-syria.html.

"Putin Podpisal Ukaz ob Ucherezdenii Voennogo Attashata pri Posolistve Rossii v Katare [Putin Signed a Decree on the Establishment of a Military Attaché Office at the Russian Embassy in Qatar]," *ITAR-Tass*, June 24, 2019. https://tass.ru/armiya-i-opk/6584844.

"Putin Zayavil o Primenenii v Sirii 215 Sovremennyh Vidov Vooruzhenii [Putin Noted that Russian Forces Used Some 215 new Types of Advanced Weapons Systems in Syria]," *Interfax*, January 30, 2018. http://www.interfax.ru/russia/597769.

"Qatari Emir in Russia to Discuss Syrian Crisis," *Al Jazeera*, March 25, 2018. https://www.aljazeera.com/news/2018/03/qatari-emir-russia-discuss-syrian-crisis-180325195253621.html.

Rahman, Fareed, "RDIF in Talks with UAE Partners for Investments," *Gulf News*, December 3, 2017. https://gulfnews.com/business/sectors/investment/rdif-in-talks-with-uae-partners-for-investments-1.2134596.

Ramani, Samuel, "Why Russia and Israel Are Cooperating in Syria," *Huffpost*, June 23, 2016. https://www.huffingtonpost.com/entry/why-russia-and-israel-are-cooperating-in-syria_us_576bdb68e4b083e0c0235e15?guccounter=1.

Rasmussen, Sune Engel, "In Syria, Foreign Powers' Scramble for Influence Intensifies," *Wall Street Journal*, February 28, 2018. https://www.wsj.com/articles/in-syria-foreign-powers-scramble-for-influence-intensifies-1519817348.

"Reports on US Training 'Ex-Terrorists' in Syria Concerning," *RT*, December 25, 2017. https://www.rt.com/news/414189-syria-terrorists-training-lavrov/.

"Reuters: Russia Apparently Deploys Forces near Libyan Border in Egypt," *RFE/RL*, March 14, 2017. https://www.rferl.org/a/russia-special-forces-libya-egypt/28368266.html.

Roblin, Sebastien, "Israeli F-16s Wiped Out a Syrian Missile Complex (Russian Didn't Fire Back)," *National Interest*, June 3, 2019. https://nationalinterest.org/blog/buzz/israeli-f-16s-wiped-out-syrian-missile-complex-russian-didn%E2%80%99t-fire-back-60732.

"Rosneft Pulls Out of $30 bln Iran Oil Project over Fears of U.S. Sanctions," *Moscow Times*, December 13, 2018. https://www.themoscowtimes.com/2018/12/13/rosneft-pulls-out-of-30-bln-iran-oil-project-over-fears-us-sanctions-media-reports-a63811.

"Rosoboroneksport Oproverg Nalichie Kontrakta na Postavku Su-35 Egiptu [Rosoboronexport Denied the Signing of a Contract for the Supply of Su-35 Fighters to Egypt]," *Interfax*, March 26, 2019. https://www.interfax.ru/russia/655788.

"Rossiiskie Bespilotniki Vedut Kruglosutochnyi Kontroli v Sirii, Zayavil Shoigu [Russian Drones Are Conducting Round-the-Clock Observation in Syria, Shoigu Said]," *RIA Novosti*, October 27, 2017. https://ria.ru/syria/20171027/1507669571.html.

"Rossiisko-Egipetskie Ekonomicheskie Otnosheniya [Russian-Egyptian Economic Relations]," *ITAR-Tass*, December 11, 2017. https://tass.ru/info/4802472.

"Rossiiskie MI-28 Osnastili Provalinoi Elektronikoi [Russian Mi-28 Equipped with Subpar Electronics]," *Lenta.ru*, November 30, 2017. https://lenta.ru/news/2017/11/30/mi28/.

"Rossia Gotova Narastit Postavki Prodovolstviya v Qatar [Russia Is Ready to Increase Food Supplies to Qatar]," *ITAR-Tass*, June 8, 2017. http://tass.ru/ekonomika/4323794.

"Rossiya Gotova Postaviti Iranu S-400, Zayavili v FSVTS [Russia Ready to Deliver S-400 to Iran, Declared Federal Service for Military-Technical Cooperation of Russia]," *RIA Novosti*, June 28, 2019. https://ria.ru/20190628/1556012154.html.

"Rossiya i Katar Vedut Peregovory po Vozmozhnym Postavkam Su-35 [Russia and Qatar Are Negotiating the Possible Supplies of Su-35 Fighters]," *ITAR-Tass*, March 1, 2018. http://tass.ru/armiya-i-opk/4999532.

"Rossiya i Qatar Ssoriatsya iz-za Rukoprikladstva [Russia and Qatar Are Quarrelling over a Physical Fight]," *Interfax*, December 5, 2011. http://www.interfax.ru/russia/220228.

"Rossiya Perevela Nekotorye Oruzheinie Eksportnye Kontrakty na Rashiot v Nationalnyh Valiutah [Russia Switched Some Arms Export Contracts for the Calculation in National Currencies]," *ITAR-Tass*, September 14, 2018. https://tass.ru/politika/5564237.

"Rossiya Postavila Saudovskoi Aravii Vooruzhenie i Voennuiu Tehniku [Russia Supplied Weapons and Military Equipment to Saudi Arabia]," *Interfax*, June 27, 2019. https://www.interfax.ru/russia/666791.

"Rossiya Protestirovala v Sirii 316 Obraztsov Vooruzhenya [Russia Tested in Syria 316 Types of Military Hardware]," *RIA Novosti*, March 11, 2019. https://ria.ru/20190311/1551688108.html.

"Rossiya Protestirovala v Sirii Yeshche 43 Obraztsa Novogo Oruzhiya [Russia Tested 43 More Types of New Weapons in Syria]," *RIA Novosti*, December 24, 2019. https://ria.ru/20191224/1562776515.html.

"Rossiya Privlekla dlya Perevozki Gruzov v Siriu Desyati Grazhdanskih Sudov [Russia Contracted Ten Civil Vessels for Cargo Transportation to Syria]," *RBC*, November 15, 2015. https://www.rbc.ru/politics/15/10/2015/561fb5539a79471d00663b1e.

"Rossiya Postavila OTRK Iskander-E v Odnu iz Stran Severnoi Afriki [Russia Has Delivered Iskander-E Ballistic Missile Systems to a Country in the MENA region]," *RIA Novosti*, November 15, 2017. https://ria.ru/defense_safety/20171115/1508832294.html.

"Rossiya Vstupila v Peregovory s Egiptom ob Ispolizovanii Voennyh Aviabaz [Russia Entered the Talks with Egypt on Use of Military Air Bases]," *Meduza*, November 30, 2017. https://meduza.io/news/2017/11/30/rossiya-vstupila-v-peregovory-s-egiptom-ob-ispolzovanii-voennyh-aviabaz.

"Rossiya Ushla ot Ispolizovaniya SWIFT i Dollara po Oruzheinym Kontraktam [Russia Abandoned the Use of SWIFT and Dollar in Arms Contracts]," *Interfax*, June 26, 2019. https://www.interfax.ru/business/666701.

"Rosoboroneksport Polnostiu Vypolnit Godovoi Plan po Eksportu Vooruzhenia [Rosoboronexport Will Fully Implement the Annual Plan for Arms Exports]," *ITAR-Tass*, November 15, 2017. http://tass.ru/armiya-i-opk/4731347.

"Russian Ambitions for Syrian Phosphates," *Syrian Observer*, August 3, 2018. https://syrianobserver.com/EN/features/19755/russian_ambitions_syrian_phosphates.html.

"Russia Accuses US of Training ex-ISIS Fighters in Syria," *New York Post*, December 27, 2017. https://nypost.com/2017/12/27/russia-accuses-us-of-training-former-islamic-state-fighters-in-syria/.

"Russian Air strikes on Syrian Targets Raise 'Grave Concerns' in US," *Financial Times*, September 30, 2015. https://www.ft.com/content/a72cee0a-674e-11e5-a57f-21b88f7d973f.

"Russian Anti-Terrorist Operation in Syria," *RT*. https://www.rt.com/trends/russia-syria-op/.

"Russia and Egypt Hold First-Ever Joint Naval Drills," *Defense News*, June 10, 2015. https://www.defensenews.com/home/2015/06/10/russia-and-egypt-hold-first-ever-joint-naval-drills/.

"Russia Bewildered at France's Statement on Syria," *AMN*, December 10, 2017. https://mobile.almasdarnews.com/article/russia-bewildered-frances-statement-syria/.

"Russian Delegation to Syria Proposes Kurdish Autonomy," *Moscow Times*, June 26, 2017. https://www.themoscowtimes.com/2017/01/26/russian-delegation-proposes-autonomy-for-syrian-kurds-a56934.

"Russia Delivers LNG to Egypt under a Contract," *ITAR-Tass*, August 4, 2017. https://tass.com/economy/959129.

"Russian-Drafted New Constitution for Syria Promises Kurds Greater Autonomy," *New Arab*, January 26, 2017. https://www.alaraby.co.uk/english/news/2017/1/26/russia-drafted-new-constitution-for-syria-promises-kurds-greater-autonomy.

"Russia to Extend Tartus and Hmeimim Military Bases in Syria," *Deutsche Welle*, December 26, 2017. http://www.dw.com/en/russia-to-extend-tartus-and-hmeimim-military-bases-in-syria/a-41938949.

"Russian Firm to Take over Syria Port for 49 Years: Damascus," *Arab News*, April 25, 2019. http://www.arabnews.com/node/1488161/middle-east.

"Russian Foreign Minister Sergey Lavrov to Hold Talks in Qatar," *Al Jazeera*, March 3, 2019. https://www.aljazeera.com/news/2019/03/russian-foreign-minister-sergey-lavrov-hold-talks-qatar-190304070458781.html.

"Russia Hopes Algeria Will Resolve Its Issues in Constructive Manner," *ITAR-Tass Russian News Agency*, March 12, 2019. https://tass.com/world/1048369.

"Russia's Intentions Behind Mediating Iran, Israel Explained," *Persia Digest*, October 7, 2018. -https://persiadigest.com/Russia's-intentions behind-mediating-Iran,-Israel-explained.

"Russian Investors Want to Reconstruct Damascus Airport," *Russia Business Today*, January 21, 2019. https://russiabusinesstoday.com/infrastructure/russian-investors-want-to-reconstruct-damascus-airport/.

"Russia Is Not a 'Fire Brigade' to Save Disintegrating Iran Deal, Says Putin," *Times of Israel*, May 16, 2019. https://www.timesofisrael.com/russia-not-fire-brigade-to-save-disintegrating-iran-deal-says-putin/.

"Russia Lends Egypt $25 billion for Dabaa Nuclear Power Plant," *Al-Monitor*, February 26, 2020. https://www.al-monitor.com/pulse/originals/2020/02/power-plant-nuclear-egypt-russia-loan.html.

"Russia's Military Offer Stalls in Lebanon, For Now," *Asia Times*, April 8, 2018. http://www.atimes.com/article/russias-military-offer-stalls-lebanon-now/.

"Russian Military Police Deployed to Saraqeb," *ITAR-Tass*, March 2, 2020. https://tass.com/defense/1125825.

"Russian Mercenaries Are Fighting in Libya, UN Diplomats Confirm," *Moscow Times*, May 7, 2020. https://www.themoscowtimes.com/2020/05/07/russian-mercenaries-are-fighting-in-libya-un-diplomats-confirm-a70204.

"Russian Mercenaries: Vagner Commanders Describe Life Inside the 'Meat Grinder,'" *Radio Free Europe*, March 14, 2018. https://www.rferl.org/a/russian-mercenaries-vagner-commanders-syria/29100402.html.

"Russian Military, UN Mission Conduct First Joint Patrol of Israeli-Syrian Border," *ITAR-Tass*, October 26, 2018. https://tass.com/world/1027954.

"Russia's New Armament Program to Focus on Precision Weapons," *ITAR-Tass*, December 27, 2017. http://tass.com/defense/983376.

"Russian Propaganda Outlets Prosper in Turkey," *Economist*, February 28, 2019.

"Russia Reacts to Claims of Iranian Missile Downing Ukrainian Plane," *Moscow Times*, January 10, 2020. https://www.themoscowtimes.com/2020/01/10/russia-reacts-to-claims-of-iranian-missile-downing-ukrainian-plane-a68859.

"Russia's Rostec to Co-develop 5th-gen Fighter with UAE," *Defense News*, February 20, 2017. https://www.defensenews.com/digital-show-dailies/idex/2017/02/20/russia-s-rostec-to-co-develop-5th-gen-fighter-with-uae.

"Russian Snipers, Missiles and Warplanes Try to Tilt Libyan Conflict," *New York Times*, November 5, 2019. https://www.nytimes.com/2019/11/05/world/middleeast/russia-libya-mercenaries.html.

"Russian-Sponsored Syrian Agency to 'Protect Government Facilities'," *Asharq Al-Awsat*, July 11 2019. https://aawsat.com/english/home/article/1808021/russian-sponsored-syrian-agency-%E2%80%98protect-government-facilities%E2%80%99.

"Russia Stance on Assad Suggests Divergence with Iran," *Reuters*, November 3, 2015. https://www.reuters.com/article/us-mideast-crisis-syria-russia/russia-stance-on-assad-suggests-divergence-with-iran-idUSKCN0SS0TY20151103.

"Russia Steps up Military Presence in Syria, Despite Putin Promise," *Fox News*, January 11, 2017. http://www.foxnews.com/world/2017/01/11/russia-steps-up-military-presence-in-syria-despite-putin-promise.html.

"Russia to Supply Turkey with Four S-400 Missile Batteries for $2.5 Billion," *Reuters*, December 27, 2017. https://www.reuters.com/article/us-russia-turkey-missiles/russia-to-supply-turkey-with-four-s-400-missile-batteries-for-2–5-billion-kommersant-idUSKBN1EL0H6.

"Russian Visitors to GCC to Increase 38 Percent by 2020," *Gulf News*, January 13, 2018. http://gulfnews.com/business/sectors/tourism/russian-visitors-to-gcc-to-increase-38-by-2020-1.2156253.

"Russia's VTB Bank Buys 19% Stake in Qatar's CQUR Bank—Ifax," *Nasdaq.com*, August 15, 2019. http://www.nasdaq.com/article/russias-vtb-bank-buys-19-stake-in-qatars-cqur-bank--ifax-20190815-00122.

"Russia Withdraws Envoy to Qatar after Attack" *Reuters*, December 5, 2011. https://af.reuters.com/article/commoditiesNews/idAFL3E7N535820111205.

Safronov, Ivan, and Svetlana Bocharova, "Ataka Dronov Pomozhet Rossii Prodat' Sistemy PVO Stranam Persidskogo Zaliva [Drone Attack Will Help Russia Sell its Air Defense Systems to Gulf Countries]," *Vedomosti*, October 2019. https://www.vedomosti.ru/politics/articles/2019/10/23/814508-ataka-dronov-pomozhet-rossii.

Safronov, Ivan, "Kakim Sprosom Polizuetsya Rossiiskoe Oruzhie Posle Sirii [What Is the Demand for Russian Weapons after Syria?]," *Kommersant*, March 28, 2016. https://www.kommersant.ru/doc/2932551.

"Saudovskaya Araviya Investiruet v Bolee Chem 25 Rossiiskih Proektov [Saudi Arabia Will Invest in More Than 25 Projects in Russia]," *RIA Novosti*, October 4, 2017. https://ria.ru/economy/20171004/1506213502.html.

Sergie, Mohammed, "The Tiny Gulf Country with a $335 Billion Global Empire," *Bloomberg*, January 11, 2017. https://www.bloomberg.com/news/articles/2017-01-11/qatar-sovereign-wealth-fund-s-335-global-empire.

Shamizi, Omid, "Iran Allows Russia to Use Airbase for Refuelling," *Anadolu Agency*, April 14, 2018. https://www.aa.com.tr/en/europe/iran-allows-russia-to-use-airbase-for-refueling/1117681.

"Shatilov, Alexey, Représentant Commercial de la Russie: 'Nous Pouvons Aider l'Algérie dans le Domaine des Hautes Technologies'," *Algerie Eco*, June 22, 2017. https://www.algerie-eco.com/2017/06/22/alexeyshatilov-representant-commercial-de-russie-pouvons-aider-lalgerie-domaine-hautes-technologies/.

Shay, Shaul, "Defenders of Friendship 2018: Egypt, Russia Conclude Joint Drills," *Israel Defense*, October 31, 2018. https://www.israeldefense.co.il/en/node/36153.

Shay, Shaul, "Exercise 'Protectors of Friendship 2' and the Egyptian-Russian Strategic Relations," *Israel Defense*, September 26, 2017. https://www.israeldefense.co.il/en/node/31239.

Sly, Liz, Anton Troianovski, and Ruth Eglash, "Russia Revives Allegations of Israeli Culpability in Downed Plane in Syria," *Washington Post*, September 23, 2018. https://www.washingtonpost.com/world/middle_east/

russia-revives-allegations-of-israeli-culpability-in-downed-plane-in-syria/2018/09/23/
ac6741de-bf36-11e8-9f4f-a1b7af255aa5_story.html?utm_term=.a3adbe20f361.

"Source: Egypt Buys 50 Russian Alligator Helicopters, Deck-Based Version May Be Supplied," *ITAR-Tass*, September, 23, 2015. http://tass.com/defense/823140.

Steinberg, Jessica, "Mother Russia Returns to Grand Duke's Jerusalem Compound," *Times of Israel*, July 13, 2017. https://www.timesofisrael.com/mother-russia-returns-to-grand-dukes-jerusalem-compound/.

Stewart, Phil, Idrees Ali, and Lin Noueihed, "Russia Appears to Deploy Forces in Egypt, Eyes on Libya Role—Sources," *Reuters*, March 13, 2017. https://www.reuters.com/article/us-usa-russia-libya-exclusive/exclusive-russia-appears-to-deploy-forces-in-egypt-eyes-on-libya-role-sources-idUSKBN16K2RY.

Suchkov, Maxim A., "How Russia Is Reading the Killing of Qassem Suleimani," *Al-Monitor*, January 3, 2020, www.al-monitor.com/pulse/originals/2020/01/russia-soleimani-iran-us-strikes-ira1.html.

Suchkov, Maxim A., "Intel: Why Russia Is Calling for Rethinking Gulf Security," *Al-Monitor*, July 24, 2019. www.al-monitor.com/pulse/originals/2019/07/intel-russia-proposal-gulf-security-iran-tensions.html.

"Syria's Bashar Assad Is Not a Perfect Leader, But Certainly Better Than Islamic State," *RT*, March 31, 2017. https://www.rt.com/op-ed/382958-assad-turkey-us-rex-tillerson/.

"Syria Death Toll 384,000 after Nine Years of War: Monitor," *RFI*, March 14, 2020. http://www.rfi.fr/en/wires/202000314-syria-death-toll-384000-after-nine-years-war-monitor.

"Syrian Government Loses 5/6th of Territory, IHS Says," *IHS Market*, August 22, 2015. http://news.ihsmarkit.com/press-release/aerospace-defense-security/syrian-government-loses-56th-territory-ihs-says.

"Syrian President Condemns West, Vows to Survive Protests," *BBC Monitoring*, January 11, 2012.

"Syria Says Russian Missile Defence System 'Ineffective'," *MEMO—Middle East Monitor*, May 1, 2020. https://www.middleeastmonitor.com/20200501-syria-says-russian-missile-defence-system-ineffective/.

"Syria War: What the Mainstream Media Isn't Telling You about Eastern Ghouta," *RT*, March 5, 2018. https://www.rt.com/op-ed/420521-syria-eastern-ghouta-aleppo-media/.

"Syrie: 'Il Faut se Rapprocher de Bachar al-Assad Pour Mieux Détruire Daesh', Dit Thierry Mariani," *RTL*, May 22, 2015. http://www.rtl.fr/actu/international/syrie-il-faut-se-rapprocher-de-bachar-al-assad-pour-mieux-detruire-daesh-dit-thierry-mariani-7778439575.

"Tensions Flare between Syrian Leader's Foreign Backers," *SFGATE*, June 9, 2018. https://www.sfgate.com/world/article/Tensions-flare-between-Syrian-leader-s-foreign-12981371.php.

"Trump Expected to Seek Putin's Help to Curb Iran's Military in Syria," *Wall Street Journal*, June 28, 2018. https://www.wsj.com/articles/trump-to-meet-russias-putin-in-finland-on-july-16-1530187901?emailToken=17a77cd4d4aa6965efbdc228b00f6a39NabkwZUR0oRaoZreVrS0uL/If1EuI9Z5nzSZZ0rb1vjZhrq11RjTZaOdRg+QMkuSBfhJ73at7urD+G2PjjBfZFYklDNqEn3iF4OKiQuLBNk%3D&reflink=article_email_share.

"Tunisie: Les Touristes Russes Arrivent en Masse," *Espace Manager*, May 27, 2019. https://www.espacemanager.com/tunisie-les-touristes-russes-arrivent-en-masse.html.

"Tunisia, Russia Contemplate Setting Up of Free Trade Area," *North Africa Post*, April 26, 2019. http://northafricapost.com/30351-tunisia-russia-contemplate-setting-up-of-free-trade-area.html.

"Turkey's Downing of Russian Warplane—What We Know," *BBC News*, December 1, 2015. http://www.bbc.com/news/world-middle-east-34912581.

"Turkey's New LNG Storage, Regasification Unit to Dock in İzmir Today," *Daily Sabah*, July 5, 2019. https://www.dailysabah.com/energy/2019/07/05/turkeys-new-lng-storage-regasification-unit-to-dock-in-izmir-today.

"Turkish 2015 Tourism Revenues," *Hürriyet Daily News*, January 29, 2016.

"Turpotok iz Rossii v Tunis Sokratilsya, no Pokazal Organicheskii Rost [The Number of Russian Tourists in Tunisia Has Decreased, But the Flow Proves Its Organic Growth]," *Association of Tour Operators*, December 28, 2017. http://www.atorus.ru/ru/main/news/press-centre/new/41799.html.

"UAE's Russian Community Is Most Active in MENA Region," *Gulf News*, January 12, 2018. https://gulfnews.com/going-out/society/uaes-russian-community-is-most-active-in-mena-region-1.2155824.

"U.N. Envoy Says Assad Is Crucial to Defusing Conflict in Syria," *New York Times*, February 13, 2015. https://www.nytimes.com/2015/02/14/world/middleeast/un-envoy-to-syria-says-assad-is-crucial-to-hopes-to-end-war.html.

"Upravlenie po Turismu Katara Prezentovalo Rossiiskoe Predstavitelstvo i Oboznachilo Prioritety [Qatar Tourism Authority Opened Representation in Russia and Outlined Its Priorities]," *Vesti.ru*, March 30, 2018. http://travel.vesti.ru/article_37356.

"US Destroying Syrian Cities Liberated from ISIS to Obstruct Pro-Assad Forces—Analyst," *RT*, October 15, 2017. https://www.rt.com/news/406751-mayadeen-syria-liberation-isis/.

"US Protecting Syria Jihadist Group—Russia's Lavrov," *BBC News*, September 30, 2016. http://www.bbc.com/news/world-europe-37520793.

"V 2019 Hadj Sovershat 20,5 tysyachi Rossiskih Musulman [In 2019, 20.5 thousand Russian Muslims Will Make the Hadj]," *ITAR-Tass*, January 16, 2019. https://tass.ru/obschestvo/6007479.

"V FSVTS Zayavili o Peregovorah s Katarom po Postavkam S-400 [FSMTC Announced Talks with Qatar on the Delivery of the S-400's]," *ITAR-Tass*, February 19, 2019. https://tass.ru/armiya-i-opk/6133932.

"V Irak Dostavlena Pervaya Partya BMP-3 [The First Batch of BMP-3's Delivered to Iraq]," *BMPD*, August 29, 2018. https://bmpd.livejournal.com/3322045.html.

"V Minoborone Raskryli Chislo Uchastnikov Voennoi Operatsii VS RF v Sirii [The Defense Ministry Revealed the Number of Participants in the Military Operation in Syria]," *Zvezda*, January 3, 2019. https://tvzvezda.ru/news/forces/content/201901031142-b4d1.htm.

'Vladimir Putin Accuses US of Backing Terrorism in Middle East', *The Guardian*, October 22, 2015. https://www.theguardian.com/world/2015/oct/22/vladimir-putin-accuses-us-backing-terrorism-middle-east.

"Vladimir Putin of Russia Calls for Coalition to Fight ISIS," *New York Times*, September 27, 2015. https://www.nytimes.com/2015/09/29/world/europe/russia-vladimir-putin-united-nations-general-assembly.html.

Von Eggert, Konstantin, "Opinion: Putin Power Games May Get Out of Hand," *DW*, January 6, 2020. https://www.dw.com/en/opinion-putins-power-games-may-get-out-of-hand/a-51907064.

Voronova, Tatiana, "Exclusive: Russian State Bank Secretly Financed Rosneft Sale after Foreign Buyers Balked," *Thomson Reuters*, November 9, 2018. https://www.reuters.com/article/us-rosneft-privatisation-exclusive/exclusive-russian-state-bank-secretly-financed-rosneft-sale-after-foreign-buyers-balked-idUSKCN1NE132.

"Vyhodtsy s Kavkaza v Ryadah IG (IGIL) [Peoples from the Caucasus in the Ranks of the IS (ISIS)]," *Kavkazski Uzel*, March 1, 2018. http://www.kavkaz-uzel.eu/articles/251513/.

Yaffa, Joshua, "How the Russian-Saudi Oil War Went Awry-For Putin Most of All," *New Yorker*, April 15, 2020. https://www.newyorker.com/news/dispatch/how-the-russian-saudi-oil-war-went-awry-for-putin-most-of-all.

Walker, Shaun, "Murder in Istanbul: Kremlin's Hand Suspected in Shooting of a Chechen," *The Guardian*, January 10, 2016. https://www.theguardian.com/world/2016/jan/10/murder-istanbul-chechen-kremlin-russia-abdulvakhid-edelgireyev.

"Washington Uses Terror Groups in Syria for Its Own Goals," *ITAR-Tass*, November 21, 2017. http://tass.com/politics/976604.

"We Can't Force Iran Out of Syria, Russia Tells Israelis," *Reuters*, July 30, 2018. https://uk.reuters.com/article/uk-mideast-crisis-syria-israel-russia/we-cant-force-iran-out-of-syria-russia-tells-israelis-idUKKBN1KK29A?il=0.

"Where Does the Syrian Regime Get Foreign Currency From?," *Enab Baladi*, July 8, 2020. https://english.enabbaladi.net/archives/2020/07/where-does-the-syrian-regime-get-foreign-currency-from/.

"Wikileaks: France Said Syrian General Killed in Regime Feud," *Naharnet*, August 25, 2011. http://www.naharnet.com/stories/en/13646-wikileaks-france-said-syrian-general-killed-in-regime-feud.

Wright, Robin, "A Tanker War in the Middle East—Again?," *New Yorker*, June 13, 2019. https://www.newyorker.com/news/our-columnists/a-tanker-war-in-the-middle-eastagain.

Wright, Robin, "Russia and Iran Deepen Ties to Challenge Trump and the United States," *New Yorker*, March 2, 2018. https://www.newyorker.com/news/news-desk/russia-and-iran-deepen-ties-to-challenge-trump-and-the-united-states.

Wroughton, Lesley, and Patricia Zengerle, "U.S. Sanctions China for Buying Russian Fighter Jets, Missiles," *Reuters*, September, 20, 2018. https://www.reuters.com/article/us-usa-russia-sanctions/u-s-sanctions-china-for-buying-russian-fighter-jets-missiles-idUSKCN1M02TP.

"Zhertvoi Fugasa Stal Rossiiskii General [The Russian General Fell Victim of IED]," *Kommersant*, March 6, 2017. https://www.kommersant.ru/doc/3235107.

Zine, Imène, "Coopération entre Deux Univeristés Tunisiennes et Leurs Homologues Russes," *L'économiste Maghrébin*, April 4, 2018. https://www.leconomistemaghrebin.com/2018/04/04/cooperation-universite-tunis-manar-sfax-russes/.

Journal Articles, Chapters from Edited Volumes and Theses

Baev, Pavel, "Turkey and Russia," in Alparslan Özerdem and Matthew Whiting (eds.), *The Routledge Handbook of Turkish Politics*. London: Routledge, 2019, 413–24.

Bogdanov, Mikhail, "Russian-Egyptian Relations at the Turn of the Centuries," *Asia i Afrika Segodnya*, no. 12 (2013): 2–3.

Bourguiba, Habib, "Nationalism: Antidote to Communism," *Foreign Affairs*, 35, no. 4 (July 1957): 646–53.

Chernayev, Anatolii, "Iz Vospominanii: Brezhnev i Gorbachev" [From Memoirs: Brezhnev and Gorbachev], Polis, no. 3 (2012): 165.

Copp, John W., "Egypt and the Soviet Union, 1953–1970" (Master's Thesis, Portland State University, 1986), 121. https://pdxscholar.library.pdx.edu/cgi/viewcontent.cgi?article=4806&context=open_access_etds.

Freedman, Robert O., "Russia and the Middle East: The Primakov era," *Middle East Review of International Affairs* 2, no. 2 (May 1998): 1–8. http://www.rubincenter.org/meria/1998/05/freedman.pdf.

Ginat, Rami, "The Soviet Union and Egypt, 1947–1955" (Ph.D. Thesis, London School of Economics, 1991), 24.

Katz, Mark N., "Implications of the Georgian Crisis for Israel, Iran, and the West," *Middle East Review of International Affairs* 12, no. 4 (December 2008): 4–5. http://mars.gmu.edu/bitstream/handle/1920/5585/Meria_katz_Dec_2008.pdf?sequence=1&isAllowed=y.

Katz, Mark N., "Putin's Pro-Israel Policy," *Middle East Quarterly* 12, no. 1 (Winter 2005): 51–9. https://www.meforum.org/articles/2005/putin-s-pro-israel-policy.

Katz, Mark N., "Russia and Algeria: Partners or Competitors?," *Middle East Policy Council* 14, no. 4 (Winter 2017). http://www.mepc.org/journal/russia-and-algeria-partners-or-competitors.

Kınıklıoğlu, Suat, and Valeriy Morkva, "An Anatomy of Russian-Turkish Relations," *Journal of Southeast European and Black Sea Studies* 7, no. 1 (2007): 533–53.

Makienko, Konstantin, "Rossiiskii Eksport Vooruzhenii v 2014–2018 gg.: Stagnatsya, Rost Riskov, Uhudshenie Vneshnei Sredy [Russian Arms Exports in 2014–2018: Stagnation, Increased Risks, External Factors]," *Export Vooruzheniy* 2 (2019): 9.

Margold, Stella, "Agrarian Land Reform in Egypt," *The American Journal of Economics and Sociology* 17, no. 1 (October 1957): 9–19.

Marten, Kimberly, "Russia's Use of Semi-State Security Forces: The Case of the Wagner Group," *Post-Soviet Affairs* 35, no. 3 (2019): 181–204.

Minin, Nikita, and Tomas Vlcek, "Determinants and Considerations of Rosatom's External Strategy," *Energy Strategy Reviews*, 17 (2017): 37–44.

Nation, R. Craig, "The Sources of Soviet Involvement in the Middle East: Threat or Opportunity?," in Mark V. Kauppi and R. Craig Nation (eds.), *The Soviet Union and the Middle East in the 1980s*. Lexington: Lexington Books, 1983, 59–60.

Sayigh, Yezid, and Avi Shlaim, "Introduction," in Yezid Sayigh and Avi Shlaim (eds.), *The Cold War and the Middle East*. Oxford: Clarendon Press, 1997, 3.

Seale, Patrick, "Syria," in Yezid Sayigh and Avi Shlaim (eds.), *The Cold War and the Middle East*. Oxford: Clarendon Press, 1997, 38–77.

Zinin, Yuriy, "Is the Red October Legacy Still Traceable across the Middle East?," *New Eastern Outlook*, January 31, 2018. https://journal-neo.org/2018/01/31/is-the-red-october-legacy-still-traceble-across-the-middle-east/.

Books

Barabanov, Mikhail, Konstantin Makienko, Ruslan Pukhov and Aleksandr Rybas, *Voenno-Tehnicheskoe Sotrudnichestvo Rossii s Zarubezhnymi Gosudarstvami: Analiz Rynkov* [Military-Technical Cooperation between Russia and Foreign Countries: A Market Analysis]. Moscow: Nauka, 2008.

Bechev, Dimitar, *Rival Power: Russia in Southeast Europe*. New Haven: Yale University Press, 2017.

Bergman, Ronen, *Rise and Kill First: The Secret History of Israel's Targeted Assassinations*. London: John Murray, 2018.

Çağaptay, Soner, *Erdoğan's Empire: Turkey and the Politics of the Middle East*. London: Bloomsbury, 2019.

Freedman, Robert O., *Soviet Policy towards the Middle East since 1970*. New York: Praeger, 1982.

Golan, Galia, *Soviet Policies in the Middle East: From World War II to Gorbachev*. Cambridge: Cambridge University Press, 1990.

Gordon, Joel, *Nasser's Blessed Movement: Egypt's Free Officers and the July Revolution*. Oxford: Oxford University Press, 1992.

Grinevskii, Oleg, *Tainy Sovetskoi Diplomatii* [The Secrets of Soviet Diplomacy]. Moscow: Vagrius, 2000.

Heikal, Mohamed, *The Sphinx and the Commissar: The Rise and Fall of Soviet Influence in the Middle East*. New York: Harper and Row, 1978.

Kirişci, Kemal, Turkey, and the West, *Faultlines in a Troubled Alliance*. Washington, DC: Brookings Institution, 2017.

Larrabee, F. Stephen, and Ian Lesser, *Turkish Foreign Policy in an Age of Uncertainty*. Santa Monica: RAND, 2003, Ch. 4.

Lucas, Scott, *Britain and Suez: The Lion's Last Roar*. Manchester: Manchester University Press, 1996.

McFaul, Michael, *From Cold War to Hot Peace*. New York: Houghton, Miffin, Harcourt, 2018.

Naumkin, Vitaliy, *Nesostoyavsheesya Partniorstvo. Sovetskaya Diplomatya v Saudovskoi Araviy mezhdu Mirovymi Voynami* [Failed Partnership. Soviet Diplomacy in Saudi Arabia between World Wars]. Moscow: Aspekt Press, 2018.

Nizammedin, Talal, *Putin's New Order in the Middle East*. London: Hurst, 2013.

Nove, Alec, and J. A. Newth, *The Soviet Middle East. A Model for Development?* London: Allen & Unwin, 1967.

Özcan, Gençer, Evren Balta, and Burç Beşgül (eds.), *Kuşku ile Komşuluk. Türkiye ve Rusya İlişkilerinde Değişen Dinamıklar*. İstanbul: İletişim, 2017.

Philips, Christopher, *The Battle for Syria: International Rivalry in the New Middle East*. New Haven: Yale University Press, 2016.

Podtserob, Alexey, *Rossia i Arabskii Mir* [Russia and Arab World]. Moscow: MGIMO Universitet, 2015.

Primakov, Yevgeny, *Confidentially: The Middle East on Stage and Behind the Curtains*. Moscow: Rossijskaya Gazeta, 2012.

Primakov, Yevgeny, *Russia and the Arabs: Behind the Scenes in the Middle East from the Cold War to the Present*. New York: Basic Books, 2009.

Ro'I, Yacov, and Boris Morozov, *The Soviet Union and the 1967 Six Day War*. Palo Alto: Stanford University Press, 2008.

Trenin, Dmitri, *What Is Russia Up to in the Middle East?* Cambridge: Polity, 2018.

Vinogradov, Arkadii, *Nepridumannaya Siria* [Syria in Real Life]. Moscow: Mezhdunarodnye Otnoshenia, 2017.

Zolotarev, Vladimir, *Rossia (SSSR) v Lokalnyh Voinah* [Russia (USSR) in Local Wars]. Moscow: Kuchkovo Pole, 2000.

Index